Clement Scott

Round about the Islands

Or Sunny Spots Near Home

Clement Scott

Round about the Islands
Or Sunny Spots Near Home

ISBN/EAN: 9783744746939

Printed in Europe, USA, Canada, Australia, Japan

Cover: Foto ©Andreas Hilbeck / pixelio.de

More available books at **www.hansebooks.com**

ROUND ABOUT THE ISLANDS:

OR,

SUNNY SPOTS NEAR HOME.

BY

CLEMENT W. SCOTT.

LONDON:
TINSLEY BROTHERS, 8, CATHERINE STREET, STRAND.
1874.

ROUND ABOUT THE ISLANDS:

OR,

SUNNY SPOTS NEAR HOME.

BY

CLEMENT W. SCOTT.

"Summer isles of Eden lying in dark-purple spheres of sea."
TENNYSON. *Locksley Hall.*

FRONTISPIECE AND VIGNETTE BY GEORGE DU MAURIER.

LONDON:
TINSLEY BROTHERS, 8, CATHERINE STREET, STRAND.
1874.

LOAN STACK

I Dedicate this Book

TO MY FRIENDS.

C. W. S.

"L'amitié c'est l'amour sans ailes."

PREFACE.

In obedience to the request of many warm friends, I have collected and arranged these very imperfect sketches of frequent holiday rambles round our summer islands near home. Now in a car through the Connemara District of Ireland : now on the yellow sands or under the white cliffs of the Isle of Thanet : now among the wild flowers or over the downs of the Isle of Wight : now hither and thither through the cornfields or on the seashore of our own England : now exploring the deserted Hayling ; and now cast, like a lonely Robinson Crusoe, upon the shores of Sark, I have hurriedly written as I rushed along, offering my humble devotion at the altar of nature and enjoying a short holiday with the enthusiasm of a schoolboy.

Many of these letters were sent home day by day through the old-fashioned medium of the post, but not a few were scribbled in country post-offices at sunset and despatched to London by telegraph. Their imperfections are, I am well aware, sufficiently transparent, but let it be kindly remembered they are not the deliberate work of an essayist in his sanctum, but the unripe fruit of a running pen. To me they are bound by memories of walks, talks, rambles and scrambles shared with many of my faithful friends, and if in presenting these letters to the public in a collected form I can suggest in any way the rare delight of a combination of freedom, scenery and sympathy, I shall have risked obvious criticism but added one more happy recollection to those here enshrined.

Even in so eminently a realistic and unenthusiastic age as this I am yet confident there are hearts alive to the influence of sea and sunshine; field and flower; health and happiness; and some lips may be uncurled even when so imperfect an attempt is made to express the reaction after hard work, afforded by long days among our summer Islands.

CLEMENT SCOTT.

ST. JOHN'S WOOD,
    Christmas, 1873.

CONTENTS.

	PAGE
ON A CAR THROUGH CONNEMARA	1
BESIDE THE "MELANCHOLY OCEAN"	24
A PILGRIMAGE TO BLARNEY	36
ON THE ROAD TO KILLARNEY	46
LIFE AT KILLARNEY	56
COLLEEN BAWN LAND	65
AT THE YORKSHIRE SPA	76
SCARBOROUGH'S SUNDIAL	83
THE HAPPY ISLAND	100
A DESERTED ISLAND	134
OZONE-LAND	144
ON THE ROAD TO GOODWOOD	154
ALONG THE UNDERCLIFF	172
THE FALL OF THE LEAF	184
PUTTING ON THE PAINT	194
A JOURNEY EN ZIGZAG	203
AFTER DARK	214
THE SORROWS OF SARK	222
BEFORE THE BATTLE	245
LONDON IN THE DARK	254

The "Afternoon Dorking"	263
The Round of the Clock	274
Among the Roses	281
Among the Ruins	291
A Grumble about Inns	298
At the Academy	304
"Down among the Coals"	313
The Last Man in London	321
In the Heart of the Earth	329
Home!	348

ROUND ABOUT THE ISLANDS.

ON A CAR THROUGH CONNEMARA.

It is nearly three o'clock in the morning when, with a vigorous pull at the bell of the Railway Hotel, at Westport, I arouse the semi-somnolent porter, and at that unholy hour ask for the traveller's privilege of a bed.

This is the commencement of my Connemara trip. It had been such baking weather in Dublin all day, that I determined to take the night mail to the West; and I can offer tourist no better advice than to trust to the good offices of the Midland Great Western Railway at the Broadstone terminus if he would travel through the wildest and most romantic country that imagination can picture or pen can describe. In the cosy carriages of the Midland Great Western you can sleep like a top. In the clean sweet sheets of the comfortable Hotel at Westport you can finish the remainder of the night in delicious comfort, lulled by a waterfall which is distinctly heard through the open window, and only occasionally reminded of a new and strange scene by the sharp stroke of the Catholic chapel clock, on the other side of the avenue of trees over the way. We all know the delightful fascination of waking in a new town.

In London we keep dozing, if we can, as late as Robin and Richard, those "two pretty men" who "stayed in bed till the clock struck ten;" but here in Westport, notwithstanding the half-feverish and dissipated railway journey, when you sleep with one eye shut and one eye open, when you are shaken up for tickets at the wrong time, and when you are rash enough to smoke with a determination which is praiseworthy but not healthful—why, you wake up at seven o'clock and have your tub—and feel an uncontrollable impulse to see the town, to explore Westport before breakfast, to find out the course of that sleep-giving waterfall, and discover whence came that smell of new-cut hay which filled the bedroom hours ago with delicious fragrance.

I had an idea, when I looked at Westport on the map, and when I thought of the bold coast of the West of Ireland, that the best hotel in Westport would be situated on the edge of a rock facing the sea—that I should get a plunge into salt water before breakfast, and watch the long roll of the Atlantic before the car was harnessed. But all these sea dreams were soon destined to vanish. The sea may be discovered some miles away; Clew Bay is a fact of which lazy excursionists may be aware; and there is Achill Island, which looks so lovely in the pictures in my guide-book, that I am almost tempted to give up the car and find out the sea, wherever it may be. But Westport is Westport all the same. It is a desolate, dreary Irish town. I am told in the guide-book that "on the market-day it presents a very gay and animated appearance." I was there on a market-day, and I found an old grey pony laden with peat, and a dozen old women in scarlet Galway petticoats chattering in the market-square. It was the park of the Marquis of Sligo, adjacent to my hotel, which provided me with the whiff of new-mown hay; but when I have chuckled over the eccentricity of the monument to a certain Mr. Glendinning, in the centre of the principal street, and discovered that the said Glendinning was an agent not unconnected with the Sligo estates—when I have marvelled at the hovels and the uncontrollable dirt even of the High Street of Westport—I think it is time to put my luggage on the yellow car that is harnessing at the door of the hotel.

And now the fun commences. The car is a stout conveyance, built on the Irish principle, back to back, but carrying six on each side, and as much luggage as can be stowed away in a capacious well or packed up behind the double row of passengers. It is just the day for a journey in the open air. It has rained since seven in the morning, it is true; but happily, at ten o'clock, the rain has ceased, and the air is heavy with the scent of flowers. So away we go up the steep street of Westport in the double-horsed yellow car, and in less than half-an-hour we are in the heart of the mountains. Your guide-book will tell you that one side of the car enjoys a special privilege of scenery, and on the day of my travel a party had telegraphed from Dublin to secure the pretty side; but upon my honour I consider this a stretch of enthusiasm. What one side loses the other gains. If you keep your eyes open you can be delighted with a succession of rarely magnificent views.

How can I rapidly and effectively describe the strange awe inspired by the wild mountain scenery? If the mountains ran merely on the right hand and on the left, you might be bored with the monotony of the hills. But they occur in wild irregularity, now in perpendicular ranges, now at right angles, but everywhere mountains; now hidden in the clouds, now pure green under the sunlight, now dark purple under a passing cloud. The further we get, the wilder and more desolate the scenery becomes. We meet peasants, all barefoot, trudging to the market town, and even in rags they are picturesque. The scarlet petticoat hangs in graceful folds, and there is an artistic method of arranging the bright shawl about the head and shoulders which commends itself to the stranger in this wild country. There are carts filled with peat, villagers on horseback and on foot, all passing us; but the eye is constantly strained and the imagination quickened with the delights of an ever-changing scene. We have heard of the rude Irish cabin, reared but a few feet from the ground; of the pigs and turkeys, the geese and chickens, the dogs and children, all sharing the same roof with the parents. Here they are then: the pigs grunting their content, the turkeys gobbling about the turf, the geese and chickens perpetually grubbing in the road, the dogs well fed and loud of voice to protect the simple tenement, and the children, bright of eye and firm of flesh, splendid specimens of poverty, revelling as all children will revel when their feet are bare and there is black Irish mud to dabble in.

While so intent on the pigs and children, the red-petticoated peasantry and the peat stackers of County Mayo which we shall soon leave, a rock-capped mountain called Croagh Patrick has been left behind; a mountain which tempts Young Oxford to its summit, and which boasts a holy well, thousands of feet above the level of the sea—a cure, the car driver assured me, for sore eyes, rheumatism, chronic complaints, and worldly misery, and an attraction for good Catholics from as far away as America, when twice a year the devotion of the Stations of the Cross is practised there, and mass is said on rude altars erected among the clouds. The scenery is now relieved by a pure sheet of water, along the side of which we travel to Leenane, a peaceful hamlet resting under the blue hills and overlooking a calm and unruffled lake. This is a place of all others which would tempt a traveller to rest. But here I am compelled to pause and wonder at the want of enterprise in this exquisite land.

"Man wants but little here below, nor wants that little long;" but he does want a little comfort. In a Connemara trip I do not look for luxuries; I do not require salmon cutlets and Geisler's champagne; but I demand the produce of the country carefully cooked and palatable, and comfortable inns which would have delighted the poet Shenstone. But what do I find in Connemara? High prices, and anything but comfort; and there is besides a sad untidiness about these western highland inns which will disgust all but enthusiasts. Arrived at last at Glendalough I find something like comfort; but my experiences on more than one occasion have been very much the reverse. If I were in deserted regions I should not grumble. But here is a railway company giving cheap coupons and every facility—here are bookmakers tempting the public by telling them the trip can be done for six guineas, here is the public sensible enough to come and revel in this superb scenery and intoxicating mountain air, and yet an enterprising Irishman has not been discovered to lift the inns, not into grandeur or modern splendour, but into simple cleanliness and taste.

I have walked with the same faithful friend with whom I now travel through Brittany and Normandy, through the unknown villages of South Wales, but I have never met with such wretched hotel accommodation. It is an insult to Connemara that she should be so ill served up. A cosy inn at the end of a long day is a treasure not yet to be found in a region where enthusiasts do congregate in spite of the inns. Let me not be misunderstood. I would not have missed seeing the interminable mountains, the peaceful lakes, the desolate, dreary wastes, the bold magnificence of Killery Bay, the cultivation of fair Kylemore, the peasants, the hovels, the original view of Irish Western Highland life, for all the discomfort and night-misery in the world. But there may be some who come to Connemara with not so much philosophy, and who, notwithstanding the impressions caused by the scene, may in a bold commercial spirit demand their money's-worth for their money all the same. And quite right too.

But now it would appear as if my sorrows were coming to an end. Indisposed to travel on to Galway without a halt, I was enticed by the beauties of Glendalough, as described by a young engineer who meditates running a railway from Galway to Clifden. I was told that Oughterard would be a good halt. My companions at the breakfast table fought over the advantages of Maam and Cong; and, still unsettled, I started by the public car from my night's resting-place. The wild beauty of Ballinahinch, with its reminiscences of Lever, its castle on the island on the lake, its marble home among the trees, unsettled my resolve to push on. The calm retreat of Glendalough decided me. Here was an inn with a lawn sloping to the lake, with mountains opposite, and trees all round us. Here were valleys of ferns and dells of blackberries, the very place of all others to loll about, to smoke and talk and gather flowers. I stopped the car at the other side of the lake, and bade the boatman ferry me over to this peaceful home. At the window of a sunny inn, overlooking a lawn sloping to the lake, overlooking the unrippled water, overlooked by the awful mountains, I sit and write; and I hope to be ferried over the lake in a few minutes to catch a certain post-cart which will take my letter to regions of civilization where a post-office exists. I am planted here in a colony of fishermen, learned in flies, brown trout, and salmon. They are in the air all day, but at nine o'clock we eat our dinner: and by-and-by I propose to tell you something of our life at this delightful fishing inn on the Lake at Glendalough.

On the Lake Glendalough.

Vevey and Montreux, Lausanne and Ouchy must, in some respects, bow before the delicious calm of Glendalough; one of the most beautiful lakes in the Connemara district, and the head-quarters of the enthusiasts who patronize the Ballinahinch Fishery. It is just the place I had longed to see. A white inn nestling in a delightful wood, a lawn covered with blue hydrangeas sloping to the lake, the celebrated Twelve Pin Mountains frowning at you from the other side of the water, and everywhere an utter calm and stillness impossible to describe. Life at Glendalough is curious enough. I would advise all who go there to get themselves posted in the slang of the angler, to learn some of the mysteries of winches and hackles, and, if they do not fish, to pretend at least some familiarity with the art.

The fishermen who come to Glendalough come to fish, to live upon fish, to talk fish, and if they worship anything it must be Dagon the fish god. The fate of a Ministry, the prospects of a country, the merits of a book, the flora of a district, the beauty of a landscape, are to the fishermen of Glendalough mere idle words. You may tempt them with a leading question on any one subject save fish, and, having mildly kicked at it, they return to their beloved theme. Get up at six o'clock in the morning, try to get out of the hall for a walk into the wood, and you will be tripped up by tangles of fishing lines festooned from chair to chair, and wound from hat-stand to door-handle. You will wander through an avenue of landing-nets, and pick your way through a puzzle of baskets. The fishermen eat fish for breakfast, catch fish and cook them for luncheon, consume more fish at dinner, and talk fish steadily until bedtime. There are queer characters, of course, in such a place. One fisherman owns that he has quite lost his head on the subject of salmon. Mountains, woods, and ferns are to him absurdities. He has set his heart on destroying the " wily salmon," and to this object he has devoted his life. He has purchased a horse, he has hired a man; he has been two months at Glendalough; he rises at seven, and departs with his faithful slave to the desolate lakes of this extraordinary country; he returns to the nine o'clock *table d'hôte* with the same old story that he has caught his trout for luncheon, which Man Friday has cooked in the camp-kettle, but that the "wily salmon" has not yet been captured.

The mere tourist is at Glendalough looked down upon with supreme contempt. The man who would come to explore the mountains or bathe in the lake—the woman who, with basket and trowel, would hunt for and find the maidenhair fern and the Mediterranean heath, specimens of which are to be obtained in the Connemara district—are looked upon by the Glendalough fishermen as lunatics. The servants of the establishment are taught to eye the tourist with distrust; and, if you have not pluck enough when alone to shut yourself up in your shell and listen, or to make up a party of sufficient strength to conquer the fishermen at dinner-time, there are hours at Glendalough which may weary you. Breakfast at Glendalough is at eight sharp, and after breakfast the scene at the hotel door is well worth study. The black horse is saddled for the Captain. The faithful "Eliza," whose praises are both written and sung in every page of the visitors' book, and who, luckily for the fishermen, takes upon her shoulders the sole management of Mr. Mullarkey's important inn, has been busy since daybreak packing up luncheon baskets for each of the cars, now ready harnessed at the door; and a dozen sturdy and sun-burnt rustics of the district loll about like the guides at Chamounix, prepared to lead the Captain's horse, to drive the clergyman's car, to guide the pedestrian fishermen to Lough Inagh, or across the mountains to Leenane, or to row the hotel boat to some spot where there are ripples on the lake and the white trout will rise.

It must not be imagined that the Ballinahinch Fishery is open to every one who comes to Connemara with rod and line. A good round sum—half a guinea a day, I believe—is demanded from every rod by the directors of the Company in London which owns this delightful property; and at an early hour every morning the steward of the estate comes to the hotel to post his water bailiffs, and to map out the various lakes for the several anglers. Between the hours of nine and nine—nine o'clock in the morning, when the last fisherman departs, and nine o'clock at night, when the most desperate angler returns—the sunny inn on the blue lake is pleasant enough for snubbed tourists like myself. An authority whose opinion should surely have some weight—Mr. Tom Taylor —deliberately declares in the visitors' book that Glendalough is the very place for "honeymooners." I am not prepared to dispute the fact, and possibly when my turn comes I may fly with her I love to the lake by the mountain brow. Two lovers wandering in the tangle of the Glendalough wood, or rowing on the bosom of the Glendalough lake, would certainly make a pretty picture—such a picture as Mr. Tom Taylor evidently had imagined when he painted it in the pages of the visitors' book. If I wanted perfect rest I would come to Glendalough. If I had a three-volume novel to finish, or were recovering from a nervous complaint caused by living in a first floor in the Strand, or opposite a popular cab-stand; if I had been crossed in love, or had suffered a disappointment which made me hate my fellow-creatures; or if, as now, I desired to enjoy a holiday, I would come to Glendalough.

Morning at Glendalough. We will take the mountain at the back, up the cool wood, through the soft mosses, tracing the course of the mountain stream where the ferns grow, till we get out on to a wild and desolate plain. You look around and see nothing but mountains and marsh land and lakes of every shape and size. The cabin which was to have guided you is lost; the dog who jumped out at you has ceased to bark; and having tramped on without thinking where you were going or how you would get back, you find that you are lost. You make a desperate start, and are cut off by a bog; you scramble over stone walls, and plunge knee-deep in the heather; you disturb the little white mountain sheep, but you appear to be getting no nearer the fern-valley or the pleasant wood. It is ever the same. Mountains everywhere; new lakes, fresh marsh land, stone

ON A CAR THROUGH CONNEMARA.

walls at every turn, and a scent of miles of heather. Patience is at last rewarded. Torn and splashed, stung with midges and horseflies, laden with specimens of fern and heather, with hands and nails ink-black with grubbing in the damp earth, but with an appetite which speaks volumes in favour of Glendalough air, the quiet inn is reached at last. Still not a sound, save the whistling of barefooted Pat Sullivan, who suns himself all day in the boat at the foot of the lawn, and the droning of the bees among the flowers before the window.

Afternoon at Glendalough. The heat becomes intense, almost stopping the energy of Pat Sullivan in the boat, and driving you away, first from the room where you were attempting to write, next from a dream over a pocket Horace on the lawn, afterwards, in consequence of the midges, from the shelter of the trees. There is no one about—not a boat is on the lake; the servants are all dozing in the kitchen. Glendalough is as still as death. A happy thought suggests a scramble down the wood; and then in an instant your clothes are off, and you are swimming over to the fern island in the tepid water of the lake. You neglect the caution of the Royal Humane Society, and remain in the water far beyond the allotted period; for in the water alone you are free from the attacks of insects and from the rays of the burning sun.

Evening at Glendalough. You get Pat Sullivan to stop his interminable whistling and row you about on the lake. The sun is sinking, and the changing shadows on the mountains are not the least of the glories of the delightful day. Mr. Ruskin should be here to describe the colour of the sunset at Glendalough. Mr. C. J. Lewis should attend to paint it with his poetical brush. I saw sunset effects at Glendalough which made me long to enchant hither the artists by whom they would have been so much appreciated. Gradually as we row the sun has vanished behind the hills; the golden glitter on the water has gone out; the little man with the oars is getting weary; for the first time to-day the air is chill, and there are lights in the dining-room windows. The fishermen have returned, and, poor fellows, they must not be kept waiting.

I did not come to Connemara, however, to idle away my time at fishing boxes, but to ride about on cars: and this rash experiment of mine has endangered my chances of ever getting on. I am told in the morning that the public car will pass the cross road at ten o'clock, but I have as much chance of getting a place as I have of catching a salmon. However, nothing venture nothing win; so, when Master Pat Sullivan has ferried me across the lake to the tune of "Savourneen Deelish," in a particularly minor key, I sit upon my portmanteau, by the side of a dusty road, speculating on my hideous fate if the public car is really full. I cannot stand for another day the piscatorial "shop" of Glendalough. I have been lazy long enough. But how am I to get on, with no car to be obtained for love or money, and irritating *impedimenta*? It grows very exciting, and with the aid of a field-glass I look towards the bend of the cross-roads, where the car will presently be seen. Each minute seems an hour. Every cloud of dust makes my heart palpitate like that of Sister Ann in the legend of "Blue Beard." At last the yellow conveyance is seen a good half-mile away, and when my barefooted attendant nudges me, and, with a knowing wink, says, "Bedad, sir, it's full," I feel inclined to stop his whistling for ever.

Round the hill goes the car; now it is in sight, now it is lost again, until the ugly truth of Master Sullivan's statement is confirmed, and my miserable face touches the tender chord in the heart of the good-natured passengers and the sympathetic driver. They make room somehow. Children are taken on to maternal laps; my portmanteau is strapped up somewhere; and, perched on a grateful though rickety seat, I go on my way rejoicing, and commence what turns out to be the most interesting portion of my journey on the car.

Ennis, County Clare.

People are pleased to differ in selecting *the* point of beauty in the Connemara ride; and I must own that they may well pause before making a selection. There are some who will vote for the bleak desolation of the district under Croagh Patrick; many will choose the majestic beauty of Leenane; others will decide for the Killeries; many for the pretty cultivation of Kylemore; and not a few for the bold high land under the Twelve Pins Mountains.

But, for a ride of varied scenery and constantly occurring incident, I record my verdict in favour of the road between the Recess Hotel and the Spanish town of Galway, where we leave the car and take to the train again. This road is to me so interesting, because passing along it no one can fail to notice the gradual change from barren wilds to smiling civilization. As the car rattles along the hard, smooth road, and as hour after hour passes by, the land appears to melt from waste into promise. At ten o'clock you are driving by mud cabins, with the ragged, scarlet-kirtled mother at the door—the inevitable plaid shawl about her shoulders—hunting out her troop of ragged children to run four miles after the car in the hope of earning a penny. At three the cabin is a cottage, with flowers in the window and a crop of corn at the back; and the children stand gazing at the door, too proud a race of little Irish Castilians to beg from any one.

Between the cross roads to Maam and the pretty village of Oughterard I find most begging and beauty. Tourists on the cars encourage the begging by starting a scramble for coppers; and, had it not been for the encouragement of the said tourists, we should not have had pursuing us, for at least a mile and a half, a bonny Irish maid of eighteen, blue-eyed and bare-legged, pretending to offer coarse stockings for sale, but in reality enjoying a scamper with the boys, and ready to fight in the dust with any of them for a penny. From the box-seat of the car you can see the effect of the penny-throwing system. Directly the car is sighted, down from the hills, and away from every field far and near, each cabin contributes to the race its complement of children—lovely children they are, well-fed and nurtured, in many instances stamped with a refinement and delicacy unknown among our lower orders, and capable of running like young greyhounds. Waiting at stiles and under hedgerows, they get well forward at the beginning, make one bound into the road, and do their two or three Irish miles without panting or turning a hair, chatting and pleading all the way.

Their condition is wonderful, and the girls in every race outstrip the boys. There is one face I shall not easily forget; it is that of a little girl—nine years old, I should say—a child with long brown curls, and a pair of soft blue Irish eyes set in a face almost perfect in every feature. Her arms and legs were bare; and if she followed us an inch, the distance she raced must have been two miles and a half. I can see her now, her arms well to her sides, bounding with a wonderful stride over stone-heaps and grass-mounds like a young antelope. She did not beg exactly, but occasionally came near to the car and gave one irresistible look up at the passengers. The little one was an artist.

She knew at once by the motion of a hand when the coppers were coming, and the instant they fell on the road they were swept up by Miss Blue Eyes almost without a change in her stride. That child would make a fortune at Lillie Bridge, and might be matched advantageously against many a good runner, though her condition no doubt depends on the pure mountain air she breathes. I wondered as I drove along where the Connemara men are to be found. In some districts there are apparently no fields to till—at any rate, the men are nowhere to be seen. A few old fellows are dotted about, and boys with worn old-men faces struggle on for a few hundred yards behind the car; but the women and the girls of Connemara appear to enjoy a monopoly of strength and beauty.

I have told you before of the excellent condition of the Connemara mountain roads, and of the bold little Irish horses racing gallantly along from stage to stage with a heavy load of passengers and luggage at their backs. You can best judge of the pace by now and then walking smartly up a steep hill, and attempting to cover some ground before the car overtakes you; but very few such walks are possible. The botanist must make haste in selecting his specimens, the geologist must crack away desperately with his hammer, unless he wishes to be left behind in a wilderness till the next day's car overtakes him. It was during one of these hurried walks, that I came upon a subject for Mr. Israels, the pathetic painter of cottage life. On the very wildest portion of our path I found one of the Highland cottages, and a strange curiosity induced me to peep inside. I cannot hope to describe the desolation of the scene where the hovel stood. There was not a cabin visible for miles around. The familiar pig and family of chickens were absent from this lonely home. A tall blue mountain cast a gloomy shadow on the mud roof, but the door stood open—and, as I have said, curiosity tempted me to look in. I wished to see how the peasants lived and how the peat burned, and to ascertain if the pig really did grunt by the side of the children. Any excuse would do. I had lost my way, or desired a glass of water. With some hesitation I stood on the threshold, and looked into the darkened cabin. It was apparently empty, so I ventured further. Then, for the first time, I saw something covered up with rags in a corner, and suddenly a gaunt woman in black rose up, and lifting up her bare arms, uttered a piercing wail. It was a woman watching over a dead body, and I had disturbed her in her grief. There was no time for explanation or conjecture. The car overtook me, and I was obliged to hurry off, having seen the picture, and nothing more. Who the watcher was, and whom she had lost—how assistance ever came, and where she was to bury her dead, cut off from the world in this desolate land—are questions to which I shall never receive an answer.

It was well, perhaps, that a short time after this

we came upon a smiling landscape; and we were all delighted with a succession of views which reminded me of scene-drops by Mr. Telbin. I always thought before that these theatrical landscapes were due entirely to the imagination of the scenic artist. You know exactly the scenery I mean: in the distance a mountain range, a suspicion of forest, a very blue lake, a meadow here and there, an occasional cottage, and an utter absence of inhabitants. Over and over again I saw Mr. Telbin's scenery on the road from Oughterard to Galway, for here cultivation begins in real earnest.

We see real trees and real houses. We pass gentlemen's country houses and drive down shady lanes, and there is a suggestion of life which tells us that the Connemara car-ride is almost at at end. Westport and Galway are the extreme points, and we are now within a few miles of Galway. Some miles before reaching our Ultima Thule, while still in the region of desolation, a mishap occurs which somewhat interferes with the jollity of our day. It speaks volumes in favour of a trip on an Irish car that ladies are able to drive apparently without fatigue, from half-past eight in the morning until four o'clock in the afternoon, with only an occasional halt of five minutes.

The stage from Clifden to Galway is desperate even for a strong woman; but add to the length of the journey, a burning August sun which refuses to be kept off by any umbrella, and a hunger which time does not allow you to alleviate—and you must not look upon sunstrokes and fainting fits as impossibilities. In point of fact a lady fainted on the car; and an Irish car going at full speed to catch the four o'clock train at Galway is not the most convenient place in the world for such an incident. Providentially, we were provided with a flask of brandy, and a kind Irish doctor—is it not somewhat extraordinary to notice how the converse of the rule about policemen obtains with regard to doctors? Wherever you go, whatever happens, a doctor is sure to be on or very near the spot. It was an awkward predicament.

The driver was bound to catch the train at Galway, and there was not a minute to spare. The patient required a recumbent position, and every seat on the car was occupied. A happy halt to change horses enabled the doctor to improvise a couch; so the fainting lady took the seat, and the passengers, by standing on the foot-board, performed an act of kindness, and kept off the sun. In this fashion we were whirled past still lakes, fringed with waving rushes, reminding the traveller of Mr. Millais's Academy landscape; through a sunny district foretelling the approach of a town; past groups of picturesque peasants in bright costumes, returning from Galway market, who stood affrighted at what appeared to be a pleasure car used for the moment as a temporary hearse. It must have surprised these simple and superstitious peasants to see the poor lady stretched out on the seat, her head supported in her daughter's lap, and anxiety painted on more than one face.

But there is no time to answer questions or reply to the kindly offers of assistance. Galway is reached at last. Round we go by the Moorish archways—over the bridge of the river, where the salmon are caught by anglers from the walls—through as foreign a market-place, both in point of colour and architecture, as I have ever seen—till we reach the station, and, in a hurry to get a sandwich and a seat in the train, are pestered to buy bags of Galway herrings and dozens of those delicious diminutive Irish lobsters, insultingly called prawns in Dublin. Now here is another example of want of enterprise in this strange land. I have already told you how nature does everything for Connemara, and the innkeepers very little—how the public comes, and refuses to be driven away even by discomfort. But would any one have believed that day after day, from May to October, the Connemara car comes into Galway at four o'clock with a load of starving passengers—men, women, and children who may have tasted nothing but dry biscuit since breakfast, and yet the Galway refreshment-room could provide no more promising food than whisky and gingerbread nuts? There was not a sandwich to be had, not even the bread without the meat. In the land of pig there was not a pork-pie. They were not eaten out, but they had never been there. It had never struck any human being in Galway to provide nourishment for starving tourists. "But are you never asked for sandwiches? Are they not often applied for? Does not the car frequently arrive close upon four, giving no time for a visit to the hotel?" "Shure, and it does." "But why then not fill the refreshment-room with appetizing things?" "Bedad, I don't know." This is the only answer you ever get—an answer given with a delightful smile which makes one ashamed of a little temper increased by the sharp pangs of hunger.

A feverish desire to press forward urged me from Galway in the hope of reaching Cork somehow or other. My through ticket booked me to Athenry, and once there I found myself in a hornets' nest. There is a short line from Athenry to Ennis owned by another company, and the system at Athenry is to know nothing. The train starts from the opposite platform, but nobody knows anything. They hardly know of the existence of Ennis, while Limerick and Cork are difficulties with which they do not attempt to grapple. Vigorous language, however, carries me on, and I find myself, on a lovely evening, at Ennis. But there are reasons not unconnected with considerations of personal comfort why I cannot remain at Ennis. I have done Connemara on a car; and now I will do the County Clare on the same vehicle. To-morrow I will make a pilgrimage to the sea. By hook or by crook I will smell the Atlantic in the morning, and inhale the sea breezes at the Cliffs of Moher.

BESIDE THE "MELANCHOLY OCEAN."

Atlantic Hotel, Miltown Malbay, August 17.

I HAVE arrived at the sea at last. I am writing in an old rambling inn situated at the very edge of the County Clare. I bathed not two hours ago in the Atlantic Ocean, and the next parish is America. We have rocks here, and caves; we have miles of grass cliff; we have a mighty expanse of sea, and not a ship to be seen on it; we have sands, and children who dig all day, and sprain their ankles by jumping from rock to rock in search of crabs and anemones; and we have pretty girls who play croquet on the huge semicircular grass plat in front of this long white hotel by the sea, who twine their arms about one another's waists, and race and romp among the hay, apparently intoxicated with ozone. But it must not be imagined that I have pitched my tent in a modern hotel at a fashionable watering-place. We are miles and miles away from a railway. We are sixteen miles distant from anywhere, and it is only by means of a jaunting car and a good horse that I shall ever get on again southward to the Killarney district where I am due by-and-by. The long, huge-roomed, wind-swept, sea-kissed inn at which I have arrived, and where I am extremely comfortable, is unlike any hostelry I have ever come across; and though my worthy host, and his fair daughter, and his estimable son-in-law tell me heart-rending tales of the utter desolation and misery of the place in winter, of the Atlantic waves which wash over the house, whose traces are still to be seen upon the walls and passages—though these good folk naturally, no doubt, long for the time when the railway will come within a mile—I would not have one room of the Atlantic Hotel altered, or one modern villa introduced to ruin the character of a "village on the cliff" which would delight the heart and inspire the pen of Miss Thackeray.

The town of Miltown Malbay is two miles distant from this place, and possesses some clean, prosperous-looking houses and a handsome cruciform church, the interior of which presented an extremely picturesque sight on the sunny Tuesday morning dedicated to the Feast of the Assumption, when the peasants attended early mass in such numbers that the nave and aisles of the church would not hold them, and the surplus crowd was compelled to kneel outside against the walls, and in the long cool grass among the graves. The Atlantic Hotel—such a name ought to make the fortune of an inn—is built within a foot or so of the sea. If you are in a ground-floor bedroom you can hear the waves rolling up to the wall just under your window; and in the morning you have nothing to do but open a back door and take a header off the rocks, making the same use of your inn as you would of a bathing machine. The visitors who come to the Atlantic come purely for health and fresh air, and not to show off their new boots and Dolly Varden dresses. We do not dress here a dozen times a day; but we eat an enormous breakfast, then go down to the shore, and sit upon a huge projection of slate rock, where the pleasant summer sea, sleepy and oily under the burning sun, is irritated by the jags and spars and splinters of the rocks, and boils up into fury.

When weary of this, we wander on to the grass cliff, where they are making hay in August—so cruel has been the rain this summer; and we rest in a field which is said to be the burying-place of many a body that came to invade Ireland in a Spanish Armada, and was tossed ashore on the very slate rocks which keep irritating the waveless sea. Restless again, we watch a family of pretty children, boys and girls, paddling about the rocks, naked to the knee, and flinging great pebbles into the water, to the huge delight of a black retriever, who is never weary of plunging after stones which he knows he will not find, apparently for the sole purpose of turning his tail indignantly to every wave which comes rolling in and threatens to stop Neptune's progress.

Or another wandering fit comes over us, and we take a boat and row over to Mutton Island, where we fish and chat and read and smoke and dream again; till, before we are aware of it, the travellers have returned from a car-drive to the celebrated sulphur and iron springs of Lisdoonvarna. This is a place some sixteen miles off, where accommodation, according to all accounts, is remarkably limited, but where such extraordinary cures have lately been effected, that the Irish medical profession keeps on sending patient after patient to Lisdoonvarna; which, however, does not consider that the time has come to build hotels and provide amusements and offer dainty lodgings to the affected and the hypochondriacal who love spas, and who, for the sake of the twin-springs of sulphur and iron issuing from the rocks side by side at Lisdoonvarna, threaten eventually to take the place by storm. We change our dresses for dinner at the Atlantic, because it is cool and refreshing so to do; and we are only interrupted in our ante-prandial game at croquet on the lawn, with the pretty girls in white muslin, by a cry of "A ship in full sail!" which excites the Atlantic Hotel as much as would the appearance of the Channel Fleet, and, luckily for us, directs our attention westward, where we behold a superb sunset, and see the ship in full sail bathed in a glory of red and purple and gold. Dinner at the Atlantic is wisely postponed until after the sun has gone down, and the air is chill. We shut out the day with regret, and light the moderator lamps; and as in our long dinner-room the floor is uncarpeted, as there is a piano and a player in the room, as the day after dinner is yet young, and as our spirits are irrepressible, why—we dance until midnight, and persuade the servants to wind up with a regular Irish jig.

But perhaps you will wonder how I ever managed to find my way to the sea at all, buried, as I was, in Ennis, and apparently destined to mope and groan in an uninviting town, half-starved and out of temper. I had not known until I inquired, the immense advantage of the Irish car system. Wherever you are in Ireland, in town or village, in desolate regions or thickly-populated districts, you can always get a car —a mail-car possibly, but a private car certainly— for next to nothing. The cars are firm enough; they will carry any amount of luggage; the horses, though not pretty to look at, are "good 'uns to go;" and the charge for the accommodation is sixpence a mile, with a "pour-boire" for the driver. One horse thinks nothing of twenty Irish miles (about twenty-four English); and if you wish to go further you can be passed on by another car at any stage. This information had to be wormed out gradually at Ennis; where a traveller is a god-send, and I discovered a mysterious freemasonry between car-drivers and inn-keepers. With a sigh of relief, however, I saw the luggage eventually packed up, and in a few minutes more the head of the Irish horse was turned seaward. There is not much interest in the County Clare as far as Inistymon, except the important fact that hereabouts the male peasants dress like Mr. Falconer in the play. Ever since I came to Ireland I have been longing to see the conventional costume, the felt hat, the tail coat with lappet pockets, the corduroy knee-breeches, and the blue worsted stockings—in a word, the stage Irishman. The Dublin car-drivers are certainly like Mr. Boucicault in the "Colleen Bawn;" but I wanted to see Mr. Falconer dressed for "Innisfallen" and "Eileen Oge." I did not find him either in Dublin or in the Connemara district; but directly I came to County Clare, there he was to the life, though without the shillelagh—for he does not take this useful "property" out for a walk with him. Inistymon was asleep, for the sun was so hot that it threatened to melt the caravan of waxworks which broiled in the market-place. Mrs. Jarley was nowhere to be seen, and I suppose that Little Nell was picking buttercups and purple foxgloves in the meadows. Lahinch, the first seaside village we came to, suffered so much from drunkenness and dirt that the good-natured horse agreed to tug the car up the hill towards Hag's Head Promontory and the grandly awful Cliffs of Moher.

Before the car turned in at the lodge gates of Birchfield House, lately owned by Mr. O'Brien— who appears to have been a king in this part of the country, and for whom the driver assured me that the lads would willingly have died on account of his good deeds—the cars laden with villagers, the groups of pedestrians, the waggons crowded with women and children wending their way up the hill, persuaded me that something unusual was going on. It was a pilgrimage to St. Bridget's Well, and for miles and miles away the peasants were coming to "do their rounds" at the holy fountain on Mr. O'Brien's estate. The village belief is, that this loved master of theirs, when threatened with blindness, was cured by prayer and an application of water from the well. At any rate, Mr. O'Brien planted the cave round with flowers and shrubs, and erected stone crosses and little altars in the grounds; and there he and his family lie buried, within a stone's-throw of the mysterious fountain. It is not necessary to go as far as Ober-Ammergau or travel on the Continent, to visit Spain or spend an Easter in Rome, if one would behold the fervid devotion of the peasantry.

The scene at that fountain of St. Bridget, on the road to the Cliffs of Moher, I shall never forget. The pictures were of surpassing interest. You turn off from the roadway by steps into the sacred grove where the water-cave will be found; and having passed by a rude stone bench, on which rest rows of dusty shoes and stockings, you come upon a still pool, to which the peasants descend to wash their feet before commencing their devotions. I could hardly believe that I was on soil which England owns. There was an Eastern glamour about the scene. The burning, intense sun, the gorgeous colours of the peasant costumes, the washing of the feet in the pool formed by an overflow from the well, and thus, according to the peasantry, possessing some mysterious properties; the fervent prayers, as men and women on their knees prostrated themselves on their way up the grass to the stone cross at the top of the hill; the simplicity with which, with eyes downcast and hands clasped in prayer, they went round and round the cross, kissing it at every turn; the meekness with which they entered the cave, still on their knees, and went up to receive the tin of water from the hands of an aged and wrinkled woman at the well; the evident belief and the unquestionable power of the devotion—were these sights seen and these things done in a part of the British dominions, in the nineteenth century, by a people bound to us for evil or for good? They were seen by my eyes in the County Clare, and they may be seen a dozen times a year by any one who cares to visit Ireland.

I spoke just now merely of peasants—poor creatures with sore eyes and wounded limbs, the halt, the maimed, and the blind, the deformed, and the grievously sick—who found their way to St. Bridget's Well, and who, having stowed away their shoes and stockings under the stone bench, washed the dust from their feet, and commenced their devotions before drinking the water. There were scores of peasants, it is true, but those who were not peasants visited the well, and washed their feet in the pool by the side of the humblest. Well-dressed young women, girls in fashionable bonnets and white piqué dresses, with clean white petticoats and high-heeled boots, by no manner of means distressing to look at, sat on the stone bench and made bare their legs and feet, going down to the pool like the rest, and doing their ablution preparatory to prayer. Whatever may be said about the superstition that inspired the ceremony, the earnestness and the intention of those who took part in it were most unmistakable, and lifted the performance into a pathetic dignity.

I cannot say if all these simple people really thought that the actual water would cure diseases, as manifold as they are puzzling to science. It may be that they were content with putting up the prayer for relief of their own and their friends' distresses. I merely give the picture, and let others interpret it. But before I leave it, I should much like to declare with how much humility, with how little affectation, with what complete absence of any trace of consciousness or Phariseeism, the whole ceremony was carried out from end to end. The last scene I saw was, even from the colour point of view alone, well worth studying. I had returned from a visit to the O'Brien grave, and stood at the back of the cross, looking down the grass hill upon the grove in which the well stands. The sun was in its full glory, and streamed down the slope of intense green upon the face of a grey-haired old woman commencing her journey on her knees. A scarlet handkerchief was folded round her head, and her dress was of bright colours, beautifully blended. She was pressing a crucifix to her heart, looking with intense rapture on the cross, and evidently praying from the very bottom of her heart.

Altogether, the scene at the well was curious, indescribable, and not without its impressiveness.

The Mr. O'Brien whose praises the villagers are never tired of singing had—unlike a certain landlord who, owning property on the Dover Heights, implores the public to walk "as near the edge of the cliff as possible"—railed round and flagged and walled in the dizzy heights of Moher, which fairly equal in grandeur and awe-inspiring effect the boldest part of the Cornish coast. You look down sheer into the sea a giddy distance of 650 feet, listening to the shriek of the innumerable sea-birds—now resting on the bosom of the blue-green water, now fluttering like butterflies, to their nests in the fissures of the perpendicular and awful cliff.

Away in the far distance, on one side, you can see the Twelve Pins Mountains, which were so near to me a day or so ago; and in front, with a good glass, you can pick out the lighthouse, and an occasional cottage on the melancholy islands of Arran—where, by-the-bye, they manufacture excellent potheen, a liquor by no means to be despised. And now would you hear the true story of the goat, on an unapproachable rock among the Cliffs of Moher? Some years ago an adventurous spirit, with the aid of a rope, lowered from the cliff down to a grass-grown projection of rock a harmless goat, who has lived there in peace, and still lives to this very day. A little boy was very anxious to show me this lion of Moher; so at last, after a

D

diligent scrutiny, we detected the long-bearded old gentleman behind a stone which protects him from the wind, and there he makes his bed. Human hand can never reach the wretched animal now. But he seems fat and jolly enough, feeding on the grass with which he is well provided, and scampering about on the dangerous rock promontory. For seven years, at any rate, he has braved summer sun and winter storm; and when I saw him rise and shake himself after his nap he did not appear to have the smallest intention of committing suicide, or of being gathered to his fathers just yet. I grieve, however, to remark that he is a villain, this goat of the Cliff of Moher. He is a murderer, I am ashamed to say. One day some one with a tender heart, pitying his loneliness, let down a Nanny goat to cheer him in his solitude. But the cruel brute lost his temper, and resisted the interference. He put down his head, gave a butt forward, and hurled poor Nanny into the depths below! I have left few places with so much regret as the grass height above the Cliffs of Moher, where, however burning the sun, there are pleasant breezes coming across the sea, and where the lapping of water against the cliffs, the roar of a wave rushing into one of the caverns at the foot of the rock, and the shriek of the sea-fowl form a wild and not unpleasant discord.

But we had to get on to Miltown Malbay, and to ask for a lodging at the Atlantic Hotel; so I put the car once more in requisition, and made speed thitherward, listening to more anecdotes from Pat, the driver, about Mr. O'Brien—all delivered in that peculiar melancholy tone which I find among the humbler orders here. One particular story related to the Birchfield Races, got up by Mr. O'Brien to amuse his tenantry, when he organized a special police force out of his own dependents, and made a Spartan law against drunkenness and whisky. Every drunken man was immediately tied up with whipcord, by friends or relatives, and thrown like a beast into a field, there to lie until he was sober. This summary punishment for drunkenness tickled my driver immensely, and he almost forgot his melancholy so far as to give a grim chuckle. How I escaped sunstroke during that long journey to Miltown Malbay I know not; for I had never felt such heat. However, Pat kept his promise of rapid work; and the first signs of civilization—the muslin dresses on the croquet lawn—did not make me indisposed to cheerful anticipations from my visit to the Hotel "contiguous to the melancholy Ocean."

A PILGRIMAGE TO BLARNEY.

Cork.

I HOPE some day, when such a blessing as the telegraph is looked upon as an antiquated invention, that a genius will be found to give us a means for instantaneously registering our travelling impressions, and sending them home fresh as they come upon us. In the hurry and bustle of scampering from one place to another, much must be forgotten and much more omitted; for beauty caps beauty, and one superb scene is obliterated by another. In a long car-drive, for instance, when a succession of delightful pictures passes before your eyes during a forty-mile journey, how pleasant it would be to stop occasionally at a telegraph post on the road, and breathe home a description of the last half-hour!

I am now compelled to compress into a short space scenes and impressions which deserve a little volume. You last heard from me when I was dreaming about the rocks on the coast of the County Clare, and looking across the Atlantic Ocean. What have I done since then? I have travelled up the Shannon—a glorious river—in a pig-boat, and had an opportunity of a study of the physiognomy of the clean white Irish porker, which would not have been lost on Mr. Britton Riviere. I must own, however, that the fun of the embarkation of 300 pigs at Tarbert—when a third of them, instead of coming on board, "rushed down a steep place into the sea," and swam about so contentedly in the harbour, that I am shaken in my belief about the suicidal action of the swimming pig; to say nothing of another third, which made an obstinate rush in a different direction, and ran off for the Irish mountains, pursued by a little army of shrieking drovers—was certainly counteracted by the noise and the smell of the companions of Ulysses, as they lay huddled together fighting, biting, snarling, and snorting in the fore-part of the steamer Rosa.

I have bought lace at Limerick, and seen the fine young oarsmen of that gifted town practising for the silver cup given at the Glenbrook Regatta. I have heard the bells of Shandon, and marvelled how Father Prout could have been inspired by an old church tower in a dirty street, when I, and I dare say thousands more who admire the good priest's most musical lyric, had imagined that Shandon steeple would be found nestling in the woods which so much adorn that poetical and perfect river—the river Lee. I have taken a car, and, after a drive through the lovely scenery which creeps up to the city of Cork and hedges it in—north, south, east, and west—I have kissed the Blarney Stone, and wandered all by myself, not dogged by tourists, or pestered with guides, through the shady groves of

Blarney. I have enjoyed a Turkish bath in the grounds of a fairy colony which will be found among the woods on St. Ann's hill. I have sailed upon the "silver Lee," past the palaces and villas of the Cork merchants, past the summer hotels, and baths and pleasure-houses of a city by the sea, down to Queenstown, capable of accommodating the whole Channel Fleet in her noble harbour—a spot daily watered with the tears of Irish emigrants, daily blessed by travellers at the end of their journey, and wanderers come home at last.

I have seen a worthy officer despatch a tug full of emigrants, with their beds and their bundles, their tin pots and frying-pans, dry-eyed, and apparently very jolly, as they were bound to be, having the good luck to be booked to America by a vessel which has advantages of its own, and a crew to boot so jovial and full of anecdote, that I confess I was tempted to forget all about my enjoyments, and to secrete myself in some sly corner until the good ship had got well out to sea. In the company of two sharp Cork detectives, I have examined this emigrant vessel, from bowsprit to rudder, peeped into cabins, dived into the hold, surveyed the first-class passengers, chaffed the steerage folks, rummaged among the coals and behind the boxes, in the hope of unearthing a certain young gentleman who was "wanted" for being too intimately connected with the contents of a certain till—but who, despite the vigilance of the Cork detectives, got off safely to America, if he happened to be on board the vessel after all. I have seen Haulbowline and its storehouses; and I have been rowed across to Spike Island, where the convicts may be seen dragging blocks of stone up the steep incline to the prison, where they appear to be kept according to an admirable system, and where their sad punishment is tempered with as much kindness and consideration, as can be shown without interfering with the strict letter of the law.

The good city of Cork is in the very heart of lovely scenery, and the head-quarters for excursions, which should never be neglected by travellers bound for Killarney. Cork, in fact, for travellers, means Imperial Hotel, and Imperial Hotel means here good management. An enterprising gentleman whose name is sufficiently well-known on both sides of the Atlantic, by some wonderful tact which he possesses enables travellers to or from America to make a rush while the steamer is at Queenstown, and "do" Blarney and the Cork scenery before the vessel is off again; who, by such luxuries as a ladies' drawing-room, with piano, periodicals, and bouquets of flowers, delights the fair sex; and by a sly passage from the hotel into the Cork Commercial Rooms, where the latest telegraphic news is recorded, and every newspaper in the kingdom is found, makes the Imperial, so far as men are concerned, at once an hotel, a club, and a place of business. I think it was Judge Haliburton who summed up Cork in the following pointed fashion: " If you are an admirer of beautiful scenery, go to the Cove of Cork; if you want a good hotel, go to the Imperial; if you want good tobacco, go to the smoking-room there. I may add, also, you may find more than good pipes and cigars; for you will meet with a vast deal of amusement, as some droll fellows do congregate there." Sam Slick was perfectly right.

The Imperial is a feature well known to tourists and business men; and here, in my onslaught on Irish want of enterprise, I am fairly disarmed. Put yourself into the hands of the manager in the morning, and he will map you out a jolly day enough; and when the gong sounds for the *table d'hôte*, at half-past six, it will be your own fault if you do not spend a merry evening—first at the dinner-table, in the noble concert-room, enjoying the society of refined women passing to or from Killarney, or possibly on their way to America; afterwards in the drawing-room among the books and at the piano; and, before retiring, in the cosmopolitan smoking-room, where Irish wits, officers quartered in Cork, travellers, tourists, townsmen, and good fellows open out, and, with anecdote and experience, postpone until unholy hours a visit to the comfortable Cork beds.

I have already hinted my disappointment at not finding Shandon steeple, situated in a picturesque spot on the river Lee. Certain theories in connexion with the Blarney Stone were also in due time driven to the winds. Some one surely had told me that to kiss the Blarney Stone it was necessary to mount the rickety staircase of a ruined tower, and, having attained the top, to be held out from a window in an ignominious and dangerous position by the heels. I think I remember a tragic paragraph which went the round of the papers, and told us all how Mr. Sothern saved Mr. Toole, or Mr. Toole rescued Mr. Addison, when, by some hideous mischance, the side-spring boot of one of these favourite comedians came off in the hands of a luckless guide, during the osculatory process in connexion with the Blarney Stone.

I nerved myself accordingly for the encounter. For the sake of the privilege of kissing any lips which have not come in contact with the stone, and of acquiring a certain bold and chivalric manner which, I am led to believe, is not altogether distasteful to pretty girls, I was prepared to be held over any giddy height by my hair or my heels. Merely using the precaution of wearing lace-ups instead of side-springs, I made my will, wrote out farewell instructions, and took a car to Blarney. But judge of my surprise when, instead of being led to a giddy height, a cellar door was opened by "a nurse of ninety years," and, among old ladders and scaffolding, pickaxes and shovels, I was shown a lump of stone-cornice lying neglected in a heap of rubbish. Severely the old lady looked upon me, and ordered me on my knees to kiss the stone.

I protested. I doubted her story. I implored to be taken upstairs. I asked about the head and heels anecdote. I demanded if there was not another stone, some rock above, which should be kissed, instead of the uninviting lump. She looked upon me with supreme contempt. She asked me scornfully if I did not know that the Blarney Stone had fallen down from the tower—its constitution undermined, I expect, by the immorality of its life.

When, the romance quite knocked out of me, I shirked the three kisses for myself and the three proxy kisses for any friend at home, who might be desirous of the blessings attendant on the ceremony, the dame waxed wroth. Slamming the tower door, she placed her back against it, and vowed vengeance against me if I were heretical enough to disbelieve the virtues of the stone-cornice, or sufficiently impious to leave Blarney without one kiss. Thus threatened, I obeyed; and from this moment let the "merry maids of England" beware. I am now a privileged person, and I have every intention of exercising my privileges. Of the wild legends about the Blarney neighbourhood there appears to be no end. A communicative car-driver was anxious to impress on my mind the wonderful virtue of the water of the Holy Lake; a stream which, according to my friend, is visited by wealthy landed proprietors who are not blessed with any offspring. I hesitate to record in detail the particular instance which he adduced; but the story, as told by Pat with all its minutiæ, would exactly suit the doggrel poets who provide for the music-halls, the ballads so deservedly execrated.

Wandering among the woods fresh painted with green by the heavy rains, which found me out at Cork, and seem to be playing away during the waits between the acts of summer weather, I came across the happy family which dwells on St. Ann's-hill. When I was a child they used to tell me a romantic legend about a lonely traveller who, wandering through a wood, suddenly came upon an enchanted marble palace, surrounded by rose gardens, within whose walls he found singing and dancing and perpetual delight. In a certain sense this childish dream was realized in the Blarney neighbourhood. There was once upon a time a certain Dr. Barter, who, with Mr. David Urquhart, first started the Turkish Baths which proved to be such a wonderful blessing to many of us. Up among the trees on St. Ann's-hill, in a warm and sheltered spot, Dr. Barter, at immense expense, built a Turkish Bath on the best and most elaborate principle, marble within and without, decorated with coloured lounges, festooned with polychromed hangings, adorned with tapestry and needlework; a bath with painted windows, throwing rays of colours on the marble; a bath which would tempt you to the "sudarium" if you were in perfect health and in thorough exercise. This was the marble palace that I discovered in the wood; and I was not long in ascertaining that Dr. Barter's bath is the centre of a village *ornée*, built in a luxurious flower-garden. It is called a "hydropathic establishment;" but this long-sounding title gives no idea of the pretty colony of St. Ann's. Wherever I turned I met a rose-covered cottage, or a summer-house; the "establishment" is built on the terraces of a hill, and I cannot imagine a more delightful spot for the nervous or hard-worked.

A large farm is attached, which supplies meat, butter, eggs, and everything that can be desired in the way of eatables. There is a croquet lawn for the ladies, a library and reading-rooms provided with every paper and periodical. Cars and carriages, saddle-horses and driving-horses, can be sent round to the door after five minutes' notice. And then, for the robust in health, there is a river full of trout and salmon, a pack of hounds or so meeting in the immediate neighbourhood in the winter, and several billiard and bagatelle tables. What more can man or woman desire, save a post-office, and the use of the telegraph wire? There they are, then, in a Swiss cottage at the entrance to the wood. The object of the establishment is to restore health and to promote cheerfulness and good temper. I am told the society at St. Ann's is most charming, and seeing as I did pretty girls playing croquet on the lawn, children romping at the swing, old gentlemen smoking under the trees, Indian officers finishing a game at billiards, a party starting for a ride, Sybarites dozing over a cup of coffee and cigarette, the bath just over, flirtations in the wood, anglers setting out to fish —and peeping as I did into Dr. Barter's cabinet of curiosities, a cottage all low lounge and bow window, all corner and easy chair, a miniature temple adorned with china and knickknacks, and dedicated to the studious—it was with regret I turned my back on the enchanted palace, and denied myself the pleasure of accepting an invitation and enjoying the society at St. Ann's.

ON THE ROAD TO KILLARNEY.

Glengariff.

THACKERAY, when asked which was really the most beautiful of several Irish lakes, summed up the matter in the following admirable fashion: "When at the smaller lake, we agreed that it was more beautiful than the large one; then when we came back, we said, 'No! the large lake is the more beautiful;' and so, at every point we stopped, we determined that that particular spot was the prettiest in the whole lake. The fact is, and I don't care to own it, *they are too handsome.* As for a man coming from his desk in London, or Dublin, and seeing 'the whole lake in a day,' he is an ass for his pains. A child doing a sum in addition, might as well read the whole multiplication table, and fancy he had it by heart."

I am at this moment precisely in the position of the author of the "Irish Sketch Book." By some lucky chance, I have proceeded from charm to beauty, and whenever I have made any comparisons the new love has had a considerable advantage over the old. Wearied with a week in Dublin, and still clogged with the London dust, I thought that nothing could exceed the beauty of Powerscourt and the Dargle. Driving through Connemara, and resting at Glandalough, I declared emphatically that no scenery could surpass that on which my eye rested.

But then I had not driven from Macroon to Glengariff, through the wild and striking pass of Cuminer, with its two walls of rugged rock and its mountain torrent leaping down into the valley. I had not skirted the bright blue Bay of Bantry, with its mountains, its white-sailed fishing boats, and its smell of sea breezes coming up to you sweetened, after passing over acres of yellow gorse and purple heather; and I had not discovered Glengariff, my last new love, for whose dear sake I throw over Glandalough and all the lovely spots I have seen— so charming is its situation, so peaceful its seclusion, and so primitive its life.

I shall not in the guide-book fashion tell you about the position of Mrs. Eccles's hotel, right on the sea, and with a view of innumerable islands, castles, and mountains; or of its immediate proximity to Lord Bantry's Cottage in the wood, which can be reached only by passing rushing salmon streams, over rustic bridges, and by making acquaintance with innumerable waterfalls. At Glengariff you are reminded of Oban and Bettwsycoed; you get a bit of Windermere from the front window, and a scrap of Lynton on your way to church. At Glengariff we do not grow ordinary hips and haws in our hedges; we soar far above the dignity of wild honeysuckle and dog roses. Our hedgerows here are made of fuchsia, and the bushes of blue hydrangeas are as common as privet.

At Glengariff we rise at half-past three in the morning to catch bream behind the islands, commanded so to do by a black-eyed fisher lad, who is on confidential terms with the boots of the inn, and, having discovered our sleeping room, keeps on flinging gravel up at the window, which comes in at the top, hits us on the nose, and finally induces us to believe there is a greater charm in bream than in bed.

We bathe at eight, when the bream refuse to bite, or we are tired of hauling any more of them into the boat; and all day long we "potter" about the sea, enjoying a sunny lotos-eater dream, and pretending to catch mackerel from the stern. Meanwhile the promising model for Mr. J. C. Hook, R.A., sculls us about from point to point, and prevents us from dozing, with ludicrous ancedotes about the miseries of the last German waiter at the little Inn, who was set upon and half murdered by the "lads of the village," because he obstinately refused to espouse the cause of the French. In the evening, when the sun has gone down, the fishermen and villagers, sit and smoke on the low wall opposite the inn door, and after a little persuasion the only fiddler in all Glengariff takes his chair under a tree, a friend lights up the scene with a guttering tallow candle, and the cook and the baker, the celebrated "Richard," boots at the hotel, boat-owner, land proprietor, and possessor of no fewer than two hundred sweethearts—I have this on the authority of black-eyed Johnnie, who is the Quasimodo to this fascinating Frollo—with one of the girls of Glengariff, the fisher lads with the chambermaids, "take the floor," and such a jig commences in the dusty road, with such steps, such time, and such inimitable grace, that I long for the assistance of the lungs of a Strand gallery, to cheer on the dancers and keep them at it till they drop.

This praise of Glengariff is the most disinterested thing I have ever done, and I tremble to think of the accumulated wrath which will be poured on my unfortunate head when I disclose the great secret of the Killarney tour. I say disinterested, because, of course, I shall go to Glengariff again, and I do not wish one stick or stone of the place altered. I should like it to remain as it now is. I fear much wrath, because the beauty of Glengariff is not sufficiently known, and at this moment the secret is in the possession of a few. The guide-books merely mention it casually. Tourists think of the twice forty-two miles of car-driving, and rattle round to Killarney by rail.

Neither guide-books nor tourists have yet ascertained the fact that a forty-two mile car-drive, in the admirable cars provided on this route, through this delicious air, with scenery changing at every turn, with halts for luncheon on the road, with opportunities for taking short cuts, and for a dozen miles walk if you choose, is far less fatiguing—I have canvassed the ladies, and obtained their unanimous opinion on this point—than a half-day journey by rail. There is a social charm connected with a car-drive appreciated by all but the utterly selfish; and there is a brisk health-giving tone acquired by the journey, which, according to my view, is simply invaluable. When I am met with the objection, "Oh! but it takes two days on the road, and nothing is finer than Killarney;" I can only answer, "Have you walked up the Pass of Cuminer? Have you taken advantage of the halt at Guoganebarra, to see the lovely mountain lake, where on an island is the hermitage in which lived St. Fionn Barr? Have you seen the Bay of Bantry from the Glengariff road? If not, pray do not say you have seen Ireland's beauties." But there I have let the cat out of the bag. The Oxford and Cambridge reading parties will, I trust, no longer keep Glengariff all to themselves. Mrs. Roche will be compelled to make her beautiful Inn as elastic as on the celebrated night, when Mr. Cook brought round a large party of American knights, to see Ireland with "all the effects turned on." Mrs. Eccles must add another wing to her pretty house, which will always be popular as a private box from which Glengariff life is seen; and the car proprietor must be prepared for any emergency, and when one car is full at a stage, send on another. The best feather which can be stuck in the cap of Glengariff is the simple truth, that tourists on the orthodox round, are constantly known to remain here a fortnight, where they had originally intended to rest a night.

The same incidents occur on the Glengariff car road as in Connemara, with this exception—in

County Cork begging on the road is made an art, in Connemara it is mainly a matter of fun. You can at once detect the difference in civilization. The Connemara children had no notion of doing anything but run with the car and beg. The Cork girls and boys make up fanciful bouquets of wild flowers; they pelt the travellers with posies, and slyly pitch a water-lily, or some heather, into a lady's lap, after the fashion of the flower-girls in Milan. But besides these pretty tricks, they make more ghastly appeals to public sympathy. Unfortunate boys with twisted legs and deformed limbs, scramble up the hill on crutches with painful eagerness; blind men led by pretty girls come shuffling after the car. Each artifice meets with its reward. The flower-girls get pence, the blind men sixpences, and the cripples shillings; and during the tourist season you may be sure the schoolmaster has hard work to get his scholars together, for when money comes in so fast there is a disinclination on the part of parents to teach their children that begging is not a very edifying trade. The nearer you get to Killarney the worse the begging becomes; and though I own, when the children are pretty and fascinating, plucky and active, it is extremely difficult to practise what you preach, it is heartily to be wished that tourists would cease to encourage the trade of begging— which is interesting no doubt, but becomes in time an abominable nuisance.

We have been favoured lately with the most extraordinary freaks of weather. On alternate days, we smile and growl. A scorching August sun one day, bronzing your neck and taking the skin off your unfortunate nose; the next day bitter cold, a violent wind, and every mountain covered with a veil of cloud and drenching mist. When I drove to Glengariff through a wild flower garden, forty-two miles long, the colours of land and sea were so perfect, the heat was so grateful, the bees and dragon-flies were enjoying such races over the hills, that we could scarcely believe it would ever rain again. Just as by the side of a winter fire you cannot think of "ornaments for your fire stoves" without a shudder, so in the sun, you laugh at the storm and rain. When the fiddler had done, and the jig was over, I went out on the water before going to bed.

A perfect night. The rudder-course was marked by a phosphorescent streak. As the oar dipped it made a sparkle in the water; and if you plunged your hand in the sea, the wavelets glittered over your fingers like diamonds. But change the scene to the middle of the night: the windows rattle against the rickety frames, and almost drive you mad with the irritating noise; the window-blind, which had been left half up, finds its way out at the top, and flaps dismally, like a torn sail; a tempest of rain lashes every pane, and the wind comes down from the mountains, and shrieks round the house. The sea, so calm an hour or so ago, is maddened. Change the scene again to the morning: the mountains have disappeared; the roadway is strewed with blossoms from the fuchsia hedge, and bunches of scarlet berry from the mountain ash. Up higher in the village, at midday, is a scene which I had imagined only occurred in novels or on the stage.

The rain is still beating pitilessly into the valley; the streams from the mountains are swollen, and sweep down the fern and the grass as they roar over the boulders on their way to the sea; the villagers are huddling under walls, and under hedges, outside the rude chapel at the cross-roads. It is surely late for mass at this hour? It is; but you must remember the priest has to ride sixteen miles across the mountains, and it is the custom for the congregation to wait for their pastor outside the chapel-door. You cannot see many hundred yards up the mountain-road, because of the blinding mist; but at last a tall figure, on a black horse, is recognised. This is the signal for a rush forward. Half a dozen villagers go to the horse's head, and every one seems anxious for a word with, or a blessing from, the good man as he makes his way to the chapel-door. He is wet through to the skin, yet there is no time for a change before mass; still I hope some hospitable farmer has a cut of the joint, and a glass of punch, ready for the Father when service is over, for nothing has passed between his lips this morning. Once more, please, change the scene. In an instant a broad blue patch of sky tells us, that we shall get our walk after all. Every mountain is unveiled. The scene is set as in the first act, when I drove into Glengariff. The fern-lanes, on the road to Lord Bantry's cottage, are like a hothouse; and the effects of sunlight seen through the openings of dripping leaves, fully make up for a disturbed night and a soaked jacket.

Have I left anything unnoted which will tempt the holiday-maker to take the Glengariff road, when he travels towards Killarney? Nothing, I think, but the originality of the Inn-life at Glengariff. There is nothing "stuck-up," or modern, about the Bantry Bay Hotel. Every one talks to every one else. The fisher boys loll about the door, and chaff the visitors. The visitors wander in and out, from one room to the other, chatting to the hostess and her sister; and Richard, the idol of the village, and the witty Sam Weller of the establishment, is quite a feature in Glengariff society. I have told you of Richard's fascination, and his Mormonite wealth of sweethearts; but I have not told you that besides owning vessels, running races with the village boys, joining in their amusements, and making himself popular, he is reported to have a ready wit. It is whispered that once upon a time, when some swell London footmen were located for a season at the Inn by the sea, Richard, with a very grave face, offered to instruct John and Jeames in the art of rowing, and sent them finally across the bay—to a chorus of laughter from the lads—with the blades of the oars in their hands, and the handles wildly knocking about the waves. Further, it is recorded in the Glengariff jest book, that when a stupid vulgar millionnaire put up at the simple seaside-inn, and made a ridiculous fuss about the absence of grouse for dinner, Richard with a sly twinkle, protested that they were in the room. "Where are the grouse, sir?" said Locuples, indignantly. "There, sir," replied Richard, pointing to a case of stuffed birds, which may be seen over the sideboard of the Glengariff Inn. The lover of game made no more complaints at Glengariff. But let me add that, with all this chaff and banter between villagers and visitors, hostess and servants—with all this in-and-out, unconventional, happy-go-life—there is an absence altogether of familiarity or forgetfulness. Life at Glengariff is original, and its originality is its charm.

LIFE AT KILLARNEY.

Killarney.

I HAVE arrived at Killarney at last, and am quite determined to make no comparisons whatever. It is the fashion here to squabble and compare. The Scotchmen will not hear Killarney mentioned in the same breath with their beloved lochs. A faded English girl at Cork snubbed me for considering that the Irish lakes should not be put out of court because Windermere is lovely. Welshmen consider they have quite as beautiful bits in the land of the leek; and Americans make a dead rush through the orthodox Killarney trips, and are perpetually reminding you that there is scenery quite as fine in other corners of the earth. May I humbly ask what all this has to do with me? I do not come to Killarney to contrast Mangerton with Snowdon, to compare the Torc Waterfall with the Staubbach, to measure the lower lake with Coniston Water, to pit Muckross Abbey against Tintern, or to sneer at the neighbouring Paradises owned by Mr. Herbert and Lord Castlerosse, because there are such places in the world as Trentham, Studley, Alton, and Longleat. It is distressing to me that the tourist is not more eclectic in his tastes, and that I am not allowed to eat my dinner at the *table d'hôte*, to lounge about the flower-garden at the Victoria, to join a party at the Gap of Dunloe, without being pestered with these irritating comparisons. It is the fashion, it is the craze, to take a bird's-eye view of this superb place, and then to knock off a decision. Now, if any one at Killarney has a right to be hypercritical and unenthusiastic, to look the place over in a cool and deliberate manner, and to compare Ireland with Ireland—I am surely that person. I have come here gorged with beautiful scenery. My brain is almost dizzy, after a course of views and panoramas. Mountain and lakes, wild hills and waterfalls, woods and acres of heather, views in the sun and landscapes in the rain, sunsets and sunrises—I have seen them all. In my greediness, I have sometimes wished for a day in St. Giles's, or a walk round St. Patrick's Cathedral, just to relish all the more the next course of nature.

I have fancied with Mr. Swinburne that "I shall never be friends again with roses," so satiated am I with the scent of flowers. I did not come to Killarney straight from desk and papers, a lean and hungry traveller prepared to swallow the first thing that was set before me, and to admire everything because the holidays had commenced, and it was summer-time. I came here an epicure, a connoisseur, and a critic. Here is Killarney, then; and to pick holes in it would be on my part intolerable affectation. Winding round the lovely Glengariff road under the tree-covered Torc Mountain, and catching the first full view of the lake panorama—being introduced at one burst to the Purple Mountain, to the upper, middle, and lower lakes, to the Eagle's Nest, where the bugler was waking the echoes as I passed—I was startled, and nothing more. Was this, then, the Killarney about which so much has been written? Was there no more? Was this all? Such thoughts as these are inevitable, when you have allowed your imagination to run away with you. But they soon wear off at Killarney. I never was at a place which so thoroughly grows upon one. Its first surprise soon yields to affection. At Muckross you are hesitating, and on the lawn of the Victoria Hotel you are conquered.

Let me now say something about Killarney life, postponing the trips for another occasion; for I have no intention of doing Killarney in one day, or indeed of leaving anything undone, so fearful are the penalties which I should incur, according to the superstitious doctrine of guides and boatmen, who are not altogether disinterested in the matter of strict observance of Killarney ritual. As I neared Killarney, having fought my way through a chattering gang of bog-oak ornament sellers, girls with huge baskets and a great power of talk, girls who swarm about you like flies, pelting you with bracelets and brooches, and paper-cutters, and who by their importunities render a walk at Killarney almost an impossibility—having mercifully escaped unhurt, after running the gauntlet down an avenue of old women, armed with bottles of whisky, jugs of goat's milk, and wooden bowls prepared to kill one on the spot with an awful compound, fancifully termed "mountain dew," of which, did you obey the commands of the old women, you would consume some gallons between breakfast and dinner time—I discovered that I was in a new set altogether.

I have travelled many hundred miles during the past few weeks, under a burning sun, with companions who have elected to wear all kinds of head coverings, from the tall white hat to the black billycock; with good fellows who have apparently suffered no inconvenience from the sun's rays, and have not even thought it worth while to resort to the expedient of the humble cabbage-leaf in the crown. But at Killarney I find it is the thing to decorate your hat of straw, or felt, with " a puggaree;" and that strong-bearded men do not disdain the somewhat feminine affectation of wisps of cambric, or muslin, down their brawny backs. Wherever you turn you see these semi-Indian cap-covers; and possibly, I am not the only person who has noticed the spread of the puggaree fever, and the adoption of a fashion which I am certain is suggested by vanity rather than by necessity. At Killarney the men allow the muslin to stream half-way down their backs; and, poor dear fellows! they are so afraid of their pretty complexions, that they swathe their faces in veils, and are as careful not to burn their noses as the young ladies in Westbourne Grove.

At the police-station on the Glengariff Road I met the first instalment of these veiled young gentlemen, and I declare that I longed to tear the trumpery from their faces and to tell them that, according to scientific men, the sun is no hotter now than it was ten years ago—that time, at any rate, when boys played cricket all August in a flannel cap, when men walked easily in a straw hat, and when both boys and men rather prided themselves when they came home from a holiday excursion with face and neck well-coloured by the sun. What have men to do with veils?

There never was a place where pleasure is taken in such a delightfully indolent fashion as at Killarney. You select your hotel—no easy matter, I can assure you, when you have to decide, like Paris, between the claims of such formidable rivals as the cosy village inn at Muckross, the excellent and well-conducted establishment at the railway, and the picturesque Victoria, with its flower-garden and paddock extending to the very waters of the lake. Say, however, that you have finally decided on the Victoria, won over by the fascination of sleeping in a room overlooking lake and mountain, of being in the very best position for excursions on the morrow, and not indisposed to ramble after dinner among the ferns in the estate of Lord Castlerosse, which touches the Victoria lawn—say that you are in no way inconvenienced by a distance of two miles from town and railway—then you have nothing to do but select a room, and permit yourself to be handed about. There is no haggling here with guides and porters, with car-drivers and boatmen; you are not annoyed with touts, and you have not to expend any vital force in making clever bargains. The hotel takes you in, and does for you. Cars, boatmen in their pretty uniform, boats, ponies, guides, buglers, all belong to the hotels, and you know to a sixpence before you start what a day's outing will cost. There is every desire, of course, to give you assistance in making up parties; so if you meet some one particularly nice at the *table d'hôte*, or commence a desperate flirtation during the carpet-dance in the ladies' drawing-room, it is the easiest thing in the world to take the landlady into your confidence, and you will find next morning that you are starting on a picnic without the trouble of getting it up, with luncheon packed in a hamper, and not the slightest fear of absent salt or missing corkscrew.

At Killarney I begin for the first time to see life and get an opportunity of studying character. Here are the bride and bridegroom, whose names are easily ascertained by a quick look at the direction on the very new luggage, and a study of the recent marriages in the paper; the nervous, uncommunicative couple who seem afraid of one another, and who never speak above a whisper; and the dreadfully spoony pair of turtle-doves who actually, in a public *salle-à-*

manger, at breakfast, and at nine o'clock in the morning, sit eating their breakfast with affectionate intervals of hand-squeezing. Here you see the youth escaping from his tutor, to play croquet with a fair-haired girl with a soft voice—just one turn with two balls apiece, during the sunny half-hour before the bell rings to warn the Victoria society to dress for dinner; and I assure you they do dress for dinner with a vengeance at Killarney. Serges and hollands are stripped off, and one marvels how muslins can be preserved crisp and faultless as they appear, when extricated from the travelling trunk, and sweeping down the dining-room just as seven o'clock has arrived. Miserable is the life of the pedestrian who has only a knapsack and no black coat; wretched the existence of the faithful wife who has obeyed the commands of her lord, and brought the largest amount of finery in the smallest possible space; for there are certain visitors at Killarney who, at dinner time, view a grey tweed jacket on a man's back, or a travelling costume neatly arranged on a lady, with as much horror as the Oxford undergraduates bestow at the apparition of a man in a red tie or a white hat at Commemoration time. I was in luck's way; for I possessed a black coat, which saved me from the sneers of the ladies in pink, blue, and mauve, the girls in muslin, the wives in silks and diamonds, and the old ladies in black satin; but I must own that I was not prepared to see the golden youths of Killarney present themselves in elaborate evening dress, all white tie and shirt-front. I discovered subsequently that this was a red-letter day at the Victoria. It was the farewell evening of the largest party the Victoria had seen this year; and some enthusiastic youth had contrived to arrange a carpet dance in the drawing-room after dinner. And they did dance with a will; none of your stupid sauntering through a "first set" or Lancers, but arms round the waist whenever there was an opportunity, perpetual galopades, and the most frantic steps and twists I have ever beheld. There was no end to the revelry that night. Ladies who had been taught by foreign masters obliged with Italian airs; sentimental young girls warbled Irish ballads; the funny man sat down and gave a comic song, which was rapturously applauded; and, as there appeared to be not the slightest objection on the part of mammas and chaperones, to moonlight rambles in the gardens between the dances, or sudden absences from the drawing-room, varying from half-an-hour to an hour, I shrewdly suspect that the Victoria will next year be liberally patronized by married couples, who will no doubt have a lingering affection for the spot, where Edwin opened his heart to Angelina, and Letitia—an old hand—for the fifteenth time put on an engaged ring. How long the dances would have lasted had not the piano finally given way, its constitution thoroughly undermined with repeated doses of "The Blue Danube," "Ah, non guinge," and the "Little Wee Dog," I cannot say; but when every note in the instrument had become dumb, the merry party broke up.

To-morrow I am booked on the manager's slate for the Gap of Dunloe. I have taken stock of the whole company, and naturally have views on the subject of my companions. I wonder if a certain blue-eyed girl has done the Gap, or if she is booked for Dinish with her grey-haired father. I wonder if that lady who talked so well and so much to the point at dinner-time, has been everywhere and is going home. I wonder if my companions will be old or young, thin or fat. I wonder if I shall have to play gooseberry to the bride and bridegroom, who squeeze hands at breakfast. But 'tis no good wondering, except for the sake of encouraging a little excitement. I shall know all about it to-morrow morning. I have acquired a dreadful habit of imbibing whisky-punch in this country, which gives one delicious dreams. My "night-cap." over, I shall go to bed.

COLLEEN BAWN LAND.

Killarney.

WITH every desire to appreciate the scenery at the Adelphi—scenery, by-the-bye, which first gave me a faint and glimmering notion of Colleen Bawn Land—on the whole I prefer the real thing. I have seen and satisfied myself with the beauty of the surroundings of Miss Eily O'Connor's home. I know now exactly where Myles-na-Coppaleen, that whisky-loving rascal, used to keep his store, in a rocky cave under one of the islands on the lake, called "The O'Donoghue's Stables." I have fixed on a spot for the parsonage of Father Tom. I know every inch of the road that Master Hardress Cregan was in the habit of travelling in order to enjoy those secret meetings with Eily; and if the flaxen-haired Ann Chute was in the habit of joining in a chase of the red deer about the woods under Mangerton and the Torc Mountain, she must indeed have been an experienced sportswoman. Though I have not yet met with green riding-habits, after the pattern adopted by Mrs. Mellon, or with Irish maidens of the lower orders, nearly so attractive as Mrs. Boucicault, I have made a point of studying Muckross Abbey by moonlight; and I must say, after seeing the "gentle moon" rise on a calm night over the Killarney Lakes, that the "Adelphi moon," so well known in dramatic annals, have been somewhat unfairly treated. I beg leave to state that, calendar or no calendar, there was most certainly an Irish moon at Killarney; and a more theatrical moon, excepting that it did not "wobble," I have seldom seen.

I am prepared to call witnesses in proof of the existence of this Killarney moon—men who walked with me under the "lamp above" towards Muckross, and girls who, at the second carpet-dance in the hotel, were not at all pleased with the illumination. They were either unromantic to begin with, or, if romantic, preferred after a valse those gloomy walks in the Victoria grounds towards a certain summer-house, the whereabouts of which I will not divulge, rather than a gay promenade when chaperones, jealous sisters, spiteful old maids, and even those nuisances fathers and brothers, are "brought out into the moonbames." But I have to tell of the expeditions I have taken since that first Victoria dance, when undying friendships were made, and we arranged to picnic at the Gap of Dunloe. As I said before, the picnic is arranged from first to last without any trouble on the visitor's part. We eat our morning meal at the fine bow-window, overlooking lake and mountain, and do what we are told. While we are consuming a huge Oxford breakfast, with fish, flesh, fowl, eggs—to say nothing of "squish," which they understand at my hotel as well as at Brasenose, and a final and comforting draught of bitter beer—the slaves of the kitchen are cutting, apparently by machinery, mountains of sandwiches for the various excursionists assembled at the hotel; and packing them up, together with other good things, and a choice selection from the wine card, in the hotel luncheon-baskets, which are as necessary items of Killarney hotel furniture as bells and baths.

When we assemble in the hall, the manager gives a signal to the slave of the stables, who proceeds to whistle. Immediately, as if by magic, appear at the door the waggonettes, cars and traps, which are to take us to the foot of the Gap. Directly we are seated, a signal is given to the galley-slaves, who, at the very instant the horses start, seize up the boat flags, which are carefully and jealously selected according to the nationality of the party, and proceed down to the landing-stage—or they will never get the boats against the head-wind across the three lakes, to Lord Brandon's Cottage, in time to meet us. This is something like system; and as we are making our way along the fine Valentia Road, following the posts and the wires of the Atlantic cable, I may have an opportunity perhaps for a mild growl.

I have told you before of my first day's experience with the bog-oak ornament sellers, and the venders of compound essence of bile in the shape of goat's milk and whisky; but all that was a perfect joke to the pesterings and importunities we encountered before we got back from the Gap of Dunloe. It is not too much to say that these petty tradespeople—these crawling, whining children who race after the traps through the villages—these firers of cannon—these tellers of ridiculous stories, do their utmost to ruin a most delightful trip. There surely are some people in the world who in such scenery as this like to be quiet for a little, to think for themselves, and to be left alone. But this is exactly the thing that is not permitted. From morning till night you are bullied for money, or worried with pointless stories, framed merely for the purpose of talk. You are hardly clear of the hotel-gates before the girls with the baskets are at you, pouring out a distressing catalogue of the trumpery contents of their basket—girls fleet of foot, who refuse to be shaken off, and absolutely shut their ears, when the verdict of "No" is pronounced. I suppose it never strikes these strange girls that no one, ignorant of the interior of Bedlam, would be disposed to start on a day's outing, laden with paper-cutters, deers' feet, work-boxes, and needle-books. They are without reason and unreasonable. One of our picnicking young ladies, who had suffered in her time, played the basket-girls a pretty trick, and partly saved our carriage from annoyance. Before she started she armed herself against the enemy. She studded herself with bog-oak brooches, and made her arms black with bracelets. She twisted paper-cutters, German fashion, into her back-hair, and she made her little brother carry a snuff-box made of a deer's foot. Directly the enemy approached, she lifted up her shawl and flashed the wealth of bog-oak in the face of the assailants. In most cases they slunk back terrified, but occasionally they had the pertinacity to turn from the clever girl to some meek and inoffensive man, who was ordered to buy presents for the sweetheart he did not possess, and toys for the infants awaiting him in the dim future. And, it must be remembered, these basket-girls are not rare exceptions on the road. For miles and miles you are saying " No," and entreating them to be off, with what civility and chaff you can for the moment muster. But one takes up the running after the other, and it is a case of " one down and t'other come on," all the way to Kate Kearney's Cottage. Pray do not imagine, however, that the hallowing influence of the beautiful creature's dwelling rids you of her irrepressible sex. Quite the contrary. You are supposed to drink Kate Kearney's health in a bowlful of mountain dew. Fancy goat's milk and whisky while you are digesting the Victoria breakfast, eggs, " squish," bitter ale, and all! Having escaped or not from the clutches of these withered Hebes, you are handed over to the children, who would certainly draw tears from the eyes of members of metropolitan or provincial school-boards. The simplicity of these young rascals is quite touching. They do not beg—oh dear! no; to beg they would be ashamed. If you believe them they are starving, but not for bread. They hunger for education; they pine for literature. They gather little nosegays of buttercups and heather; they present you with feathers and wild-flowers; and the only return they ask is, "A penny to buy a book." Who that has the great cause of education at heart can refuse so simple a request? So the ratepayers and the taxpayers, touched by the imploring looks of the little savages, and determined to make these weeds acquainted with Mavor and Mangnall, fling down nobly their shillings and sixpences, for the books which are to be such a godsend in the wilderness—alas! the coin is immediately transferred to the till of the village sweetstuff shop, or to the box on the top of the family dresser. Such is life.

But think not that at the entrance of the famous Gap of Dunloe, and at this early hour of the morning, you have shaken off the enemy. The cars and carriages have gone back, it is true. The girls have mounted the ponies, which are ready waiting for them at the last cottage in the Gap, and the men have just got into their walking stride, when a halt is called. Without asking your leave, or making any bargain whatever, a ragged fellow rushes out from a bush, and gives a "ya-hoop;" which seems to me a queer compound between the screech of a hyena in the Zoological Gardens, and the gibbering of an incarcerated and violent lunatic. This discordant and fiendish noise comes back to you hideously from the awful mountains opposite, and sixpence is demanded for what is facetiously called an echo. But that is not all. The ragged son of the ragged father, "on yonder rock reclining," without any warning of what he is about to do, applies a match to the touch-hole of a cannon. There is a flash, a report, a rumble among the mountains, irritated at having their mighty calm disturbed in this ridiculous manner— and sixpence more is demanded for the "best echo in the Gap." It is somewhat hard, I must say, to pay a shilling for being disturbed out of a reverie, for hearing a screech which was anything but desirable, and for being startled by a report which you would have paid half-a-crown to avoid. But if you object, you are told that no one has ever yet gone through the Gap without submitting to and paying for the annoyance of the Gap; so you merely smile in a ghastly manner, pay your shilling, and pass on. Once more you begin to think and admire. You are fascinated with the bold height of the mountains, and you feel a very pigmy striding under it.

You would like to have been here when in the winter time the frost cracked that mighty block, and sent it tumbling down, bringing with it trees and bushes, till it leaped the stony path, and found a resting-place in the bed of the watercourse. You are tempted to clamber up the rocks and bound from stone to stone like a chamois, just to peep at the picture that artist is painting, perched overhead in a superb position, quietly smoking, and doing his work under a sun-umbrella. You picture the Gap when the rains have swollen the stream, and a mighty river comes roaring through the arches of the bridges in the pass, and finds its way somehow into the lakes below. But they will not let you be. The guide tells you for the thousandth time, " That is the Purple Mountain"—a stereotyped announcement which is dragged in directly there is peace for a minute. I may be peculiar, but I must honestly own that my pleasure is not enhanced by learning the name of every mountain or hill. Be it the Sugarloaf, or the Devil's Mother, or the O'Donoghue's Easy Chair, or Macgillicuddy's Footstool ; to me it is a bold and magnificent mountain, and I do not wish to be a dozen times hindered from thinking by twelve announcements of the same vastly interesting fact. When the guide, who will not be shaken off, but sticks deliberately at your heels, determined to give you a day's annoyance for a day's pay, has fallen back after another allusion to the Purple Mountain, a shrill, weak old voice, and a squeaky fiddle, warn you that round the next rock you will be stopped again. The blind old man of the Gap, is feebly endeavouring to warble out, "The Meeting of the Waters," and you charitably pull out sixpence to prevent the rupture of a blood-vessel. More girls with more ornaments and more hags with more milk, dog you to the top of the Gap, and follow at your heels in relays, until you leave the ponies at the gate of the grounds, where Lord Brandon's Cottage is situated ; and with enthusiasm pay twopence to be admitted to a cool green haven of trees and flowers, where " the wicked cease from troubling, and the weary are at rest."

The wind is freshening up, and the boatmen have evidently had a hard tug up the rapids of the "Old Weir Bridge." At any rate, they have not arrived; and now, for the first time, we can enjoy delicious and uninterrupted ease. Come and lie down on this tongue of green land which stretches out into the lake, and enjoy to the full a perfect scene. Come here, ye who sneer at Killarney and declare it a mistake— a district over-praised. Are you converted now, lying full length on this pleasant grass, listening to the gentle plashing of the blue water over the smooth pebbles, looking far away at the tree-covered Torc range on the one hand, on the wooded heights of the Eagle's Nest on the other, attempting to count the innumerable islands bright with the rare green of the arbutus, brilliant with the scarlet berry of the mountain ash? The boat is not yet in sight. "Oh! how delightful," as Mr. Molloy's song says, to be free of touts and beggars, to be released for a sunny half-hour from the instructing guides who are as much a nuisance as the pedant in "Sandford and Merton!" It is a pretty picture, as we lie here in the sun waiting for the boat. Enjoyment, as well as hunger, keeps us quiet. Some doze, some sketch, many are absorbed, and those who will flirt and talk, are so over-awed by the beauty of the scene that they do their flirting and talking in a whisper. But here come the blue-jackets! There is a shout, because, as well as the boats, they bring the luncheon baskets, and after that tramp through the Gap, our early breakfast has long since been forgotten. They land us on a cool tree-covered island; but who does not know what a picnic is like with pleasant women and jolly men? The only way to stop the mouths of the boatmen, whose duty I find is to instruct as well as to row, is to set them also to work upon the sandwiches and the beer, in order that we may enjoy ourselves in our own fashion, until they ply their oars again. Once in the boat, we know pretty well what to expect. We shall have to christen islands, the price of such privilege being a bottle of whisky. We shall have to bet bottles of whisky with the boatmen about the proper course out of the Upper Lake; we shall have to hear childish stories in connexion with every tree and stone; and the only moment's peace we shall get is when the "Old Weir Bridge" is in sight, and our white-ducked friends have to attend to business instead of pleasure—for they must have their wits about them, in order to cease rowing at the exact instant, and, catching the full flow of the stream, rush the boat with the torrent in safety and in style. Round we go by the Dinish Island, under the haunts of bold red deer on the Lower Lake, until we make straight for Innisfallen, and linger there among the ruins, until the afternoon is far advanced, and it is time to hurry across to the hotel to dress for dinner.

I am in luck's way about the weather. If I had turned on effects with a tap, like a theatrical prompter, I could not have done better with the Gap excursion. A dark looking cloudy morning for the Gap itself, with gloomy shadows clinging about the cold grey stones, and a thick heavy-looking background, for a wild and desolate scene. A bright midday, and a burning sun for the halt at the Upper Lake, and the picnic on the island. A sunny, gusty afternoon, the wind blowing about the forests of trees, and ruffling the surface of the vast Lower Lake, making waves and white horses as we sail across the open waters for home. A calm still evening for the rest on Innisfallen Island. What more could any one desire, save that peace to enjoy scenery, which at Killarney and in a land of anecdote is apparently impossible?

AT THE YORKSHIRE SPA.

Scarborough.

THIS is indeed the haven where I would be, a scene of endless summer and perpetual delight. I have no intention of talking like an old hand. A man who has never visited Scarborough ought, no doubt, to be thoroughly ashamed of himself; and I am that man. But Scarborough, like an affectionate mother, has taken me into her arms, and given me of her best. This beautiful lady, "faultily faultless," has condescended to show me her jewels, and to deck herself out for me in gorgeous apparel. It is not sufficient that I have an August sun to burn me by day; that I have groves to ramble in, and flowers to delight me; that my ears are delighted with music, and my eyes dazzled with beauty. Scarborough has added to her gifts a moon, which has been set in precisely the correct position for the Spa scenery; a moon rising red out of the water the very instant we light our cigars on the balcony after dinner; a moon whose praises shall be sung when nightfall comes. But Scarborough is a cruel and exacting mistress. We are all her slaves, and she has imperiously demanded, whilst we wait upon her, dance attendance, and wander hither and thither as she wills, that we put aside pens, ink, and paper, and give ourselves entirely up to her society. It is a mystery to me how any one does business in summer-time at Scarborough; how it is that the shops continue open, and that men and women go to their daily work; since one minute away from the sun, and the flowers, and the sea, is a minute lost. Take my own case: Unless I commit an assault, and get locked up; unless I bribe some one to shut me in a cellar, or light a candle in the dead of the night and take out my writing case, how is it possible for me to turn away when this lovely lady beckons me! When you are in the air, you must lounge and dream; when you are indoors, you must eat, or look out of window. There never was such a fascinating spot.

I am not astonished that the gazette of visitors fills a large-sized newspaper; that every hotel is full; that you must carry a camp stool with you if you desire to sit in the evening at the Spa; that a rumour is already afloat about the prudent purchase of another slice of undercliff, in order to extend the flower garden and relieve the crowded promenade; and that harrowing stories reach my ears of visitors who, out of mercy to hard-worked servants, take a turn at boot-cleaning. My wonder is how any one can stay away. Look at Scarborough from any point you like, and at any hour, and where can you find her equal? Behold her as I see her now at seven o'clock in the morning—the only moment I can spare from the side of her I love—with the sun bursting out of a haze of heat, and making a golden glitter on the water; the red-sailed fishing-boats putting out to sea, and the waves discoursing their fascinating music, which has lulled me all night and given me delicious dreams. Behold her all quiet, save for the early bathers, towel in hand, hurrying briskly along the cliff. It is cruel of me, faithful friends in London, friends at the desk and at the mill, to talk like this; but we shall have such a day, or I am much mistaken. Behold my mistress, as I shall see her later on, when bath and breakfast are over, down at the Spa, where the flowers grow, where the band of Herr Meyer Lutz, most talented of conductors, attempts in vain to drown the everlasting music of the sea. Behold her waited on by the prettiest girls and the fairest women collected from the United Kingdom. Behold her in the afternoon, when we take novel or romance under our arm, and hide ourselves in some snug corner of the wood, in some sly summer-house, or cosy arbour, shadowed by the trees as green as in spring-time. Behold her later still, when the piqué dresses are exchanged for silk, when the breeze blows cool off the sea, when the moon rises out of the water a ball of fire, and the girls, who seem to understand colour, go down the cliff in wraps of scarlet, and blue, and gold. Behold her, latest of all, when the two bands clash out together, when you turn from the dazzle of gas, and dress, and eyes, to the other side of this wonderful picture, where the moon, so cruelly calm, looks down upon the revelry, and, with bitter sarcasm, throws a pure light upon the cold wet beach, where lovers wander, and upon the mournful solitude of the distant caves.

It has been said—and most unfairly said—that Scarborough is a haughty and fashionable tyrant, compelling a change of dress a dozen times a day, and forcing us to take our pleasure painfully. But the fact of the matter is, Scarborough does nothing of the kind. Her amusements are so varied, and her position so perfect, that the monotonous absurdity of a promenade along so many hundred yards of cliff, or pier, at stated hours of the day, does not exist here. There never was a place where you could more thoroughly do as you please. Unless you like you need not be seen. You can hide yourself in the wood with a book, or display yourself morning or evening on the Spa. You can toil up to the old ruined castle, and watch the gulls and pleasure boats, sheltered from the sun among the rocks, and under the grassy cliff. You can picnic at Hackness, or ride in the opposite direction. You can visit M. Sarony's studio, or explore the red-tiled fishing-village, or play cricket, or fish for whiting. You can take a stall at the theatre, and in the Spa saloon a spirited *entrepreneur* provides you with a new entertainment every evening. You can dance until five in the morning, or you can go to bed.

I shall have to tell you by-and-by of our charming society at the Crown, of the popularity of our noble president, of our efforts—and successful efforts—to eclipse the brilliancy of the Grand, and to soar proudly above the Royal; how the Prince of Wales would give anything to catch the charm of one of our picnics; and, as to our balls, how they are, during our present admirable dictatorship, the talk of all Scarborough. I shall have some notes of a picnic at Hackness, one bright and memorable morning when, after taking compassion on and giving a seat to a "Castaway," after bestowing an irresistible invitation to the Buccaneer, by whom it was promptly accepted, Amy Robsart drove off in a waggonette with Mary Netley—laughing, of course—by her side, and Sydney Daryl surveying—out of his eyeglass, of course—his precious charges from a dignified position on the box. You remember in the play these two were married; and, in the interests of "society," I am bound to declare in the most emphatic manner that they are doing their best to live happily ever afterwards. I may whisper possibly that it is reported here, in well-informed circles, that a certain Russian Prince from Tottenham Court Road, a few days ago actually sat down to dinner, and was made much of at the Grand, and that last night, on the Spa, I saw the Esmeralda of the old Strand burlesque days, chatting with the mistress of the youngest theatre in London. I could hardly believe my eyes when they rested on a most popular character, a wandering "Black Sheep" I left some weeks ago drinking whisky-punch in a monastery in the county of Wicklow; but here he is as large as life, fuller than ever of ancedote, and apparently none the worse for his acquaintance with the monastic cellar.

I flattered myself just now that it was a clever trick to get up early, so that the pleasures of the day might not be interfered with—to sit down and write, disturbed only by the snoring of my next-door neighbour, and to appear at breakfast with a weight off my mind. However I have acted foolishly. Instead of drawing down the blinds, closing the curtains, and lighting the candle, I have dragged the writing-table in front of the window, facing the busiest part of the cliff, the greenest acre of the wood, and the boldest and most magnificent stretch of sea. The consequence is that instead of working, instead of saying half I had to say, I have done little else but look out of the window. Some hours ago, when the fish-boy was the only human being visible, and there was a curtain of mist over the water, I steadily resisted temptation, and kept my eyes away. It was galling enough, it is true, when Sydney Daryl and the Black Sheep, uttering mysterious cries, went by swinging their bathing towels, and I was compelled to sit and stare at them putting out to sea in a boat for a dive and a swim. But at this moment, when early Scarborough has apparently breakfasted, the fascination of out-of-door life is too great to be resisted. The sea has retreated, and at least a dozen bathing-machines are out. I can see regiments of children digging on the sands, and I remember that I promised the "sweetest little maid that ever crowed for kisses" that I would come down some morning and build her a castle, a tunnel, and a railway station. Two very pretty girls, with whom I danced at the Crown ball last night, dressed in Baden towelling, of exactly the same shade as their hair, which this morning— how strange!—has escaped from the captivity of net and hairpin, and is tumbling down in disorder, have taken up their position on a seat exactly opposite my window. I see they pretend to read, but I rather believe I promised to join them in a ramble, and they expect me. A messenger has just come up to say that the President of our Hotel has got up a riding party, and will I be one of the number? Two men I particularly wanted to see have this instant lighted their cigars and turned down the cliff towards the Spa. A very large dog has stretched himself out on the grass and wants patting. The sun is getting hotter and hotter, and the itinerant bands are commencing in front of the house. I can stand it no longer. I cannot write a word. Will you please excuse me?

SCARBOROUGH'S SUNDIAL.

Pereunt et imputantur. This is the motto on Scarborough's sundial; but while the pleasant hours are passing away, and just before they are reckoned up against us, let me attempt to sketch the pictures which may be seen here from hour to hour. I presume you have a faint idea of this wonderful summer lounge. You can see in imagination a bright blue bay with the Enoch Arden fishing-village, a queer little harbour and pier, many red-roofed cottages suggesting a picture by Mr. Hemy, and a ruined castle topping the heights at one end of the horn of the crescent. You can follow the line of the semicircle till you are stopped by the stately Grand Hotel which shuts out the green trees of the valley between Scarborough north and south. You can travel along the viaduct till you come to the entrance of the mazy grounds designed by Sir Joseph Paxton; and then you can wander among the ferns and flowers, down quiet paths, through miniature avenues, covering the whole face of the cliff. Suddenly you arrive on the gravelled terrace of the Spa, where the lounging rooms, concert-rooms, refreshment-halls, and balconies suggest the favourite old tables of Ems, and are an improvement on the virtuous casinos of

Ostend and Dieppe. On the broad terrace of the Spa you can listen at high tide to the bold waves breaking against the terrace embankment; and at low tide you can grasp the mighty stretch of sand where the children dig, the horses race, the visitors bathe, and where John Leech's little jockeys, with their jackets of scarlet and blue, are the only drivers for the low carriages which follow in procession along the sea margin. In the distance on the right are the rocks where the sea anemones are found; and scattered all over the bay are the pleasure vessels and herring-boats which make Scarborough, in sunlight and in moonlight, so intensely picturesque. Paint in the idle vessels in the harbour; the toy steamers making for Filey and Whitby; the bathing machines on the strand; and the white houses fringing the cliff from the Prince of Wales Hotel at one end, to the grey old castle walls at the other, and you have a view of South Scarborough.

Eleven o'clock.—We cannot rise very early at Scarborough, for night after night, at one hotel or other, we are invited to a carpet-dance or a subscription ball—the former certainly not to be despised, and the latter much appreciated by dancers, for the music is good and the floor well waxed. But the bath is over, and the breakfast is done. As you stroll about the cliff outside the Crown Hotel, you can hear distinctly the strains of the first selection by the band of Herr Meyer Lutz. All the paths on cliff and pleasure-ground are filled with women in bright toilettes proceeding to the Spa. Over the viaduct they come in crowds from the Grand and the Royal; down the serpentine paths and break-neck steps they follow from the Prince of Wales and the Crown. It is a libel to say that Scarborough is outrageously dressed. I expected to find Trouville out-Trouvilled, a showy burlesque of the extravagance of Dieppe and St. Malo; but I was altogether wrong. Eccentricity is exceptional. Among fifteen thousand visitors, you may expect to find some nonsensical whim of shape or colour; but Scarborough as I find it—I am unable to make comparisons—should be complimented on its rich simplicity and admirable taste. Of course there will be cynics asking what these strong men and healthy women do here among the flower-beds, walking up and down everlastingly along this gravelled path; dressing to captivate and talking to be praised; preferring the music of Rossini and the songs of Mendelssohn, the melody of Meyer Lutz and the valse tunes of Germany; to the rushing of the waves, the healthy exercise of climbing, and the romp of seaside life?

I cannot answer. I can only declare that the sands and the rocks, the seaweed and the paddling, the musical sea and the fishing life of Scarborough are left to the nurserymaids and the children; while mamma and papa, the lover and the beloved, the brave soldier and the bronzed cricketer, the hard-worked London barrister and the member of Parliament come to the Spa promenade and appreciate nature from a distance.

Extremes meet on the Scarborough Spa. There never was such a levelling, such a mixing of oil and water. Here is a Liberal M.P., of energy and intellect, one of the most prominent men of last session, and the head-master of the largest school-board, arm in arm with a Conservative agent, and apparently enjoying his society. Here is a novelist and dramatic author offering a cigar to a reviewer of books and plays; the couple interchanging stories which cause such immoderate laughter that the Spa is somewhat shocked. Here is a popular lady, who has done more than any other in her generation for English comedy, both as actress and as reader, shaking hands with the tragic heroine of Drury Lane. Here is a monologue entertainer digging the ribs of an artist in polylogue. A very celebrated London solicitor goes home to lunch with the principal of a rival firm. An officer of Volunteers is admitted to the hallowed circle composed of the inevitable military set, indulging in talk more vapid than usual; and the two most beautiful women on the Spa—both from London, and not unknown to many of us—are apparently on the best and most confidential terms. It is not difficult for any one who has studied promenade life, though only at the Botanical broadwalk or during a Saturday afternoon at the Crystal Palace, to dash in the colour when such an outline as this is presented. The scandal of the Grand is conveyed to the willing ears of the Crown. Last night's ball is discussed, and to-morrow's picnic arranged. The histories of the ladies, which have before been written at some length in the columns of the daily newspapers, are affectionately annotated by their friends and admirers. Not a soul escapes. Scandal dances from lip to lip. Every engagement is promptly gazetted, and every rejection is published as regularly as the visitors' list. The sporting men, who have come over here in hundreds to await Doncaster, buy up every journal which contains a line of sporting intelligence, and discuss from morning till night the merits and demerits, the whispers and the "shaves" concerning King of the Forest and Bothwell, Hannah and Albert Victor. The cricketers —and we have brave cricketers on the Spa, sunning themselves before the great visitors' match of Monday —stroll about discussing cricket news. For the thousandth time we hear that there is not much partridge-shooting, because the corn is not yet cut; and that the lord of the manor is, as usual, preserving his birds for the Royal visit. Add to all this the love-making and the laughing, the sneering and the whispering, the chatter of the Hyde Park *flâneurs*, who know everybody and everybody's business; throw in the sweep of the dresses along the path and the pleasant band music—and you have a scene which, however reprehensible, is unquestionably fascinating.

One o'clock.—We will lunch at the Grand to-day, for I should like you to see the noble circular dining-room where we danced the other night, when it was filled with the visitors. You must know that at Scarborough we take our meals together. The coffee-room society is extremely small. We breakfast and we lunch, we dine and we drink our tea together; and it is owing to the family gatherings that we are all so friendly. From these are elected the hotel-presidents, and many jolly rides and picnics, sailing and fishing expeditions, are arranged as well as the nightly dance. The Scarborough air has a wonderful appetizing effect; for what is discreetly called luncheon, is in reality a sound children's dinner—hot meat and cold meat, plenty of vegetables, and unlimited beer. There is hardly time for a chat on the terrace of the Grand, where the children are playing and being spoiled; or for a peep into the great drawing-room, where, in cosy corners, ladies have already let the novel fall and are taking a siesta; or for a glance at the telegrams posted in the vast hall; or for a visit to the smoking-room, where, on this summer afternoon, in full sight of the boats and the sea, a whist-table is at work. We must be out and about.

Two o'clock.—Just as at Blarney you must kiss the stone; as on St. Michael's Mount you must clamber into the chair; as in Rome, if you desire to return again, you must drink the waters of a certain fountain, so in Scarborough you need not descend into the bear-pit and poison yourself with iron water unless you are rash; but one thing you must do—you must have your photograph taken. With Sarony's unvisited, Scarborough is undone; and I can assure you that when you have mounted the Scarborough steeps for the twentieth time to-day, it is not unpleasant to turn from the burning cliff to the cool shade of the mansion of Mr. Sarony. Here you have photographs in a princely style. If you are interested in photography as an art, the manager will possibly take you round the vast establishment, and explain to you in full the carbon process, the mystery of autotype, and the trick of albumenizing—all of which may be seen at Sarony's; an establishment which is growing so fast that the time may come when Sarony's Square will be roofed over, so fond are Scarborough visitors of taking themselves home in their pockets. Sarony's has come to be looked on as an afternoon lounge; and, if you do not wish to come under the harrow, there is no objection to a stroll through the galleries to see Mr. Barker's Academy pictures and to recognise your friends.

Four o'clock.—Scarborough is very quiet now. Most of the ladies are dozing. Some are away riding at Hackness or coming home from Filey and Scalby. The fly-men and pony-boys are stupid with the sun; and the Spa is quite deserted, save in the quiet corners among the ferns, where the irrepressible novel-reader is at work, and the tatter is plying her busy needle. I have a great desire to see what the view is like from the ruined castle. According to the formation of the coast, it seems as if there might be another bay. Judge of my surprise when, having toiled up the steep and mounted on a wall, I found not only another bay but another Scarborough. A north Scarborough this, with a cliff and a conventional semicircle of houses, and a pier where the freshest breezes in all Scarborough are found. It is a Scarborough destitute of Spa, but containing what looks like a ruined cliff garden, an hotel all to itself, and a new set of residents altogether. Half the people in the south do not know the existence of the north; and the folks who reside at the north, talk in an injured tone about the compliment which is paid them when their shores are visited. Yet the peace and retirement of the quarter are much appreciated, if one may judge from the well-filled lodging-houses, and the general happy look of the place.

No Man's Land is the best place for a good breeze, and a superb view when the tide is up. By No Man's Land I mean the grass-covered promontory between north and south, where the volunteers are practising rifle-shooting, and where the rocks and caves looking seaward are used by lovers who have, strange to say, escaped from home, and very naturally prefer such a scene as this to shopping in the town. I like looking down on the sea from a height; and on this No Man's Land the idler can be so hidden that he cannot see a house; there is nothing before you or around you but calm blue water, disturbed occasionally by a herring-boat putting out, or a little steamer fussing home with excursionists.

Five o'clock.—The romantic lovers and the lotos-eaters must cease love-making and dreaming, and leave the cliff in time to shop before dinner. This is distinctly the thing to do. A sleep and a cup of tea have worked wonders with the ladies, who were dragged up the Spa hill, by the aid of arms and sticks before luncheon. Here they are in their afternoon dresses, playing with the jewellery at Bright's, which they cannot .buy, and contenting themselves with the purchase of such gloves and fal-lals as may be requisite for the evening dance. It is quite as exciting an hour for the men as the women. While the fair sex is trying on rings and bracelets, purchasing lace cuffs, and doing various shopping, the men are crowding to Theakston's, for the London papers have arrived. Here also you can dip into the latest novel, turn over the newest box of books, order your light literature for the week, take your stall for the theatre, or engage a place for one of the entertainments which keep the Spa alive when the evening is advanced.

Oh! the delight of a London paper when you are away from home! I don't believe the man who never reads a letter or a paper on his holiday. Look at the men, with bundles of journals under their arms, neglecting the women-kind, and reading eagerly as they saunter to table-d'hôte, which is sharp at six everywhere in Scarborough. While we dine the sun sinks, flashing into your eyes at soup-time; but at pudding-time it is quite gone. The sundial therefore is useless. What remains of Scarborough life must be seen by moonlight.

People pretend to differ about the object of a

visit to the sea, but at heart they are all agreed. If you are enthusiastic about Scarborough, for instance—if you praise the society, the gaiety, the abandonment and recklessness, the walks and the drives, the picnic parties and the riding excursions, the dreamy music on the Spa, the good-will and heartiness which appear to embrace this summer nook, causing the coldest Englishman to unbend and making one large family of Scarborough, on Spa and on sand, on a bench in the gardens, on a rout-seat in a ball-room, or in the particularly cosy and pleasant smoking-room at the Crown—you will be met with the old arguments about the meaning of the sea-side, about the secret of the sea.

You will hear the stale old platitudes about the delights of lolling all day on the beach and pitching pebbles into the ocean; the pleasure of worn shooting-jackets and battered hats; the delicious indolence over a maddening novel—the same nursemaids, the same distracting children, the same uninteresting girls hovering around you from morning till night. You will be told of the charms of calm and rest, of the folly of dissipation, the idiocy of dancing; and, when you quote Scarborough, you will have Whitby flung in your teeth. Who, they will ask, would be dressing and promenading, shopping and dancing, picnicking and pleasuring among the ten thousand at Scarborough, when they can dig and moon, sleep and throw pebbles, fish and go through a process of tanning away at Whitby?

Here then I venture to put forward my unassailable position. At Scarborough you can enjoy the calm and indulge in the racket; whereas at other places, which shall be nameless, you are a candidate for Bedlam when the sun goes down. Let me come to a practical illustration. Does Whitby ever visit Scarborough? Is Broadstairs—that haven of unbroken peace—never caught revelling at Margate or Ramsgate? Very often, I warrant you, when the sun sinks and the humble lodging is insupportable. At Scarborough you are not hedged in by mile after mile of open road or blinding chalk. When you venture outside the limits of the town you can get a pleasant tree and refreshing shade. At Scarborough you can be as quiet as you choose or as dissipated as you like. With Scarborough for your head-quarters, you can doze at Filey, fish in the open sea, ride, disappear, vanish for hours, compose poems among the rocks. You can walk yourself into a fever, separate yourself from your fellow-creatures from daybreak to sunset. But returning to dinner, that most comforting meal, and the after-smoke, that most soothing indulgence, you will find your fellow-creatures, your world and your society, your music and dancing, your dissipated lamps among the sleepy flowers, your moon upon the water, your lovers on the beach, your entertainment in the saloon, and your chat upon the terrace—delights of which Broadstairs after some trouble gets an occasional taste, but for which Littlehampton and Felixstowe moan miserably. Don't tell me of the pleasures of your quiet seaside places; of the ecstacy of isolation and the rapture of the one walk, the one pier, the one "stony British stare" from morning till night; the impossibility of getting an introduction to anybody; the sisters compelled to stick by the brothers; the heavy family dinner, and the still heavier family tea—don't tell me that all this is right, and that the plan of Scarborough is radically wrong. Ask the mothers with the pretty daughters, the handsome and impecunious sons, the blessed fathers with quivers "full of them," the dashing widows, the prancers, the young men and maidens, old men and children—the types in the Scarborough ten thousand. They know well enough that Scarborough acts on a very different principle. People do not marry and give in marriage by walking up and down a pier staring at one another, by pretending to read seated on an uncomfortable stony beach all the time casting sheep's eyes, by meeting accidentally in the circulating library, or by lounging like a burglar in front of a house, longing to be introduced to the wearer of a figured muslin.

All this is a wrong system, conducive to rude health possibly, but not to relief from anxiety. The Scarborough plan is quite different. At Scarborough, in our hotel, we adopt the club smoking-room rule. We belong to the same society, and therefore we may talk. We elect a president to sit at the top of our table and say grace before our meat, to arrange our amusements, and to play the *rôle* of a refined matrimonial agent. We do not choose a grumpy old fogy who has the gout and can't lead a cotillon; but that wonderful man who invariably turns up, and who has a charm and a way with him which are irresistible—the kind of fellow boys would worship and University men idolize. He is courteous and cultivated, witty without being coarse, boy-like and not frivolous—a brawny, broad-backed young Englishman, who is called "an old boy" affectionately. The president it is who, with his staff, spends so much time among the bottles in the little parlour behind the glass windows, with the pretty bookkeeper—holding back the pen of the ready writer from entries of brandies and sodas, early luncheons and late breakfasts.

All this, be it noted, is done under pretence of organizing picnics, and dividing some expensive folly among the male members of the society, but in reality of testing the value of a curious brown mixture of curaçoa and brandy. It is the president who pooh-poohs distance and forbids reserve, who keeps the conversation going at dinner, and is the admirable master of the revels at a dance. How, indeed, is dulness possible at such a spot, and how can any anxiety as to introductions exist? When the Crown meets the Grand night after night; when the Royal embraces the Prince of Wales; when, if you are in the unhappy position of knowing no one, the sum of five shillings will admit you to an hotel dance; when partners and chaperones, the waltzer and the waltzed, do not separate after a happy evening, but meet next morning among the flowers or under the rocks; when there are common picnics to which you do not need to bring anything but wit and good temper—how can you be two days at Scarborough without having made a host of friends? The difficulty is not to get introductions, but to avoid persecution. When you are led up to a particularly bad partner, who can neither dance nor talk, who scrambles away with you instead of steering properly to the tune of the "Blauen Donau," you have surely done your duty when you have turned on the requisite amount of small talk, and led her gracefully to her seat. It is too bad to be victimized next morning on the Spa terrace, and doomed to take turns innumerable with a most uninteresting young person. I know a young lady at this moment who is in a worse plight still. Unless rumour lies—and rumour is never known to have done any such thing—she is at the same moment engaged to a delegate from each hotel in Scarborough, and her art is to play one off against the other, to avoid meeting them all at the same moment, and to keep a watchful eye upon any other eligible who may meanwhile arrive in Scarborough. The rapid manner in which young people are engaged and disengaged at Scarborough is startling. The preliminaries usually being arranged before the desirability of the union is inquired into, it follows as a matter of course that in a few hours' time the contract is cancelled. But there is no attempt at sulking or despairing; there is no leaving the hated spot and the detested rival, the false girl and the cruel parent. The rejected and the jilt remain on the best of terms; they talk, walk, and ride together just as if nothing had happened; and occasionally, by dint of patience and good temper, an old flame is rekindled, and the disconsolate of to-day is made happy a week or so after.

But it is not in the sunlight that the secret of Scarborough is told. When the day is bright, fresh air is fresh air, and sea is sea. Scarborough, beautiful as she is, must have many rivals when the sun shines. Standing by Scarborough's sundial, I have told you of the hours, how they pass, how one enjoyment is succeeded by another, how rest is difficult and *ennui* impossible; but before the Scarborough night my pen is powerless.

I might hurry you in a scrambling fashion through the Hackness outing, when Rebecca flies from the cathedral city and Isaac of York, and takes to picnicking as a prelude to harder work; when this same Rebecca, startling in her versatility, is at one moment engaged in dissecting a chicken-leg or extricating the sweet contents of a lobster's claw, and the next, with eyes starting out of her head and fists clenched, bounds across a barrier of bottles, making the greenwood echo with her appalling and tragic cry, "Mercy on us! there's a spider!" I might show you

Miss Polly Eccles, who will apparently be a romp till the end of the chapter, preparing for her incarceration in the "little house at Stangate," by a race through brier and brushwood up the stiffest of Yorkshire hills, away from the dreary dowagers who turn up their delicate noses at the echoing laughter and the shouts of Miss Polly's admirers. I might whisper of the chaff in store for the conventional picnic couple who disappear mysteriously after luncheon, and reappear with lamb-like innocence when the horses are put-to and the traps ready to start. I might lead you to an open field at the top of Hackness Hill, where a party of Bedlamites, admirably mounted, are making their steeds go through a set of Lancers circus-fashion, the musician with difficulty getting his lips in position to whistle the tune owing to the ludicrousness of the scene. But are not such eccentricities as these written in the annals of other seaside haunts, though they may not be honoured with such delightful society? It is at nightfall that Scarborough is unrivalled. Here there is no necessity to take a train in search of pleasure, or to scramble home again along a rocky road or a dangerous cliff. Your amusement is brought to your very door. Weary with your walk, tired after your romp, delightfully lazy after a good dinner, you have nothing to do but to cross the road, to find dissipation turned on with the gas.

This is just what was wanted. The men must smoke and the women must talk, the boys must sigh and the girls must flirt. Over all this gaslight and promenading, these brilliant shawls and this fascinating music, there hangs an inexpressible atmosphere of naughtiness, which possibly adds a charm to the place.

Why does the Spa—really so virtuous—look so uncommonly wicked at night? Is it not so? Can you stroll down the hill, among the little lamps sparkling like glowworms among the ferns, past the arbours and the bowers, and the quiet seats with a grand look-out over the heads of the promenaders away to sea; can you lean over the parapet of the terrace in some secluded corner, watching the Scarborough ten thousand passing backwards and forwards at your feet, with the moon overhead trying to shame out the glitter of the gas and utterly failing; can you walk round the circle when the band plays, catching a whisper here and a sigh there; can you take in all at once this beauty, moon, stars, coloured lamps, rockets bursting from every corner of the gardens on a gala night, the hush of a valse tune, the music of women's voices; and can you on a lovely summer night deny that here, after all, is Scarborough's secret and Scarborough's charm? Here is the market for the marriageable daughters, here the happy hunting-field of the match-making mother. Here night after night some one is made happy, and a dozen curse their fate. Surely this is the secret of the sea, born of its foam like Aphrodite—*c'est l'Amour!*

THE HAPPY ISLAND.

ATHANATOS!—the island without death, the place of immortality, as known by its earliest inhabitants—with us the Isle of Thanet, the Happy Island! I am told that this derivation is utterly nonsensical, and that the root of Thanet will be found in the Saxon word for a beacon. I care very little; but to me there is a charming fancy in the immortal gift of this summer island. Though the bold wind blusters round the houses on East Cliff and West, making the windows rattle at night, and enhancing the luxury of a cosy bed—though the sea is lashed up into a yeasty foam, breaking over the pier, and flinging a shower-bath of spray upon the adventurous youths and maidens leaning from the granite walls and watching the antics of the waves repelled by the solid masonry—though the tide is so high and so fierce after breakfast that the children have to eat their sandy bread-and-butter huddled up in a corner on the sands, and the bathing-machines have to be driven back into the station of the London, Chatham, and Dover Railway—though we are living in gusty, in billowy, and often, alas! rainy times—we have not yet done with the Isle of Thanet.

Some may have a fancy for being roasted on a chalk cliff, some for being grilled on the scorching sands; but now, when the bold " white horses" are on the sea, when the wind wages war on stiff hats and the drapery of young maidens, when the sun does shine as it is shining now, lighting up the horizon with a streak of gold, and bringing the white sails of the mackerel boats into relief; when the cheeks of the young are touched up with Nature's paint, and the skins of the little children are dyed a rich faint chocolate—this is the time for the Happy Island!

And do we in London grudge the title or envy the success of an old friend? There are other beauties, to be sure. We have to listen periodically to rhapsodies on Scarborough, and tales of the priceless properties of aristocratic Brighton—to sing the praises of picturesque Hastings, or of Cromer on one side of England, Llandudno on the other; but we feel unconcerned or awkward when we are introduced to such as these. The Island of Thanet is an old playfellow since our nursery days. It has been the fashion to sneer at this island within an island, to turn up noses at the mention of it, to call Margate low, Ramsgate common, and Broadstairs slow; but, strange to say, the sneering voices, regularly once a year, change their tune—the upturned noses, with the utmost punctuality, sniff periodically the sweet and health-giving breezes which play for ever about the white cliffs of the Isle. The cosmopolitanism of the region is its greatest charm; there is room and welcome for all classes. It is London's sanatarium and London's playing field. Look over London at this instant, search through every nook and corner of the vast metropolis, and you will see some trace of the Happy Island. The hard-working barrister will plead with all the greater vigour, now that he has had his Saturday to Monday at the Granville or Cliftonville. The weary Government official has enjoyed his blow upon the cliff; the workman in the factory has taken advantage of a cheap excursion; the girls in the workshops and establishments, behind counters and at the machine sending off telegrams and trying on mantles, are still flushed after their romp with the fresh air; the children, returned to the old walk in the streets and the old rest in the Parks, carry with them a broken spade or an injured bucket, a tress of dry seaweed or a decaying starfish, as a touching memento of their month in the Happy Island. Tell me where you can find a spot which has so thoroughly conquered prejudice, so risen to the occasion, as the Isle of Thanet! We hear of seaside places falling off, and others distancing them in the estimation of the public; but for the last thirty years the Happy Island has been striding on, building here, improving there, getting rid of nuisances and obstructions, conquering almost insurmountable obstacles with an iron will and an iron hand. Here is Westgate, which has arisen as if by magic on the north of the island—a neat, well-built, compact little spot, with a bold sea frontage and an intoxicating air; and Pegwell, making vigorous efforts to touch Cliff-end and join the good old town of Sandwich.

But come to the end of the old stone pier, far away to the very end, and let us take the favourite seat, sacred to the memory of innumerable novels which you and I devoured as boys—hardly ever moving the eyes from the book, except when the harbour clock struck one, and a white handkerchief from a first-floor by the flagstaff summoned us to a dinner of roast mutton and Kentish cherry-pudding. Those cherry-puddings are intimately connected with Ramsgate recollections. But do you remember the old days when railway companies did not dream of cheap tickets, and when it was necessary to come by the boat, or not at all? You cannot have forgotten the night before starting, when—as children—we were up to such monkey tricks long after the candles were extinguished, that sleep was out of the question, and we counted the hours longing for day. Then there was the journey by the *Little Western*, now lying neglected and forgotten—a "sheer hulk" for coals just below Gravesend; the campstools with pictures of worlds upon them; the funny men, and as it seems to us now, not at all the same kind of society to-day associated with the Ramsgate boat.

Then there was the town itself, with its green verandahs and not very comfortable houses, with its parched bit of Parade on the West Cliff and its scrubby bit of green on the East; a Gothic parish church with a bold tower, cutting the line of houses, a German band which tempted Ramsgate to the Parade in the evening, and a glittering, noisy place called the Bazaar, whither we repaired when the band had done, and threw with dice for work-boxes and writing-desks that we never won. So far as I can remember there were ladies who sang to us, and gentlemen who played to us, during the reckless dissipation; but I was very young and very short, and was therefore usually half-smothered by the crowd. No one, I dare say, will be surprised to hear, that as boys we enjoyed our mornings in making sand fortifications; taking an occasional turn at leap-frog over the granite posts on the pier; chaffing the vender of Chelsea buns—who turned up this morning, by-the-bye, on the sands, apparently as well as ever; and enjoying a lyrical chant invented by an extraordinary man in a velvet smoking-cap, who sold the most delicious sweets, and composed verses in honour of alicampane. This friend of my youth I have not yet rediscovered, though as I write I expect to hear his hand-bell tinkle as in the bygone days, and to see him going by with his muffin-tray, making odes to brandy-balls and dedicating stanzas to Everton toffee.

But now look up and see if you can recognise the Ramsgate of the ancient times. There are the old houses with the green verandahs, the same familiar flagstaff and the same Gothic church, the same Wellington Crescent, the same Jacob's Ladder and Augusta Stairs. But look away yonder. Regard that stately Royal Crescent, with the greensward in front of it, ringing all day to the click of the everlasting croquet-ball. Look at the Catholic Church, an old feature of Ramsgate now, though not a dozen bricks were laid in the days to which I have referred; and behind it see the Gothic Monastery and the Gothic College, and houses away again at the back, joining Pegwell and Ramsgate. The old Parade is cut up into broad, dry walks; and there is an air of comfort and stolidity which Ramsgate in the old days never knew. You must, however, come up to St. Lawrence-on-Sea, as the new district is called— if you would notice the greatest improvements. Is this pretty flower-garden, where the geraniums and calceolarias grow so well, and the tender young trees struggle so piteously with the tearing blustering wind—is this excellent promenade, where you get the best blow in all Ramsgate, the old despised East Cliff? I hardly think you would recognise old Ramsgate now, so great are the alterations, and so satisfactory is the promise of better things to come. Neither Rome nor St. Lawrence-on-Sea was built all in a day. Good houses, an hotel of distinguished proportions, a flower-garden, and a croquet lawn—which you will find inside the

Granville-gates, guarded by the stone griffins —a promenade, and a stretch of sea which cannot be surpassed : all this you know is not a bad beginning ; and if by chance some well-grounded complaints may be heard of the tortuous round by narrow streets and up steep hills which your fly takes on the way to the Granville from the station on the sands, you have only to peep over the cliff and see that a work of great difficulty is steadily advancing. The owners of the new estate have determined to make a winding road from the top of the cliff to the bottom, bringing the hotel and the railway station within two minutes of one another ; and when the raging tides permit the workmen to continue their labour in peace, the breakwater will be complete, and an inestimable gain afforded to St. Lawrence-on-Sea. It will thus be seen that Ramsgate is not asleep ; and that, true to her liberal spirit, the Happy Island offers a home to rich as well as poor, and denies her breezes to none who care to come and take advantage of them.

There never was such a fascinating hotel as the Granville. Its charm lies in its originality, and there has evidently been a desire to give us something out of the common—not a mere barrack, where you are put up and done for, but a cosy domestic dwelling-place. This is the prevailing spirit of the place. Outside it does not look like an hotel ; inside you are reminded of home. Without desiring to revive the old discussion as to the rival merits of Gothic and Italian architecture, it would surely be difficult to grumble at the faultless detail shown in every nook and corner of the Granville. Everywhere there is an absence of gimcrack. From wall-paper to stair-carpet there is the same artistic tone, extending from such a useful article as a washing-stand to the ornamentation of a stone fireplace. There is a distinct meaning in all the decoration, and there is not a rickety table or chair in the house. The comfort is great; and you eat your dinner in an elaborate banqueting hall of the early English period, which is fitted up with a stage, thoroughly adapted to theatrical performances in the winter season. There is a social charm, also, at the Granville. The homely influence of the place is more actual than suggestive. Friendships are rapidly made, the visitors soon "chum" together, and the icy reserve which is supposed to be a characteristic of the Englishman melts away at the Granville just as it vanishes in the hotels of Scarborough. In another year or so, indeed, I should not be very much surprised to see a Granville president—to be invited to a Granville expedition to Canterbury, a Granville picnic, a Granville yachting expedition, or a Granville dance. The hotel is ripe for something of the kind.

But the history of the Granville is not complete without some slight mention of the bath system, which has been started under most favourable auspices, and promises to fill the visitors' book in winter as well as summer. Have you not here, within the very walls of the Granville, but yet open to all, resident or non-resident, a Turkish bath with all the newest effects turned on? Have you not a great shampooer who won his spurs under the eye of the celebrated Dr. Barter, the father of the Turkish bath system; who relieves the monotony of the bath with quaint anecdotes and sage counsel, and has invented a system of douches so perfect and exhilarating that his pommelling and joint-cracking propensities—tortures he inflicts with Spartan determination—are forgiven for the sake of the luxurious effects attached to a Granville bath?

In the autumn of the year the Turkish bath is in great request; and as, according to the attendant's theory, the human being who neglects his Turkish bath is unfit for society, and as you cannot have too much of a good thing, the patients, thanks to the gloom of the autumn evenings, increase and multiply.

Say that your walk is over when the sun is down, and that it is chill and gloomy outside. It is too dark to read, and not sufficiently dark to justify lighting the gas. This is the time when ladies congregate in the drawing-room, and gossip over the first autumn fire before dressing for dinner. The wanderer and the outcast alike seek refuge in the Turkish bath ready to their hand. It would require a graphic pen to suggest the gloom of the Inquisition which clings about the roasting-rooms; to tell how, with the slightest effort of imagination, you can picture the red eyes of the authorized torturers glaring at you through the solemn painted glass, while the walls of the torture-chamber become hotter and hotter, and the sable attendant glides through the room grinning, as if to mock you in your torments. Far better is it to revert to the romance of the douche-room, where you experience every imaginable sensation of delight.

Picture a framework or cradle as high as a man, the bars of the frame pierced with thousands of holes, which spurt out thin streams of water, and tickle you into a delicious delirium. This done, a fire-hose directs a stream of ice-cold water upon your chest, and does its best to knock the breath out of your body. The Inquisitor next proceeds to water you with the rose of a Brobdingnagian watering-pot, and finally treats you to five minutes in the Falls of Niagara—a douche which is the concentrated essence of all the lashers on the Thames. These delightful tortures over, you are flung panting on a soft couch, there to luxuriate in Turkish cigarettes, strong coffee, and exquisite sleep, until a fiend arouses you and whispers in your ear that you have five minutes and three-quarters left to enable you to dress for dinner, and that your host is a martyr to punctuality. And what a dinner it is after such a preparation may be well imagined! I had supposed that the force of luxury could go no further than sound sleep in a comfortable bed after a long walk, a Turkish bath, an excellent dinner, several German valses, charming society, and a stirrup-cup of German love-songs feelingly expressed; and all this at the seaside, with a heavy sea and the wind howling delightfully. But I was awakened this morning by an awful presence at my bedside. The black form of a most symmetrical and muscular West Indian stood near, and beckoned mysteriously. This inventor of pleasure tortures had something else in store for me—some other hideous delight. "Nature must have its course," he whispered. "Come and be ozoned!" He would hear of no refusal, but with an awful grin again led the way to the torture-chamber. To my mind a warm bath is among the most luxurious things in the world; but what do you think of having a warm bath supplemented by a couch of the softest picked seaweed, and of being allowed to repose thereon in a warm ooze of iodine? Rapture ill-expresses the sensation. What with the warm water, the smell of the seaweed which clings about you, and the strengthening properties of the iodine that enter the pores opened by the recent Turkish bath, you get positively angry when a negro opens the door and commences an ozone shampooing process, which happily ends with the renewed tortures of the needle and Niagara douches, the water being ice-cold. And so to breakfast, with an astounding appetite.

There are some of the Granville patients, I hear, who exhibit such ferocity of appetite after the ozone bath, that it is necessary to post a waiter outside the door with a pound of beefsteak, to be ready the instant the douche is over. But, joking apart, the cures at the Granville with both baths have been most satisfactory; and it is no exaggeration to say that, under careful treatment, there has been more than one case of a cripple lifted into the hotel, yet able in a few weeks to move about on the promenade without much difficulty. The only danger is, lest the bath system should be overdone. Take my own case, for instance. When I began to write this letter the sun was shining over the sea, and all the misery of a cruel September was being forgotten in the prospect of a bright October. I had promised myself an afternoon walk along the edge of the cliff, towards Margate; but at this moment the rain is streaming down the plate-glass windows, the children have been hurried home, the Bath-chairs and the pretty girls have left the cliff. The prospect out of door is appalling. What can I do? I am sorely tempted to go downstairs and peep into the bath. If I once see the negro I shall have to surrender. But no; I will resist, and, protected by a thick greatcoat, will take my exercise in the pouring rain.

Ramsgate has played us false, but I for one can forgive so old and tried a friend. On the first day of grouse-shooting, for which we care simply nothing on this little island, whilst the sportsmen were on the moors knee-deep in the heather, Ramsgate was to have given us her annual regatta. Good Mr. Forbes had placarded the town with notices of special railway arrangements, and the minds of the boatmen on the coast were made up to pocket a few more sovereigns; the lifeboats were to have come from all the neighbouring stations, to pay a visit to the noble *Bradford*—at present, thank Heaven! rocking idly in the harbour; the crews victorious at Deal were prepared to measure strength with the Ramsgate lads, and the delightful harmony of the life here was to have been broken into by the stir and bustle of an aquatic festival; but at the last moment the dream was cruelly dispelled. I honestly declare, however, that I shall not join in the chorus of complaint, for the regatta is only a pleasure deferred.

Besides, if the original intention had been carried out, it would have prevented me from going round the dear old place, and making friends with scenes and pictures which to me are fresher and brighter than ever. There are few living Londoners, I am quite certain, familiar with this part of the country, whose memories do not take them back to Ramsgate, one of the brightest of treasured recollections. Changes and innumerable improvements have taken place in it; St. Lawrence-on-Sea has started into life. The old East Cliff Parade, where the band played on alternate evenings when many of us were children, has acquired ecclesiastical grandeur. The beautiful Granville has lifted her head out of cornfields, and a mighty tower has sprung from the gardens. Geranium-beds, croquet-lawns, and cool pavilions, heraldic lions and Gothic griffins, convent-knockers and monastic bell-pulls, everywhere architectural works of rare taste, are noticed on the very ground where years ago we plucked nosegays of poppies and other wild flowers whilst walking with our nurses close to the cliff's edge, or resting under the shadow of Sir Moses Montefiore's garden-wall. A broad chalk road to take the station flys up the cliff is, as I mentioned before, almost finished, and the railway authorities, with their station-sheds, granite embankments, and other necessary but still very ugly paraphernalia, have, it is true, to some extent spoilt our old sands, where years ago we munched our mid-day bread-and-butter, and purchased our Chelsea buns. But here are the Augusta Stairs, up which we struggled every morning, dragging at our nurse's gown; and there is the parched, brown enclosure opposite Wellington Crescent, where lads were then, and are still, playing cricket. Gazing down below, a Rip Van Winkle, rubbing his eyes after a dream of thirty odd years, would find not a stick, stone, or a house altered. The same old spade and shoe shops, the same coloured alabaster presents to be placed on the nursery mantelpiece at home, the same shell-work boxes and marvellous pincushions, the open carriages in a string round the harbour-gates, the never-to-be-forgotten fishy, shrimpy smell along the quay, and the old happy mixture of tarred rope and miscellaneous drinks and eatables. Why, what change can any one find here? The sunburnt sailors are still idling about those granite posts on the quay.

Here is the precipice over the harbour basin, which still, as of old, frightens nervous mothers. Apparently the same waiters, with white napkins under their arms, are standing on the hotel steps, making tempting offers of good joints just in cut. The traps, pony-carriages, and public conveyances are still taking up excursionists for Margate or Pegwell Bay. We miss the old cry of "Tivoli Gardens," but we hear much now of the "Hall-by-the-Sea." No change near the old flagstaff, except that "Fuller's Marine Library," where our mothers gambled for work-boxes and pianofortes, is a deserted ruin. The very same seat is beneath the old flagpole, round which blue-eyed lads and yellow-haired maidens are still romping. The old balcony still exists, where a certain laughing child, far more years ago than I, for one, care to remember, acted most successfully the part of Helen, and a Liliputian Trojan war was waged on her behalf by the urchins residing in Wellington Crescent.

I find no change in the Paragon, and but very little in the West Parade, save that the semicircle ends as it began, in a piece of refined architecture. Once upon a time the sanctuary bell rang out in a little temporary chapel among the wheat, whereas I heard to-day the "Angelus" sounded from the tower of an almost finished church. I would not give much for the man who has no sentiment of affection for his old home and school, the ancient farmhouse where he paid an annual visit to a good maiden aunt, or for the first seaside place to which he was taken—Ramsgate. The broken character of the town, and its varied frontage, with steps here, and hills there, its utter lack of uniformity, double cliff, unequalled harbour, bold pier, fisher-life, promenades, and opportunities for excursions, render it altogether unlike any other watering-place that I know of. Many coast towns have the stereotyped row of houses facing the water, conventional sea-wall, uniform sands or beach, and orthodox and ugly pier; but at Ramsgate it is possible to live amongst a dozen sets of people and see a dozen distinct views a day. For instance, the morning walk among the pretty flowers of St. Lawrence-on-Sea, when the band plays opposite the pavilion; the happy, quiet life on the Granville croquet-lawn—where the gardener shows the fallacy of the theory that plants will not thrive luxuriantly by the sea. This is altogether different to the laughing, reckless, mad-cap life down the Augusta Stairs, among the babies and bare-legged children on the sands, where you find the wandering photographer, and lie under the awnings of bathing-machines, or stroll among the niggers and ballad singers, who play their part in forming the great Ramsgate picture. The sands this morning were more throbbing with life and variety, and more picturesque than I have ever seen them. It appeared as if it would be impossible to introduce one more bench or one more baby. Every London itinerant band and organ-grinder had come down. The racecourses had emptied their Bohemian frequenters on the sands. Donkey-drivers were energetically plying their profession. Old-fashioned barrel-organs were having pitched battles with the new piano instruments which delight suburban residents on quiet evenings, the impromptu singer was dividing the pence with the pseudo-Davenport Brothers, promoted to Ramsgate from Exeter Street, Strand; and boys and girls were laughing in glee as they, with their clothes tucked up, paddled amid the tiny breakers.

In the old days every child had to be stripped after dabbling in the sea barefooted. We all remember that, irritating dab of damp petticoat against the nude leg! But what does the modern mother do? She simply binds up all the wilful clothes in a French *caleçon*, which is worn by every girl and petticoated boy over everything. The children bound thus, certainly look like Mr. Alfred Thompson's ballet-girls, so far as their striped decorations are concerned; but I really think that the good lady who hit upon this simple and happy expedient deserves as much praise as the ever-quoted and mysterious gentleman who invented the perforation of postage-stamps. And then the high tide comes up driving the nurserymaids right back into the premises of the London, Chatham, and Dover Company, chasing all the children up the breakwater, among donkeys and goat-chaises, and sending the novel-reading girls higgledy-piggledy into the shoe-shops and alabaster warehouses. But there is another life altogether on the pier. Yachts are going out sailing, and filling fast with excursionists. The men, weary of their babies, are off fishing for the day, or rowing for an hour or so; and those who enjoy a happy mean between dulness and excitement, and who spend their whole day on the breezy pier, are rewarded this morning by the excitement of the entry into port of a Norwegian barque which was caught on the Goodwins last night in a fog, and by the brave exertions of my friends the Deal sailors (about the pluckiest fellows on this dangerous coast) was tugged into Ramsgate, making water very fast, but, happily, all safe. A little further on, there is still another life; for Ramsgate, following the popular fashion, has recently started an Aquarium, which has already been visited and officially approved by the leading natural history authorities. It is a modest little structure, no doubt; for, following the example of Mr. Peggotty, some most intelligent sailors in communication with the fishermen of the port have once more made a house out of a boat. In a roomy old boat this modest little Aquarium thrives, and is already well-stocked with fish and decorated with excellent taste. The Ramsgate Aquarium does not intend to be beaten by its more commodious rivals,

I can assure you. Here several specimens of the hippocampus nod their horse's head and twist their tails round the seaweed; here we find the sulky dogfish and the lovely butterfly gurnard with its superbly-coloured fins; here we discover for the first time that the lobster has a tail of the most gorgeous ultramarine blue; and here the wrasse, the eel, the sole, the plaice, and the turbot, the hideous skate, with his comical countenance, and some superb sea-anemones delight the Ramsgate public and the excursionists. Great things come out of small beginnings, and the idea of making the Ramsgate Aquarium principally a collection of local specimens is one which will commend itself to Mr. Buckland and all fish-lovers. Don't let the Ramsgate people snub the poor little Aquarium, because it does not look showy outside, and because it is built in a boat. I for one, having enjoyed an interesting half-hour in the show, say decidedly, "Walk up, walk up!" Even now I have not nearly exhausted the delights of a Ramsgate day. I intended to have taken you round the old streets—another life again—into the famous fruit market; up on to the other cliff, where a sober life commences again, where the governess propriety is found, and where Bath-chairs and devourers of novels congregate, where the click of the croquet-ball is heard on the crescent, and the young ladies in the front drawing-rooms exercise their fingers with Thalberg and murder Liszt.

Still at Ramsgate.

"Oh! haste and leave this sacred Isle!" This is what my conscience whispers, in the words of that misogynist, St. Senanus, who actually swore a coarse oath that the "sainted sod" of the Isle of Scattery should "ne'er by woman's feet be trod." But I am ill-disposed on this occasion to listen to the whisperings of conscience. I don't like going away from anywhere; and for me, in season or out of season, Thanet Isle has a strange fascination. I feel that my holiday time is drawing to a close; that work has commenced again seriously in London; that the island is for the most part occupied by unfortunate Londoners who have been compelled to postpone their rest until the last moment—grumbling at the sun when they were caged up, and longing for one gleam now they are free; or by those who have nothing to do but to spend money and take "nips" of fresh air.

Still I must wander on. When I have completed my pilgrimage round the coast to the Margate Station, it will all be over for the year. The smell of the sea and the fresh scent of the breezes, the wild elastic feeling as you stride across the grass on the top of the cliff or pick your way among the low rocks on the shore, will be put away and locked up with summer suits until the winter is over, and the spring sun shines again. But how to leave Ramsgate now, as I take my stand, outside the Granville-gates, so blown about that I can scarcely resist the bold wind that sweeps along the cliff and bullies the steamer on its way home through the angry waves? I have owned to the delightful feeling that I ought not to be here. It is like lying in bed when you have important engagements to fulfil and had arranged to have been up and about hours ago. I feel like a schoolboy who enjoys, but yet hates, the day on which he plays truant—or like a Government clerk who does his mid-day park in the season, and braves consequences. I must wander on, and Ramsgate must be locked up for the winter. I have an irresistible longing to do that which I cannot do. I should like to mount to the top of the bold new tower at the Granville and look out to sea on one side, and over Canterbury on the other. I have a desire to turn my steps in precisely the opposite direction to that I am bound to take, to enjoy an oyster luncheon at the new Pegwell Inn, or a chat with the Kentish rustics sitting about the benches at the Sportsman Inn at Cliff End; or on again through the old town of Sandwich, away over the sand-hills to shingly Deal. I want to sit on the granite pier and talk with Isaac Jarman about his bold adventures with the lifeboat lying there in the harbour, all trim and ready for action—and it cannot be very long before it is wanted during these fierce equinoctial gales; or to take a book and sit underneath on the jetty, pretending to read while the water laps for ever against the wooden piles and platform.

Wherever I turn I am tempted. Here is a steamer about to start for Dover, and a yacht ready to take out a party for a sail, for the not very extravagant price of one shilling; or, if I choose, I can fish in a public boat, fascinated by the promise that "the fish caught will be divided among the company." Again, there is much to see on the sands—now, alas! by railway companies and embankments, wooden piles and bathing machines, reduced to a minimum of space, and hardly to be recognised as the same Ramsgate Sands Mr. Frith painted years ago. But the sands are not dull, though October has already been born. Here is the man—the afternoon man from Southampton Street, Strand—with the tame canary birds, the sleek tabby cat, and the domesticated mice which have a strange partiality for pussy's embrace; the whole entertainment terminating with a feline representation of the great fight between Sayers and Heenan. Here is a nigger troupe, with the pluck almost taken out of it, sitting idly on the scarlet cushions of the rude green benches. Here is a Cheap Jack of astounding volubility; and here is the galvanic battery by which you can be rendered intensely uncomfortable for a penny. Here is the youth in the dirty Jersey, who likes to be tied up with ropes, but apparently has not recovered that fearful "Tom Fool's knot" to which Mr. Sothern once introduced him, while some adventurous spirits, plucky to the last, are bathing yet, and giving one an opportunity of noticing that, in matters of decency, no less than in local administration, Ramsgate has turned over a new leaf, and shown signs of wise and healthy reform.

But here I could stay all day, running away like Romeo, only to return the next moment and listen to Juliet's last word. I must wander on. The best plan is not to look behind; so with a halt under the trees of the gardens of that fine old English gentleman, Sir Moses Montefiore, to listen to the colony of birds gathered here in a singing parliament from all parts of the island, because this is the sweetest spot and all is peace—and another rest at the first chine where the telegraph wires run under the sea—I make my way across the muddy fields and over the moist chalk land, till the Bleak House comes in sight and Broadstairs is reached.

Let the reader disabuse himself of the notion that because Ramsgate is building and Margate improving, because St. Lawrence-on-Sea has been born, and Cliftonville must be added to the local maps, pretty little Broadstairs has been asleep. Seen from the front, Broadstairs is little changed. I see the same cosy and well-managed hotel, the same row of pretty seaside houses—the same compact, bandbox look round about Broadstairs, in the hollow of the hill. But if you wish to see how Broadstairs has been building, you must wander up by the railway station, where neat and substantial little villas, neat and convenient, have sprung up like mushrooms. For, say what we like about the attractions of her taller sisters on the right hand and on the left, Broadstairs will always be a pet. Everything here is on a miniature scale, but everything is of the best. There is a little harbour and a little bay, a little semicircle of sand for the little ones to dig in, a little promenade, and pretty little boats. It is the watering-place of Liliput. Pray do not imagine that Broadstairs will be offended if you call her quiet. On the contrary, she prides herself on her peace. Here you can do just as you like. You can fling yourself down on the grass cliff just outside the promenade, and read undisturbed by a crowd of astonished gazers. You can sketch without interruption. You can dress as you please, and, night or day, you are soothed by a delicious and indescribable quiet. You are out of the world, and, instead of having thousands of eyes upon you, the hundreds of opera-glasses belonging to Broadstairs alone disturb your peace. And then, again, it is like playing at being at a seaside place of abnormal dulness. If you require dissipation, you can have it in a few minutes by the train either way. There are the ozone and Turkish baths of Ramsgate, together with her pier and promenade, on the one side; and on the other the billiard-tables, the jetty, the Assembly Rooms, the Hall-by-the-Sea, and the Theatre Royal of Margate. We are not all idle men. Even in holiday time some of us have, if not to work, at least to think over it; and, depend upon it, dreamy little Broadstairs, with its quiet mornings, its opportunities for getting about in the afternoon, and its starry evenings, will hold its own, notwithstanding the powerful attractions of its rivals. At any rate, the town was never in such a flourishing condition as now. Just let us look at Broadstairs for the last time before I wander on. Over there by the harbour and the pier is the suggestion of the Enoch Arden fishing life; there are the picturesque smacks, the tiny sails. No funnels or grimy smoke, no steamers or tugs, disturb the freshness of Broadstairs. It is all of the salt salty. But Broadstairs boasts her lifeboat and her reading-rooms. She has a clean bay of sand, dear to the maternal heart. There are opportunities for bathing appreciated by the athletic maiden; and, take it altogether—sand and harbour, fishing life and cliff lounge, croquet-lawn and pretty lodging—I know of no better place for the children who must dig and paddle all day, and for the parents who maintain, as it is fitting that virtuous parents should, they seek the seaside for health's sake and fresh air; but who, when the weary diggers and water-babies are curled up in little cribs asleep, are off to see their fellow-creatures on Ramsgate Pier, or to watch the young men and maidens vowed to Margate-valsing in the Assembly Rooms, or listening to the concerts in the Hall-by-the Sea.

Merry Margate.

To say that Margate is full is to convey no notion whatever of the normal condition of this wonderful spot. To say that she is merry is but faintly to express an idea of the "high jinks" carried on here from morning until the new Licensing Act cuts short the evening pleasures of the holiday-makers, and drives them sulkily to bed. On a Saturday morning we have scarcely breakfasted before early Londoners came trooping through the town, and, entering the various hotels in a nonchalant manner, ask for a bed. They are literally laughed to scorn. The impudence, says our landlady, of coming to Margate on a Saturday morning, and expecting any sheltering roof but that of a friendly bathing-machine! Why, the porters of all the hotels are seeking in highways and byways for rooms promised to "some of our very oldest customers." Good-natured hostesses, anxious to please, receive by every post a pile of letters, and each one could have filled her house a dozen times over. A garret in a public-house might be obtained as a favour for five shillings, and I was myself very nearly closing with a clean front-kitchen and a shake-down under the dresser. It was positively painful to see the heart-rending position of unprovided families who believe overmuch in the elasticity of Margate, and never dream of a previous telegram or a halfpenny post-card. Harassed mothers with children in arms and disobedient urchins dragging at their tails wended their melancholy way up streets and down streets, painfully perspiring, but suffering nobly, as all good mothers do; irritable fathers, the first to lower their flag, gave it up in despair, and sat upon a ruin of boxes at the water's edge. Knowing flymen were driven about from pillar to post, first told to explore the Marine Terrace, then taken up higher, and finally implored to exhaust the new-built region at Cliftonville. Now, let it be remembered that at this early hour, when garrets were letting for a week's wages and kitchens were at a premium, London had not really arrived at all. The London, Chatham, and Dover had not emptied its trains on the beach; the South-Eastern had scarcely contributed one family to the jetty; not a morning's boat nor a husband's boat had been spied, steaming in the offing, through the family telescope or the balcony opera-glass. It all came right in the end, however. Before the last galop had been whirled away in the dear old Assembly Rooms, before the last wild dance had been concluded at the Hall-by-the-Sea, merry Margate had been once more true to her friends, the yellow boots and the canvas shoes had been placed outside some door or other, and in parlour and drawing-room, on sofa and on chairs, in kitchen and in attic, Margate retired to rest, leaving the deserted streets to the melancholy policemen and the sea dashing against the piles of the neglected pier. And what wonder is it there is all this hubbub and confusion, this crowding in of trains and boats, this desire to be accommodated anywhere, this passion to be present on pier and jetty and in ball-room? for, let them sneer as they will, Margate has a speciality of her own, and is unlike any other place in this or any other island. Margate can only be compared to herself. She prides herself on her rare good-nature and her reckless spirits. "Take us as you find us," says Margate, in the truest spirit of hospitality. "We are a little rough, perhaps, but very jolly. There is no pride, and you will find no stuck-up notions here. We have come out for a spree, and mean to enjoy it." So the bracing air, the life, the *élan*, and the heartiness of Margate, carry her along, and make her a thousand times more popular than the proudest and most aristocratic watering-place in the world. Here all scenic effects, all beauty of coast line, all enjoyment derived from welcome pictures on sea and land are crushed out by the violent colour of the crowds about the place, and the vigorous life of the passing people. No one comes to Margate for the romantic or the beautiful. Scarcely a visitor could sketch the outline of the place from memory. Very few dream of walking as far as the Cliftonville Hotel. .

Any one proposing a walk along the cliff to enjoy the silent charm of Kingsgate and its castle, the pretty retirement of Broadstairs, or the gentle grace of Ramsgate would be considered a madman. The notion of a pilgrimage to Canterbury is put off for the first wet day. That picturesque neighbour, little Westgate-on-the-Sea, might be as far off as Scarborough for aught the Margate people care about it, and as to Reculvers or Herne Bay, they might just as well be on the coast of France. Margate does not sit down and dream or doze, but derives her enjoyment by racing and tearing along. The whole place is alive with excitement and gaiety. There are niggers and banjos in every street—you cannot stir a dozen yards without hearing a band. Bohemians and mountebanks increase and multiply on sand and cliff and parade. You may not meditate or think. You cannot get away from pleasant din of excitement. Step out of the station, already exhilarated with the joyous Margate breeze, and you must bathe instantly or be thought a muff. Go a little further, and you must take a row, or you will be for ever in the black-books of the Margate sailors. One yard in advance, you must mount a donkey and go clattering along, a whooping-boy with a whacking stick pursuing you like a demon, or you must be bundled into a basket-carriage and sent flying along dusty, treeless roads. Stroll on the jetty, you must be weighed, or must punch a buffer to test your strength, or must be borne along down the slippery steps to sail for a couple of hours, or, failing all these, must be button-holed by one of your hundred Margate friends, and introduced to some fair one sitting with her legs dangling down on the edge of the jetty. Rush with difficulty from the pier, you are immediately plunged into the confusion of the shops near the Mariners' Club.

Mount further on, you must bathe again at the Clifton Baths, buy photograph frames from an industrious man who is doomed to spend an existence in beautifying firewood, patronize more niggers, more bands, a Punch and Judy, dancing-dogs, and an entertaining monkey. No heat nor sirocco, no hurricane nor whirlwind, stops the even flow of the Margate merriment. The variety of climate at Margate is extraordinary.

It is like Bombay in the morning and the Bay of Biscay at night. The heat was positively awful when those poor houseless mothers dragged about their moaning infants. The asphalte on the jetty was softened into an inky jelly. It felt as if one were walking on a furnace in goloshes. We all left our footprints on this pliable promenade, and the ladies with high-heels were in danger of sticking there until the sun went down. The white cliff was positively dazzling against blue sea and blue sky. The stone pier almost blinded the eyes. The venerable old goats attached to the chaises put down their heads and vainly endeavoured to wriggle their roasting bodies under the little carriages. Cabmen and boatmen, ticket-porters and sailors, hanging about the jetty, were almost driven wild by a very pestilence of flies. But still Margate treated the sun's glare with consummate indifference. There were only two places in all Margate where it was possible to seek the shade—down the steps of the Jetty, within a few inches of the sea, or away in the heart of the town in good old-fashioned Cecil Square, close by the tall, red-brick houses or under the broad portico of the Margate Assembly Rooms, where George IV. loved to dance in days gone by, and where a past and forgotten Margate crowd was in the habit of discovering where the Duke of Wellington rested at the Royal Hotel, and calling the old gentleman to cheer him as he looked out from an upper window. But Margate disdained the shade and snubbed the idea of an afternoon siesta.

The Jetty steps were patronized by the few ladies here who care for their complexions, and good old Cecil Square with its recollections was left to a few old gentlemen who knew Bath and Tunbridge Wells, and, under the portico of the Royal Hotel, revived the old-fashioned watering-place scandals. Margate never rested for an instant. Though the thermometer was at fever heat, and the sun was pitiless, the Jetty must still be done, shrimps and hot tea must still be taken in those queer looking old houses overlooking the sea, with a fish-shop in the front, and behind a long parlour and a tinkling piano, donkeys must still be ridden, excursions taken, more bathing, more boats, more sails, more ceaseless laughter. Pattering by went the young men with their racket-shoes and blue-jackets, who have been so aptly termed "nautical cricketers;" in a crowd and a flutter went by the girls with their white-spotted blue dresses, and the women with those baggy, dreadful-looking yellow shoes; the chignon girls, and the girls with tall white sugar-loaf straw-hats breaking out into an agricultural splendour, poppies and corn. Never was seen such a mixture. Frock-coats and summer-coats, straw-hats and chimney-pots, pipes and cigars, good taste and bad—there was really no end to the delightful discord. And the Margate excitement does not die with the day. It increases rapidly as the sun sets. The tea and shrimps put vigour into the Margate constitution. The animal spirits become wild and ungovernable, when ordinary lovers of effect would be watching one of the most glorious sunsets. Who cares at Margate for a sunset, who knows that Turner caught many of his best effects here, or hints that Mr. Ruskin might write an essay this evening on the harmonies of colour? Margate is in high spirits. A bet has been made that a gentleman will not go from one end of the Jetty to the other in full evening dress, carrying a couple of theatrical board-bills, within a few minutes of the arrival of the Husbands' Boat; and he actually does it, preceded and followed by a dusky regiment of niggers, hastily collected from all the streets in Margate. The bet is fairly won, the Jetty peals with laughter at the extraordinary sight of the boardman in *grande tenue*, smoking a cigar and distributing playbills with lavender-gloved hands, and the only person who appears to be shocked is an old lady in a Bath-chair, who has a horror of theatres and a detestation of practical jokes. But when the husbands have been welcomed and chaffed, when the telescopes and opera-glasses have been put away; when the crowd has been bustled along—an *olla podrida* of domestic joy, chaff, curiosity, luggage, and touts—the whole scene at Margate changes suddenly and instantly. A wonderful wind, almost approaching a hurricane, springs up. The calm blue sea is lashed up into a fury of dull green waves. The outstanding boats and vessels gain the shore with difficulty, and every Margate dress, hat, coat, and cloak is powdered over with the finest dust and most irritating sand. It blows up in clouds and circles, and every eye is tortured almost to madness. Happy and hand-in-hand all day, Margate separates into two strong divisions when the sun has set and the wind blows chilly.

Half keeps to the darkened Jetty; the other half is blown about on the Pier. The Pier-half will go to the Assembly Rooms in a few minutes. The Jetty-half will patronize the Hall-by-the-Sea. Perhaps it is as well that we were off to both places as soon as possible,—for the entertainments are rich and varied, and promenading is almost impossible. What with dusty eyes and the sudden darkness, it is impossible to recognise the dearest friends; and the poor musicians in the Pier orchestra are clutching at their hats and struggling with their wilful cornets. But there must be a night even at Margate, or Margate would not show such a clean bill of health. It would be a pity to burn the candle at both ends, so we all turn in and appear only to have dropped off into a first sleep when the Margate sun comes streaming into the windows again, with the merry hum of bathers going to the beach, and the cry of the early shrimp-seller. Once more, thank goodness! is felt the first quick bound of the Margate pulses!

A DESERTED ISLAND.

Hayling.

UNLESS my memory grievously fails me, there is a picture drawn by a pleasant composer of German fairy stories of a land of peace and plenty, literally flowing with the kind of milk and honey which delights the fancy of an imaginative child. I am sure I can remember being told of a wonderful paradise, where the apples on the trees, bending the branches down with an agony of weight, called out to the passers-by to gather them; where the plums and peaches on the walls complained sadly that their sweetness was unrecognised; where the over-ripe ears of corn stooped low, humiliated by persistent neglect; and where, in the centre of a wood full of green leaves and flowers, was found a cottage with a roof of cake, windows made of barley-sugar, and bricks of gingerbread! There is no need to tell what happened in the enchanted land when the children who had wandered thither took the apples and peaches at their word, and commenced eating the barley-sugar windows—how under every plum was a wasp, under each leaf a viper, and a horrible witch lived in the confectionery castle. I shall certainly not push my comparison to that extent. But I have found an unrecognised spot, and spent the most peaceful days on a deserted island.

Within half an hour's journey of a thriving, bustling, important seaport town, smelling of rope-ends and tar, and lively with sailors—a town of dockyards and fortifications, and ships and improvements; within ten minutes of the main line of one of the most frequented railways, approached by a branch railway on one side and a ferry from the mainland on the other; looked at by the telescopes of some of our most popular watering-places and from the upper windows of a marine city, lies an island as deserted as the one discovered by Robinson Crusoe, and as beautiful as the home which so wearied Enoch Arden. "I beg your pardon, sir—this is South Hayling," says the guard of the train, as we stop suddenly, apparently because there is an obstruction on the line, and we cannot push on. No one has yet moved from his carriage. No one has attempted to come out on the silent platform, or to look round on a space of apparently uninhabited country. The conventional railway tavern is not seen. Not a tout has come here from hotel or lodging-house. There is not an omnibus, or fly, or carriage in the station-yard. The noise of the faintly-expiring steam in the diminutive engine is the sole sign of energy hereabouts.

"This is South Hayling," says the guard, and in a few minutes the passengers separate, and are lost in the mazes of a delightful island.

Some strike across the fields seaward, passing through the straw-yard of a farm, and losing themselves among the ricks and barns in search of a path under a hedgerow of wild convolvus. Others remain true to the main road, and ask at the Barley Mow in what direction the sea lies, and where they are likely to find the famous Hayling Beach, with its miles of sand and frequent opportunities for bathing. Where can we be?—in the heart of the Isle of Wight, in some of the peaceful Jersey lanes, or in the deserted pathways of Sark? There is nothing whatever to remind us of the sea. No lodgings, no houses, no shops, no activity. Here is a farmhouse peaceful and deserted—the farmer afield, the men far away at work, the mistress of the house occupied in some quiet dairy—no sound save the whistle of a single labourer in the rickyard.

The farm passed, there are still more country lanes, more trees, more wild flowers, more cornfields, until in a snug little corner some romantic and rose-covered cottage is discovered, or the dwelling-houses of the Hayling peasants, each with a garden rich in verbenas, hollyhocks, and dahlias. The land is apparently rich in produce—the orchards are heavy with apples, the gardens are full of flowers; but the silence is striking, and the peace is profound.

We come to an old church, and we rest a little, enjoying the silence under an old oak porch. We peep through the bars of the open church-door, and there is a sense of stillness as distinct as in the churchyard, where an ancient yew tree is supported by a crutch, lest it should fall and crush the old carved gravestones it has sheltered for centuries. We have not seen a soul or heard a sound, until in the distance we catch the ring of a blacksmith's forge, and hear the rumble of a farm-cart creeping through the shady lanes laden with grain. Pushing on, more farms, more cottages are found; but no seaside life. Where are the Belinda Terraces, and the Alma Villas? Where are the white walls and the green verandahs? Where are the children with their spades and fish-pails, the girls with their gipsy-hats and back-hair, the mothers with their luncheon-baskets and yellow boots? Supposing we had arrived here with a tribe of children, and a transport-cart of luggage, where should we discover the welcome bill and the accommodating landlady? These dreamy farmhouses, these silent cottages, only desire to be left alone. Where should we find a home and a welcome? Echo answers, Where? and still meditating through an opening at the head of a green lane, we see and smell the sea.

I have found at last an ideal watering-place. The beauty and romance of the Hayling lanes, with their cottages and trees, are only equalled by the freedom and expanse of the Hayling beach. A wild common of furze, suggestive of rabbits, a broad parade of green turf, calling out to the Hayling children to use it for cricket, rounders, and romps; a long row of seats facing the water, suggestive of idle mornings and the latest novel; sand to the right hand and sand to the left—broad, expansive, delightful sand, scattered over with shells and seaweed—sand that would find employment for all the digging children of Ramsgate, Margate, Westgate, and Herne Bay put together, and still leave acres to spare—sand which should be planted with archery targets, and made merry with donkeys—sand provided with bathing machines, elaborately made, and fitted with polished deal; provided also with life preservers and hot water foot-baths, according to the comfortable fashion at Trouville and Dieppe—sands from which you can see the green shores of the Isle of Wight in the distance, steamers and ships on the horizon, the busy scenes of Southsea and Portsmouth on the left hand, and on the right, unbroken, undisturbed sea. But, wonder of wonders, a deserted, melancholy, forgotten sand—a sand left to its own devices—a sand untrodden, and shells ungathered! The rabbits remain undisturbed and uneaten among the furze, the green common is as desolate as Dartmoor. Not a cricket-ball or rounder-stick is seen here, for there is apparently not a lad for the playground; the benches are empty, the sand is as deserted as Sahara; there is not a donkey or donkey-boy on the beach; and if a dozen bathers come to the bath-house a day, the proprietors congratulate themselves on a lively trade. Looking back to the sea-front, where we should find the long rows of sea-side houses, where should be built the reading and assembly rooms, and conversation houses, we discover that the best spots have been secured for private estates, and find nothing but a large, well-furnished, convenient, and homely hotel, which has taken several new houses under its protecting wing, and a terrace of lodging-houses, broken short off, as if it had changed its mind, and put off building for another occasion.

This deserted Hayling Island is to me a complete and unaccountable mystery. Here are farms full of milk and cream, eggs and butter; here are gardens full of honey and honeycomb; here are romantic walks in country lanes, or in lone cool woods; here is a common to shoot on, and only four gentlemen in South Hayling take out a shooting licence—so I discover on the old church-door; here is a field, or parade, of the Littlehampton pattern, for the lads of Hayling; here are sands and a beach, which have few equals; here is a strand, where the bathing is excellent; and, ugly reports notwithstanding, perfectly safe; here is an hotel, where they pride themselves on serving a French *déjeûner* in good style, and where the Hayling delicacies—oysters, rabbits, and mackerel—can be comfortably enjoyed; and still the seaside world turns its back upon Hayling. I am bound to say, that in attempting to discover the cause for all this neglect, this silly snubbing of wonderful natural advantages, this extraordinary determination to keep Hayling in its loneliness and despair, I find there are faults on both sides.

It is all very well to talk about romance and country lanes, a wooded island, a healthy spot, and a glorious sea beach; but none of us can live without houses; and I don't suppose, for all the oysters, rabbits, and mackerel in the world, that many of us would care to spend a month in a bathing-machine. If Hayling will not build houses, where are we to live? If Hayling will not exert herself to make herself amusing, how very few people are likely to come! Hayling with one shop, one policeman, a Havant doctor, and newspapers with all periodicals supplied by the courtesy of the hotel proprietor, can only attract very original seekers of the sea. If it is true that the train brings family after family to Hayling, ultimately compelled to leave it with regret owing to insufficient accommodation—if it is a fact that the island has been coaxed to build, but turns a deaf ear to the charmer—it is decidedly inconsistent for Hayling to talk about her sand and bathing, her health, her beauty, her charms and her lovely face, and to stand wringing her hands in despair on the margin of her deserted shore. She will receive no pity so long as she refuses to help herself. The railway helps Hayling half-way towards the construction of an English Blankenberge. Nature gives her the green woods and the splendid beach, which must be the envy of a score more popular places; but until she sets her house in order few, save enthusiasts, will linger long in this beautiful place.

They tell us that whilst Sherman House, in

Chicago, was burning, "the purchase of a new building was completed, and on the first night after the flames abated, shelter was given to some three hundred homeless heads;" we are informed that in the same marvellous city "a six-storied block of good substantial brickwork was roofed within eleven weeks of the digging of its foundations;" but in England, Hayling Island is unknown, though the sea has washed round its shores for years, and the yew-trees over the graves in its churchyard tell of its unchequered and peaceful life.

As the island now stands, it is ridiculous to believe, though with far easier approaches, Hayling can be much more popular than Sark or the Scilly Islands. The young ladies who want lovers, and the mammas haunted with matrimonial ideas; the holiday-makers who cannot rest without niggers and Punch and Judies; the fathers who are miserable without clubs and reading-rooms; the children who are in despair without donkeys and goat-carriages; the marvellous folk who think the seaside nothing unless they can face it, breathe it, and devour it all day long; the inconsistent people who think a holiday of little worth without the discomfort of small lodgings, and who would sooner live in a cellar facing the sea than in rambling apartments in a dear old farmhouse, "warm with the breath of kine," all these would of course ridicule the mention of Hayling, and laugh me to scorn for holding up my voice in support of such a place. But there are pleasure-seekers and pleasure-seekers, and we do not all get rest in the same way. Some love a hard mattress, and some cannot sleep a wink in cotton-sheets. Some gain health and strength amidst noise and confusion and indifferent lodgings; others are positively angry when one discovers and recommends a deserted island. But until Hayling plucks up strength and heart to please the million, there are hundreds of quiet people who will love her extremely well.

I have told you what you will not find on the island, but have only faintly touched upon the pretty idiosyncrasies of a pleasant home where the "weary are at rest." If the brain is fevered and excited, and the nerves are unstrung with howling children, rattling cabs, and street-organs—if London's whirl, rattle, tempest and confusion, make irritation border on frenzy, and the jingle of street-musicians, sand-songsters, photograph touts, and miscellaneous hawkers only serve to heap fuel on the raging fire—come to Hayling, and sleep and dream. If there is any soothing influence in the peace of farmyards and the lowing of cattle, the scent of rose-gardens, and the fresh, sweet smell of English country lanes, come to Hayling. If there is any pleasure in a long morning in a lonely wood, with no sound about one but the song of birds and the hum of innumerable insects; if there is any truth in the health of the island, as ascertained after a stroll round the churchyard and the quiet record of profound old age; if there is any delight in a long-deserted sand and the presence of a wide undisturbed sea; if there is any relief in mornings undisturbed and long free afternoons; if there is any cure in wonderful silence and perfect peace; if there is any relish for oysters coming in by the hundred, freshly caught in the beds hereabouts, supplemented by farmhouse bread-and-butter with honest English stout; if you can dine off a sweet dish of fish and a Hayling rabbit, smothered in onions; if rest is to be found in meditation or work to be done in silence; if a holiday home is desired where you can bathe in peace, read in quiet, walk unnoticed, and live in the oldest and most comfortable clothes; if an original spot is desired where worldliness is absent and fashion is tabooed—pause before you pass by Havant Station, and take a ticket I beg you for Hayling Island!

OZONE-LAND.

Weston-super-Mare.

THACKERAY, in his immortal ballad of "Little Billee," has described the partiality of the merchants of Bristol city for the sea; but the excellent merchants of that fine old spot, the traders in sugar and dealers in corn, the wonderful men who made fortunes in the slums about Temple Street, and in the dingy waterside-offices, no longer in couplets or in triplets pay their annual addresses to the ocean. These merchants of Bristol city no longer take a boat and go to sea, but in hundreds they rush to the ozone-bearing towns of the Bristol Channel. London has her Brighton, Liverpool and Manchester their New Brightons and Southports; so why should not good old Bristol have an outlet for her smoke, an exodus for her hard-working people? In point of fact she has many. Not down the Avon, with its picturesque bank of rock and wood on either side; not under the famous Suspension Bridge swinging wonderfully overhead; not skirting the trees overhanging Nightingale Valley, or sailing by the quaint fishing-villages, do the Bristol merchants rush from their counting-houses, and feed their constitutions with ozone. Some drive rapidly to the miniature Portishead Wood, covered and domestic.

Many more take a ticket at the Bristol and Exeter Station for Clevedon, the resting-place of Hallam, the holiday home of Coleridge, the quiet, health-giving spot, with its old church on the edge of the cliff and the end of the down, which inspired the Poet Laureate for his sweetest lyrics, and suggested the most exquisite passages of "In Memoriam." But the best half of weary Bristol, with their wives and daughters longing for a change; by far the greater number of the Bristol babes and sucklings, with their nurses and nursemaids, come helter-skelter to Weston-on-the-Sea. It is so easily done —one change on the Weston Junction, and you are here in a minute. There is no parting of husband and wife for a week, as at Ramsgate or Herne Bay; there is no Black Monday train and piping of eyes on Monday morning; no wild rejoicings when the smoke of the Husbands' Boat is seen as the sun sets on Saturday—for the Bristol merchant can catch the last train, and be at Weston for dinner; can have a swim in Weston Bay, and be in his office in time to chide the sluggard clerk; can kiss his babes morning and night, and never lose sight of his idolized ledger. If the Bristol mamma is a little faint and sick, she is packed off to a cosy Weston lodging for a week. If a Bristol baby is a trifle peeky and pale, why, what can be better than a turn in the perambulator on the esplanade facing the sea and the sand? If Charlie is outgrowing his strength he must pick it up again on

L

a pony up Worlebury Hill; and if Alice is thin and spindle-shanked, she must gain flesh, as all girls do, in some seminary for young ladies in this most scholastic of watering-places. In fact, Weston-super-Mare is the sea-lung of Bristol and the surrounding neighbourhood, the joy of the young ladies, and the general excuse for a holiday. The more Weston is known the more she is admired. The beautiful young lady grows so rapidly that she even astonishes her parents who are face to face with her every day. Strangers who only see her once a year might be excused when they express surprise at the sudden development of a pretty child into a lovely girl; but when the oldest inhabitant is startled at the growth of grey stone cottages, the multiplication of little stone walls, the complication of roads and terraces, the increase of miniature gardens and woods, and stands aghast at the altered appearance of Weston, we may well say that she has supplied a want, and is properly the subject of universal admiration. No old friend can be in Weston five minutes without noticing the wonderful change. Time was when Weston kept herself very much to the low ground overlooking the cold Brean Down and the Weston Bay; when Weston contented herself with the broad esplanade, the contemplation of mud at low tide, and of a good sea when it was high; when the town and the low sea-shore were all the joys Weston could boast; and when a flat district looked upon a flat sea. But that is all altered now.

The houses and terraces, the villas and pleasaunces, the shrubberies and flower gardens, have covered the hill and crept quietly into Worlebury Wood. The kindly lord of the manor, and possessor of so much greenery and situation, allows any one to build, and the consequence is that the charming sea from the front of Worlebury Hill is dotted all over with gables and chimneys. The builders at Weston have an eye for picturesque effect: they twist one house so as to give it an uninterrupted view of the Mendips; they turn another to make it face Brean Down; they give a third a peep of the opposite Welsh hills; one more, without interfering with the outlook of its neighbours, commands the two Channel islands, while many a cottage, buried in the heart of the greenest of woods, expresses no sorrow in the absence of sea peep or hill range, seeing that it is in perfect peace under the shadow of wonderful trees and amongst the roses and carnations of this flower-bearing district. It is as much a libel to declare that there is nothing to be seen in Weston but mud, as it is inaccurate to state that the Weston mud is impregnated with iodine. The mud is only visible for a portion of the day in a portion of the town, and, according to the authoritative statement of the best chemists, it is the presence of ozone, and not iodine, which gives Weston the first place in the Registrar-General's returns, and cures unhealthy Bristol in a week.

If Weston were a dreary bay of objectionable

mud; if the holiday-seekers stood for ever on the esplanade looking for the distant waves on the broad yellow sand; if there were nothing but the Brean Down and Knightstone, the Bristol merchants would take themselves off elsewhere. Better to dream among the green-covered graves in old Clevedon Church; better to hear the sea "break, break," on the "cold grey stones," as did Mr. Tennyson on this very spot; better to let the children exercise themselves on the Portishead donkeys, further round the Channel, than attempt to court the waves over the Weston mud, or call the breaker to the parched limestone; but, as very frequently happens, the detractors are prejudiced, and the statements are exaggerated.

Weston no more consists solely of her esplanade and her bay than is London composed entirely of Bow and Bermondsey. Come with me directly you have got out of the train, before you have seen or smelt the sea, before you have spent your money, as all seaside visitors will do, in one of the attractive seaside shops. Don't you hear the sound of the morning band? We must follow the music, for there the seaside visitors congregate. They do things in a very unconventional manner at Weston, and the house-owners hold out an almost unparalleled hospitality. The public band—the famous Italian band of Weston-super-Mare, famed throughout Somersetshire for the good taste of its music, the excellence of its performance, and the original skill of Signor

Ulrico, composer of a triumphal march worthy of Vienna—is actually playing in a gentleman's garden. Quite true. Mr. Walter Tucker, of the Grove, at Weston, bids the Italian band play under the shady trees of his paddock, places chairs and benches on the gravel path of his flower-gardens, invites the whole of Weston-super-Mare to wander promiscuously among his flower-beds and woods, whilst he himself sits under the porch in the morning sun, listening to the music and delighted at the hundreds of personal answers to his hospitable invitation. There is no more popular meeting for the band in Weston than in the lovely gardens of the Grove. When "God save the Queen" has given the signal for a courteous leave-taking, and Mr. Tucker's grounds are left alone until another bright morning comes round, or one more musical evening, then, possibly, you will make a dart down the steep hill to the sea, under the idea that Weston consists of nothing but one pretty garden, and the traditional mud-covered bay. But we can leave the mud and bay altogether, and get a good sea and a splendid breeze along the edge of Worlebury Hill, which is one of the delightful and shady walks in the neighbourhood. Nothing but mud, indeed! Do you see any mud, even at low tide, in Birnbeck Island, joined to the mainland by the pier? When you stand looking between the islands in the Channel, and feel the full embrace of the Atlantic, does this really seem like a marine compromise or half a seaside place?

As we lean over the battlements of the island, the wind blows across an unbroken sea, and fills the body with life and the nerves with strength, Is this not a real sea tumbling upon the broken coast and the jagged rock? Is this not a sea breaking upon the base of the bath-house at Knightstone, and which is seen and felt all day, though the mud still fronts the esplanade and there is melancholy in Weston Bay? There is plenty of sea at Weston as well as plenty of mud, and the reason of Weston's popularity is its sea. The cause of its health is the disinfecting ozone arising from Weston mud. It is a long lane, however, that has no turning. Weston, like all other places, has its moment. There is a time between breakfast and bedtime when Weston can laugh to scorn the pitiful libellers who rail about her pretensions and grumble about her mud.

The moment has come now as I write. I am not sitting on the pier, enjoying the Atlantic breezes. I am not wandering in the green recesses of the Worlebury Wood. I am not reading on the rocks at the foot of Knightstone, or stretching my legs across Brean Down. Here I am, writing to you on the snubbed esplanade facing the bay, said to be overfull of melancholy mud. It is a breezy, sunny afternoon, and Weston has come out refreshed with bread-and-butter and tea. The ozone is filling the place with life and laughter. Not a baby cries, and not a maiden melancholy. I see before me a broad stretch of sand, very little inferior to Dieppe or

Ostend, dotted all over with children, and clean white dresses, made merry with swings and games, all life and happiness. The muddy tract is now covered with water, sparkling in the sun. There are waves around the Knightstone peninsula, and big waves at the foot of Brean Down. The sun has left the public gardens on the hill-side; it has deserted the long rows of grey stone houses on the hill topped by the wood; it has ceased showing on the golden vane of the church steeple, but lovingly lingers still on the yellow stretch of sand, and gives its farewell embrace to the broad esplanade crowded with people.

I do not pretend to deny that Weston has still much to do in the matter of personal adornment. The time hitherto has mostly been taken up in making the place comfortable. Now that the houses have grown up like mushrooms, and the roads have multiplied, now that the hill-side is so picturesque and romantic, Weston may well divert some of her spare capital in other directions. The pier wants looking to. Birnbeck Island, which is now a cross between a burned-down railway-station and the deserted yard of an ironfoundry, should be swept and garnished. It is a pity to see schools of children taken to Weston Pier for a treat, and sent to play among bankrupt sheds and unused iron-girders. The guide-books tell me that the "buildings on the island are unfinished owing to the want of funds," and I cannot help thinking that the sooner funds are found the better. Funds are wanted for the completion of the pavilion at the end of the pier, for the decoration of Knightstone, for the repair of the seats of the esplanade, and for the general external decoration of Weston. Nature and position have done much.

They give the rocks and the hills, the peeps at the Mendips and of Wales, the Downs stretching far into the sea, the woods and their walks, the air and its health. Private enterprise and hospitality have also done very much. They open gardens to the public, put flowers at the disposal of visitors, cover the beds and rocks with colour. There might surely be a little life and activity shown at the spot where the people crowd to be near the sea. No one must run away with the idea that Weston is either dull or straitlaced. She enjoys herself quite as well as her neighbours. The excitement is not gone when the Bristol merchants have left their wives and children after breakfast, nor does it consist entirely in the evening reunion, when the lord and master returns. There is a West of England Mr. Cook, who rejoices in the name of Date, and who appears to be the great hand at excursions; he will run you over to Cardiff for a fête, or take you round to Clevedon for a flower-show, or show you the size and inhabitants of the two islands facing Weston-on-the-Sea, or organize any expedition for which Weston may be inclined. And, as to Weston herself, she never fails to hold a regatta every year, with four-oared races, duck-hunts, and greasy poles; and the entertainment-loving visitors are delighted to see the face of entertainers on the walls, and announcements of innumerable wizards, conjurors, and ventriloquists. Weston is determined to show that the charge of dulness is as untrue as the chemical theory of iodine in the Weston mud. It is a jolly little place, healthy and prosperous, gaining strength and popularity every day, full of health and activity, and a perfect godsend to poor black Bristol. We tired Londoners are glad enough of a Saturday to Monday in the Isle of Thanet, or a long Monday in Brighton, but think what a joy it must be for the Bristol men, when work is over for the day, to change from the corn-dust and the sugar-grit to the pure sweet breeze blowing from the Atlantic; to see the sunset from a bench or a chair in one of the innumerable coloured gardens; to blow away all care and a cigar on the esplanade pavement, or enjoy a summer evening on the hard sands of Weston-on-the-Sea.

ON THE ROAD TO GOODWOOD.

Bognor.

IF Sir Robert Hotham, the wealthy Southwark hatter, who has been quietly sleeping in his grave since 1799, could only come to earth again, and take a walk along a certain glorious brick promenade skirting a delightful sea, I am quite sure he would confess that he broke his poor old heart a little too soon. The story goes that this excellent citizen, having expended some thirty thousand pounds on a pet scheme for making a young Brighton opposite the fringe of rocks running parallel with the coast, died broken-hearted, partly because the public snubbed Sir Robert's scheme, and partly because the local authorities sternly refused to sanction such an abomination as Hothamville. A few years after the melancholy death of the speculative hatter, a very short time after the grass began to grow on the grave of the founder of Bognor, a sudden freak of fashion turned the attention of the public towards the innumerable advantages of one of the cleanest and brightest little spots on the South Coast. Houses sprung up to the right and to the left; pleasant little villas with green verandahs, consecrated to the morning needle or the after-dinner cigar, appeared here and there; trim little grass-covered squares began to be dotted about; each crescent and semicircular set of buildings sowed grass-seed and with careful taste planted geranium-beds round miniature fountains. The growth of the little town naturally suggested a large white hotel facing the sea, prettily situated in a pleasant garden.

The town took heart and built a long pier, after the pattern of the pier at Deal, stretching out into the sea, and an extra effort of energy completed and perfected the famous brick embankment, a good mile long, which is at once the feature and the pride of Bognor. This promenade was the finishing touch to the old daydream of Sir Robert Hotham, and on this breezy walk Bognor appears to exist from morning till night. Always dry, always scrupulously clean, fitted out with red bricks, on this firm, solid embankment, Bognor lives, and the whole of Bognor life is seen. There are lovely walks along the sands away to Pagham; there are delightful in-country rambles towards Chichester, among farms and green lanes, past straw-thatched cottages with their clusters of clambering roses, and beds of old cottage-garden flowers, foxglove and carnation, mignionette, lupin, and "old man." But Bognor cares for none of these things.

Mr. Johnson's quaint old thatched house, surrounded by green woods, within a hundred yards of the sea, may be the most picturesque estate in the country; Chichester may have a cathedral, and Goodwood a park; but Bognor has a promenade.

from which no archæological taste or seductive guide-book will tempt the happy visitors or the sunburnt children.

Broken his heart, indeed! I wish poor old Sir Robert Hotham could see Bognor in her seventy-fourth summer. I believe there is no town in all Holland so scrupulously clean. The Hague would not be ashamed of the streets, while the sea-front puts Schevening to shame. The houses, the villas, and the pavements are so white that they almost give you a headache to look at them. Every knocker and handle does credit to the energy of the Sussex housemaid. There is not a shop-front in the town which does not look as if it had just left the painter's hands; and if an army of charwomen were turned on to the Esplanade every morning with pails and scrubbing-brushes, they could not turn it out to the more complete satisfaction of the veriest old maid in the town. In fact, such is the mania for cleaning at Bognor that the sailors, instead of lounging about the beach with their hands in their pockets, or lifting the inevitable telescope to sweep a blank horizon, tar and re-tar, and then give one more tarring to the little round prawn-baskets lying all over the shingle, or to the fishing-boats high and dry upon the immaculate shore.

But the brick embankment of Bognor is the feature of the place, for here in all its phases can be seen its society and the sea. Why is it, when we turn seaward, that we give extra prices to get a bedroom facing the water, though, in all probability, we never once look out of window from the hour we go to bed to the moment we come down in the morning? How is it that we are disappointed when we are located in a side-street, and refuse to be comforted with the compromise of a bay-window? Is it not true that a seaside place on a cliff is not nearly so jolly as a seaside place on the shore? and is it not incontestable that true sea-lovers, if they could have their way, would have the spray for ever saluting their sitting-room windows? At the seaside we cannot have too much of the sea. We bathe in it, we taste the salt all day, we sit down by it, we listen to it, we are never tired of watching it, and at every meal devour some animal just taken out of it. It is this ever-presence of the ocean, it is this close communication with the waves and the sand, it is this delightful and everlasting smell of seaweed and tar and old rope, it is this near companionship of shells and weed-covered rocks which make Bognor so conspicuously jolly. There is no mounting or descending of interminable stairs. There is no ascending parched cliffs or scrambling down hideous precipices. The sea and the breeze are outside the door. Two steps take you on to the embankment, and once on the embankment you are literally on the sea. At high tide the waves come tumbling up to the wall, and rudely leaping upon the brick walk, sending the young ladies laughing away to the benches for protection, gathering up their garments in their flight.

At low tide a dozen steps take any one to the shingle and the sand among the old posts, covered with fresh seaweed, and in the midst of the spars and shells thrown up by the latest tide.

Bognor lives on her embankment, and the embankment is on the sea. There is no viaduct here between East Cliff and West Cliff. There is no hiatus, break, or separation. On the embankment sail along the pretty girls, blown about by a delicious breeze; on the embankment race the headstrong children, to the horror of anxious mothers, whose "hearts are in their mouths" lest they shall topple over and take a header on the cruel shingle below. At the side of the embankment are the fishing-boats and the prawn-baskets. The bathing-machines can be stepped into from the embankment without descending a stair. Here can be secured the service of that eminent swimming mistress "Miss Ragless," who, according to the placard, superintended for many years the natatory evolutions of young ladies at Brill's Baths, Brighton, and had the distinguished honour of making an accomplished swimmer of her Royal Highness the Duchess of Teck; here, strange to say, are descried four white benches for the special and particular "use of the Merchant Taylors' Company," and I am curious to know if the worthy master, the court, and all the generous officials of that distinguished society, on some given day or days of the year, come down to Bognor, and from these white benches address the ocean, like Demosthenes, or, in full pomp of civic magnificence, defy it like King Canute.

Out, I say, upon those inaccurate or spiteful people who declare that Bognor is dull! My guide-book talks sneeringly of that "not very lively watering-place;" and no doubt Brighton, the grandmother, and Worthing, the twin-sister of Bognor, are apt to turn up their noses at their successful relation. For the life of me, I cannot see how a seaside place with a mile or so of houses fronting the sea—with a mile or so of embankment full of life—with seats to read on, and sands to dig, with pier, promenades, and boats, with bathing-machines, and old sailors, and innumerable children—can ever be dull. There is an Assembly Room, to which wandering entertainers continually repair; the walls are everywhere decorated with the likeness of an entertainer as a dancing Zouave; there is a circulating library and a visitors' list; there are pony carriages in plenty, and the inevitable donkey.

But, as every one knows, the race week is the time for Bognor, for are there not visitors for Goodwood, and is it not possible to drive to the Duke of Richmond's Park, after having bathed off the rocks and eaten fresh-caught prawns for breakfast? To Goodwood we can repair, fresh and invigorated with the salt sea. From Goodwood we can return, and hear the pleasant waves again before bed-time. There is not an apartment to let along the whole sea-front. They are asking sixty guineas for the week for a house with nine bedrooms; and ladies of the high world, in splendid silks and noble Indian shawls, are content to lodge in little white houses which remind one of the cottages of the coast-guard. Enormous trunks, whose contents will be exposed on the beautiful Goodwood lawn, come up every minute from the station in lumbering vans, and many of them, too wide for the diminutive doorways, are dragged up to the first floor through the window.. At the Norfolk Hotel the greatest activity prevails; and the courteous old dog, who considers it a privilege to rouse himself out of the sunniest slumber, and escort every visitor to the garden gate, is so weary, after the repeated calls on his hospitality, that he has rolled himself into a long slumber on the croquet lawn,. and has evidently made up his mind to sulk until the races are over. The Bognor Pier, expectant of a visit from the Prince of Wales and the other visitors at Goodwood House, has unfurled with pomp half a dozen flags. Racing men interrupt their constitutional with periodical visits to the barometer at the pier-master's house; and, for the hundredth time, the most weather-beaten sailor on the shore has looked profoundly wise, and declared we shall have no rain while the wind remains so high.

The breeze blowing over Bognor as I write, is quite charming. It comes whistling and roaring round the clean white houses. It vexes the garments of the young ladies, when they turn their faces towards Pagham, and, if it did not bang every door and break every lock in the place, would harmonize thoroughly with Bognor's invigorating properties—a splendid sun, a cloudless sky, and a blue sea varied with white-crested waves. All looks well, lovely, and lively for the festivities. I see it has been raining at Brighton. Here we have not had a shower. Reports come of thunderstorms at Worthing. At Bognor, as yet, I have not seen a cloud. It is the fashion to say that there is not a bed to be had for love or money, that not a garret is to be purchased, that every hotel is over-full, that bathing-machines will be secured if the afternoon trains really contain the anticipated guests, and that Goodwood visitors expecting accommodation had better turn their steps in a different direction. I only believe half what I am told. I daresay we can find a corner, and certainly we shall give a welcome to all who would have the London dust blown off them before driving to the course, and all who would change suddenly from the excitement of racing to the peace of the spot where the " low downs lean to the sea."

I went over to Chichester to spend a long afternoon, and you would have been surprised to see the excitement already abroad in this quiet old cathedral town. The station was gay with drapery of scarlet and white, put up in honour of the Prince of Wales and the other Royal guests. About the terminus were hansom cabs, victorias, broughams, and more than one drag; while in the main Chichester street was a long line of London omnibuses in readiness to take the public to the Goodwood course. The sight of a string of Bayswater omnibuses, and a collection of yellow vehicles labelled "Old Ford" and "London Bridge," idly waiting for passengers, round the handsome old Market Cross at Chichester, makes a most comical contrast. But the contrast does not end with the London omnibuses. There is an air of propriety about all cathedral towns; the shopkeepers have the bland courtesy possessed by vergers' and bishops' valets; there is an ecclesiastical tone about the shop windows, and the colours in the linendrapers' are quiet and severe. Imagine the astonishment of the Sussex labourers in their smocks and scarlet neckerchiefs sitting on the stone benches of the Chichester Market Cross as they view the motley, Bohemian, rowdy crowd taking possession of the still sacred streets!

From window to window across every street down which the Prince of Wales and the Princess passed, the simple townsfolk had stretched flags of welcome. Throughout the long hot afternoon under these flags, and before the gaze of the staid cathedral shopkeepers, streamed the most chaotic and miscellaneous crowd ever seen: gipsy women with the inevitable babies on their backs, knock-'em-down proprietors on their way to the racecourse in the distant park; ostlers, stable-helpers, race-card men, queer hangers-on at race-meetings, with wonderful clothes and still more wonderful neckties, went along in crowds, some in search of lodgings, others careless what became of them, and ready to rest under the country hedges until the day broke upon one more anniversary of glorious Goodwood.

But I was talking of contrast just now. Turn, then, away from the din and riot of the approaching race-meeting, from the inn-doors with their congregation of racing men, from the pothouse doors with their crowds of half-tipsy Bohemians; turn for an instant to the calm, cool cloisters, where, sitting on a stone slab, you can look upon the enclosure called " Paradise," and gaze upon the antique cathedral, whose spire starts straight up into a calm heaven of perfect blue. There is not a soul but myself in the cloister; there is not a soul or an echo of a human being. Out of the niches and decorative work of the grand old church some bird starts occasionally, flapping his wings; but the stillness is supreme, and the cool surpassingly sweet. On the quiet graves in the centre of " Paradise," on the geraniums planted by loving hands, on the old yew trees, and on the daisy-starred grass, on the new spire, which has already almost grown to the colour of the original grey building, the sun still burns; but here in the Chichester cloister, there is not a trace of sunlight, and not a sound of human voice.

The same wonderful stillness, so strangely in contrast with the abnormally excited old town, reigns in the quiet garden by the rugged old Campanile tower, round again by the close and the various ivy-covered ecclesiastical dwellings, but most of all in the cathedral itself, where are gathered for afternoon service three county policemen, a sprinkling of canon's wives and daughters, two gentlemen whose costume has a racy tone, and many London faces, who all no doubt expected a choral service, chant by Tallis, and an anthem by Boyce, Attwood, Purcell, or Goss. But, as it happened, the Chichester Choir had a holiday, and the simple service was not illustrated by musical effects. One quiet voice held possession of the ancient cathedral, and when all was over a venerable doctor of divinity, preceded by a verger with a silver cross, was followed home in the sunset by his small congregation.

Worthing.

Midway between the two poles of racing excitement, half-way between Goodwood and Brighton, a rest after the hoarse shouting of the last few days, an oasis in the desert of din, lies a long, low, wave-washed shore, which I take to be the most innocent spot on the south coast of England. For Worthing is almost wholly given up to children and domestic joys. Here come the Chichester racing-men to wash away the dust of the race-course, to cool their excited brows, and to meet "the missus and the young uns;" here arrive the quiet racing visitors who, over-tempted, kept poor Bognor up so late and took possession of her esplanade by night instead of by day; through Worthing come the drags which for four days stood in a long line under the trees in Goodwood Park; but the occupants thereof, noticing the simplicity of the baby-covered beach, smile and pass on to Brighton.

Worthing is all for the children. It would be as monstrous to bring hither the scum of a racecourse as to swear in a nursery. Brighton and the surrounding districts are large enough to receive the turf drainage. We have no welcome here for niggers or perambulating minstrels. We have no laughter for the irrepressible medal-covered Ginger. The low-browed gipsies and the knock-'em-down men, the ragged venders of race-cards, the coat-brushers, the carriage-helps, the men and women with fearful faces and still more fearful tongues, have kindly given Worthing a wide berth.

There is nothing, believe me, Liliputian or insignificant about Worthing. Her fine, extensive, gravelled promenade has a spacious Portland Place air about it. The sands when the tide retires are like a broad yellow racecourse between shingle and sea. The roadway is as important as the King's Parade at Brighton. The houses in West Worthing look as if Lancaster Gate and Hyde Park Gardens had come out of town for a holiday. Worthing has hotels with a serious, dignified air about them— hotels where waiters in evening dress hand the salmon and the cutlet. There is a town-hall in the centre of a spotless street, with an important portico and a tone reminding one of quarter sessions. But in spite of this solemn importance, irrespective of these grown-up hotels and four-storied houses, notwithstanding these plate glass windows and the townhall, the impression left on my mind after visiting Worthing is that the place originally intended for grown-up folks and adults has been bombarded and taken by an army from Liliput. I never saw so many children or visited a seaside place where they were more tenderly cared for. They swarm upon the shingle, they dig in the sand, where mud-pies are more popular than sand castles, they paddle and puddle in the little pools about the weed-covered rocks, their feet are wet and soaking a dozen times a day, they fish for eels and dabs off the pier, where every one makes way for them, they play cricket with Ham, who is vainly waiting for the long-expected bachelor to come and take a sail with him, they are carried pick-a-back by Peggoty, who is weary of idling under the old luggers beached on the shore.

The parade by the side of the fine white houses clatters all day with the hoofs of the ponies of the children. The most popular vehicles are small pony basket-carriages. Goat-chaises are more patronized than flies, and the best use made of the breeze is to fly kites all the morning for the sake of the brown-legged little ones. I have been on the pier at

Worthing morning, noon, and night, without seeing one flirtation. Nurses and children, mothers and fathers, uncles on the shelf, and devoted maiden-aunts have it all their own way in this domestic Paradise. For the rest there are few attractions and small welcome. The children are helped first, as at the one o'clock dinner. If Strephon and Chloe paid their pennies at the wicket of the pier, and meditated an hour of soft nothings by the sad sea waves, I believe they would be told by the fatherly attendant that children were present, and immediately warned off to Brighton. Worthing obeys to the letter the old maxim concerning early rising and retiring. The day is scarcely warm before the boys are being bathed by their fathers. The breakfast things are cleared away by eight o'clock. The sands and the shingle are one long mile of nursery until one o'clock. The place is asleep all the afternoon, and by ten every light is out but that of the moon, who makes a path of pleasant light across a silent sea, and illuminates a deserted shore.

And why, let me ask, should there not be left alone round England one or two places like Worthing, where excitement is neither courted nor desired? Worthing is profoundly happy, and her inhabitants are happier still. She only wants to be left in peace and permitted to do as she likes. She has no petty ambition or feeling of rivalry. She envies neither Brighton nor Bognor. Let those who will call her "slow," and turn up their noses at her peaceful, innocent, orderly ways, but there are hundreds and thousands of people who will love Worthing all the better for the rest she gives and the dreamy indolence she suggests. There are plenty of other places where Strephon may dress and Chloe flirt. My dear sir, over there at Brighton there are billiard-rooms and conversation-houses, and sodas-and-brandies, and hacks to spin along the gay parade, and button-hole flowers for your summer suit. My dear miss, I assure you that if you take a cheap ticket to the station a few miles off, away over there where the lights shine long after Worthing is in bed, you can go round and round in a giddy whirl of promenaders on the pier, listening to Strauss and Gung'l, and Offenbach and Lecocq; you can exhibit your newest polonaise, and strut about in your latest holland costume; you can change your hat a dozen times, and ruin yourself in ribbons: you can patter about the *trottoirs* on your high-heeled boots, you will have no lack of admirers, you will be petted and coaxed to your heart's content. But be charitable and leave poor Worthing alone. This is a home for those who have done their Brighton and Scarborough years ago and want rest. It is the playground of the boys whose highest ambition is to rig a schooner, and of the girls in short petticoats who tangle their brothers' lines in the vain attempt to fish for flounders. The whole scene of Worthing is summed up in one stanza:—

> I have put my days and dreams out of mind,
>   Days that are over, dreams that are done.
> Though we seek life through we shall surely find
>   There is none of them clear to us now, not one !
> But clear are these things, the grass and the sand,
>   Where, sure as the eyes reach, ever at hand
> With lips wide open, and face burnt blind,
>   The strong sea-*babies* feast on the sun !

Up in West Worthing some handsome speculators have built some swimming-baths, which in point of taste and comfort cannot be excelled even at sister Brighton. Under the same Gothic roof are offered also that new luxury called an ozone-bath, wherein those who require luxurious rest are permitted to doze and dream, reposing the while on a soft couch of oozy seaweed. Elsewhere such methods of introducing iodine into the system may be excused, but not at Worthing; for at Worthing the whole air is impregnated with seaweed, and each breeze is laden with salt. It is the place of all others for rest and delicious idleness. After breakfast on the lawn, the book so eagerly attacked falls idly out of hands, and the morning pipe drops on the grass. We are ashamed of our own languor and abnormal laziness. We play with the shingle, and feel sleepy ; we repair to a seat on the promenade, and the warm sun makes us sleepier still; we move off, yawning, to the old boatmen, and listen vacantly to some long, monotonous tale. In desperation we take a sail, and as we are lifted along by the breeze we are rocked as in a cradle. We are burned and brown. The sun becomes hotter and hotter; and energy more impossible. We take a low pony-carriage, and are pleasantly whirled to the railway station. We purchase a newspaper, and a few minutes afterwards on the pier the sheet has fallen from our hands, and we dream that the old lady who is reading a romance to her invalid friend is Dr. Kenealy arguing with the Lord Chief Justice. After luncheon we are driven from the balcony by the sun, which streams upon the house. We take up a pen, and cannot write; postpone once more the letters due long ago; we attack a novel, and begin skipping. Positively ashamed of our indolence, scandalized at being a party to the general after-luncheon siesta, which is encouraged by the ladies and enjoyed by the baby-in-arms, a hat and stick are seized, and a walk commenced to Lancing, where the famous college stands on the hill, and there are romantic spots to explore. But the sea is rushing up on the shingle, the first waves seen in Worthing are breaking over one another, there are white crests for half a mile out across the water, now purple, now green, now blue. Each wave as it breaks at our feet contains a new tune, so we sit on the shore only for a minute, and remain simply watching the sea for more than an hour. It will be too late for Lancing, and the afternoon sun is burning hot. The presence of the sea fascinates us, and we wander back to Worthing to find shingle and promenade, pier-head and town, full once again of the children, refreshed with their tea and their sleep. Once more we sail their boats for them in the puddles, fish the little green crabs out of the pools, and mend their lines. The breeze has freshened up on the pier. It drowns the voice of the old lady, still deliberately delivering the sentences of the romance. The afternoon trains come in, and there is a brief excitement at the hotel-doors. Luggage comes out and luggage goes in. Ladies in cool muslin dresses appear on the balconies and beckon. They wave handkerchiefs, and signal us home. We hear dinner-bells all over the place. Then in turn come the evening cool, the sunset, and the calm. The band plays seriously, the lamps are lighted in Brighton across the bay, the moon comes up, and the day is done. How dreadfully slow! some will say. What an unpardonable waste of time others will observe. It may be so; but each one to his taste. When Brighton is gallivanting, and Hastings is on the move, when St. Leonard's is flirting in the moonlight, and Folkestone whirling round in a dance, the tired brains, fed with the seaweed air, are resting in a long, delicious doze—and the wearied little brown legs of the Worthing water-babies are hidden cosily under the counterpane!

ALONG THE UNDERCLIFF.

Ryde, Isle of Wight.

IT is quite certain that many of the beauties of this delightful island, now in the full perfection of flower and fruit, must be lost to the holiday-maker who has not been provided by nature with a good strong pair of legs. Engineers have done all they can with these steep hills and bold stretches of down. Roman and English road-makers have contrived to turn and twist their paths of blinding white dust among the most beautiful trees and romantic dells of the island; and speculators, by excursions, coaches, expeditions, and what not, tempt the Ryde visitor to go sight-seeing, and persuade him, no doubt, that when he has entrusted himself to their care, the Isle of Wight will have been thoroughly explored. This I venture altogether to dispute. The Isle of Wight Railway will carry you to the picturesque Brading, "close to the ridge of a noble down," will permit you to bathe at Sandown, to explore the delightful chine at Shanklin, and to see your invalid friends at Ventnor. Another short strip of baby railway from Cowes will reveal the hidden mysteries of Newport, and take the traveller very far indeed on his way to Carisbrooke Castle—one of the most interesting historical remains on the island. But the railway does no more than that. Then, how is it possible to be well posted in the beauties of the Isle of Wight without travelling like a lord, with postilions and a chaise? Well, there is a steamer which sails right round the island, and allows you just to peep at its beauties. It is thus possible to see the Needles, to get an idea of Alum Bay, and obtain an unsatisfactory running glance at the various headlands, lights, bays, and tree-covered fissures in the flowered cliff. Here there are coaches and *chars-à-banc*, and comfortable public conveyances of all kinds, which will run you through the Undercliff to Blackgang, stopping a minute here and an insignificant moment there— which will carry you off to Freshwater and the Needles Hotel, rush you through the centre of the island, and introduce you to the keep, the ivy-covered gateway, the moat, the portcullis, the grass-grown ramparts, and the popular donkey at Carisbrooke Castle.

But let not the happy visitor to this charming spot imagine for an instant that any coach, carriage, horse, trap, railway, or vehicle that was ever invented can properly be employed as the agent for discovering the charms of the Isle of Wight. As assistants they are admirable. They take you on your way; they pick you up when you are weary. But unless you go on foot how can that walk of all walks, from Bonchurch to Shanklin, be taken, through the coolest nut-groves and over the wonderful Landslip? How else is it possible to skirt the seashore, to explore the bays, to wander on the very edge of the Undercliff looking down deep into the forest of green which intervenes between the cliff and the sea, to taste the salt air on St. Catherine's Point, or ascertain properly the remarkable variety and verdure of the garden-island? It was the day of all days for a walk, as I fancied; the time of all others for making to the Downs and feasting on the sea. It would have been a deliberate and wicked waste of time to have enjoyed the freshening breeze only on Ryde Pier, and to have dawdled a day away amongst high-heeled boots and yellow novels. Once get on Ryde Pier, remember, you are done for. That fatal man who takes your twopence at the wicket gives you one look, and you are covered with a Circe enchantment. You may stop your ears as much as you like, but the Syren voices will enchant you. Once put a foot on that pier after breakfast, and the day is gone. You walk and return, you sit and doze, you are dazed with the constant passing and repassing. There is so little—and still so much—to do. A boat comes in: the boat must be watched. The newspapers arrive: they must be devoured—and, by-the-bye, is it not wonderful how very different newspapers read on Ryde Pier to what they do in the club in London? Tell me, how is it that when you are at Ryde, the little local paper has somehow the advantage over the London news. When the paper has been read, the best of the day is gone. More friends arrive—more conversation ensues. You declare you are going for a walk into the island; you are persuaded to take just another turn. Then there is a bath and a swim at the wrong time of the day. Some one proposes a row or a sail. All energy gradually oozes out of you. Luncheon time comes, and it is discovered that Ryde Pier has stolen another day.

Turn your back, then on the pier, and if very weak do not even take the tramway to the railway station, for by railway we will start on our expedition to the Undercliff. The unromantic part of the journey will soon be over, but it requires some strength of mind— when Ryde is left behind, and the blue bays of the sea are seen out of the carriage windows—not to leap out at every station. There ought to be a glorious view from that high down at Brading. Shanklin looks about the most picturesque spot in the world— the happiest combination of Devonshire and Jersey. The word Appledurcombe sounds vastly pretty, suggesting summer orchards round farm-yards; but at any rate here is Ventnor, and the train goes no farther. Resist, I pray you, the fascination of the Tally-ho and the Vectis. Do not listen to the tempting offers of the juvenile fly-drivers. Undercliff? Well, we are going there. Sandrock? You shall lunch there if all be well. Blackgang? It shall be thoroughly explored before dinner. Only, do not see all these places on the top of a coach along a dusty road.

Down the very steepest of roads, a very precipice,

we get into Ventnor, passing cosy little residences, varied in design, and, like all dwellings in the Isle of Wight, having nothing of the stereotyped lodging-house tone about them. One is a little Swiss villa, with a wooden balcony covered with an enormous purple flower, the most popular creeper hereabouts; another is a tiny Gothic cottage; a third is a miniature parsonage in its garden quite dazzling with colour. But there is no time to linger. The mammas of Ventnor are out shopping this sunny morning, and the young ladies in the blue-spotted dresses are hugging novels and campstools, going downwards to the sea. It is the cleanest, whitest, and sunniest of towns. The hotels remind one of Interlaken. The life out of doors—all guides, and donkeys, and excursioning—is eminently Swiss. But the sea and the beach, when we reach them, down a tremendous hill, are English all over!

What a delightful breeze! And what a day for a sail! as is proved by the pleasure-boats riding over the crisp waves, crested here and there with a curl of white foam. It is high tide this morning in Ventnor, and the sea is driving the children and the nursery-maids back on to the hot, white esplanade. It is all busy, pleasant, and fresh. Droves of donkeys, backed by laughing children, are struggling up that hill. Young ladies are reading under an old tent upon the sands. The bathing-machines are out, and the buoyant feeling over all Ventnor is caused surely by this pleasant breezy morning and the sun-struck waves. But we must push on—not up the hill, not along the chalky, dusty road, not where the carriages and *chars-à-banc* roll along, but by the path at the foot of the Undercliff, over the sea.

It is necessary here to explain the peculiarity of the Undercliff scenery. On the side of the island, between the cliff proper and the smaller elevation immediately overhanging the sea is the loveliest wood and garden. Here is hidden Bonchurch, here nestles St. Lawrence; among these noble trees, and in the heart of this flower-garden, is the National Hospital for Consumption, its chapel nearly built, and the new house almost finished. So we choose the path skirting the sea cliff, and have on our right hand the whole wealth of the Undercliff scenery. I know of no walk more pleasant and exhilarating on a breezy day than on the edge of such a steep, but of all such walks this is distinctly the most picturesque. It is never the same picture for an instant. Now down chalk steps between bushes of blackberry blossom, now under banks of wild thyme, so sweet that all the bees on the island have left the carnation beds and foxgloves for it, now brushing through narrow paths of meadow-sweet, now up again and across a stretch of turf, now round a corner and through a ripe cornfield fringed with poppies. It is all colour, and the flowers grow to the very water's edge. The boulders of stone flung up here and there are covered with orange lichen, and the mass of luxuriant wild-flowers is varied by bushes and bunches of scarlet berry.

But the Undercliff scenery on the right hand is no less beautiful than the flowers our feet are crushing. No house or castle is staring or exposed, as on the Rhine, for the trees assert themselves, and allow us at most the sight of a chimney, a tower, a gable, an oriel window, or half a croquet-lawn. Houses were never so perfectly situated. Trees, flowers, lawns, and sea view. What better properties than these could any house-owner require? So on, the breeze still blowing in our faces, the sea still purple, the wild-flowers still luxuriant, the Undercliff still green, round by tiny sandy bays, past the white cottages of the coast-guard, the Niton Lighthouse at St. Catharine's appears in sight, and we make up the hill for the Sandrock Hotel. A low thatched roof, a verandah covered with ivy, the supports thick with creepers, a sloping lawn without a daisy or a leaf left upon it, a cool wilderness at the back of the house, rustic seats in odd corners where the sea can be seen—this is where the pedestrians come to lunch, and the honeymooners' stay. Entomologists drop in with their knapsacks and butterfly nets. The Blackgang coach stops at this paradise, and the sunburnt passengers rest for an instant under the cool verandah. There is no excitement of passengers, or bustle of hotel-life, or waiters with creaking-boots, or desire to get rid of you as soon as possible and make room for some one else. It is all calm and deliciously cool. The hotel is as quiet as a Devonshire vicarage on a summer afternoon. The garden is deserted, save by the bees, and the only sign of life is when a couple of honeymoon lovers move off from the look-out by the sea and are soon lost in the recesses of the silent wood. An aged gardener is sweeping up the leaves as they fall, a solitary pedestrian is dozing in the little coffee-room opening with French windows on to the verandah.

No place is better adapted for moony meditation than the garden of the Sandrock Hotel. It requires an effort to break this pleasant charm. You want one more turn in the garden, just one more pipe on that rustic bench, one more loll upon the lawn and upward look to the cloudless sky. But Blackgang must be visited, and then we can walk back over the Undercliff scenery at the edge of the down. This is, perhaps, better than all. You get a cross-ways breeze, a blow from the down and a blow from the sea. The barren down is deserted save by the screaming plover. You peep down into the Undercliff over the trees and see little patches of lawn and garden, tired croquet players, ladies coming out of the house in their morning dresses. You look farther on and notice the sea-cliff path you took in the morning, and beyond the sea, blue everywhere save where one bank of cloud makes a deep purple patch upon the water. The fading afternoon and the sinking sun bring out the colour on all sides. The trees make long shadows, the labourers are returning from work, the bees are droning home. This journey is well planned, for we shall get to Bonchurch when the sun is setting, and see the "Shadow of the Cross." On, then, through Ventnor again, along the side of the down until we descend into one of the most peaceful and romantic spots of the island.

Nearly thirty years ago was buried in the pretty graveyard at Bonchurch the graceful author of "The Distant Hills"—the friend of all children for having composed the allegory of "The Old Man's Home." But the best-known work of the Rev. William Adams is the "Shadow of the Cross;" so his friends, keeping up the poetical fancy, arranged an iron cross so skilfully on the good clergyman's tomb, that when the sun sets the cross shadow might fall upon the turf, and keep green the memory of the author who wrote so charmingly of the end of life. Thirty years have passed, and still the clergyman's grave is decorated with flowers; roses and fuchsias and geraniums encircle it, and still we see the "shadow of the cross."

What a delightful place to rest, within sound of the sea, in this churchyard on the hill, under the shade of the tiny grey stone church—the smallest, save St. Lawrence, in the island, and possibly in any island that can be mentioned. The small "God's arce," with its crown and monument, is affectionately cared for. Nearly every grave has its cross of flowers, arranged after the Bonchurch fashion. Every corner of the churchyard is planted with choice shrubs and flowers. Could not some loving hand extend the same kindness to the church itself, and relieve it from its cold whitewashed walls and its damp mould-eaten appearance? The green moss-grown bordering at the foot of the walls, the tumble-down and barn-like appearance of the miniature church, the common kitchen chairs in the sanctuary, and the rickety communion table do not harmonize well with the neatness and perfect taste of the church-yard, the resting place of so many young people cut off by consumption before they could reach Ventnor, where they might have lingered a little among the myrtles and by the sea. There is probably no cottage in all Bonchurch—one of the most romantic and pleasant villages I have ever seen—so poorly furnished as the church which gives its name to the village.

A hundred times to-day I have longed to linger and rest—the surest sign of a successful journey—among the corn at the edge of the Undercliff, among the meadow-sweet and blackberry bloom close by the sea; at Blackgang, where for once on the island there is a sense of vastness and majesty; at the Sandrock Hotel, silently in a pure and peaceful English garden; on the down, where the wind is so keen that it lifts one along at every stride; here looking down on little Bonchurch among the trees, when the sun is sinking, and the day is nearly done. But the day is not quite over. Let us leave the sketchers in that little field above the church, catching the most poetical hour in Bonchurch. Let us leave the little children of the village wandering, finger on lip, among the flowers and the tombstones, and whispering as they pass from mound to mound. The day is not yet over, and the journey is not yet done. Off, then, once more, meeting the Shanklin people coming out for their evening walk, over the Landslip through that wonderful mile of nut-grove, where we find the light playing all kinds of odd tricks with the overhanging branches, and where Mr. Walker, thanks to the presence of groups of seaside girls romping through the nut-garden, might discover a dozen subjects at hand. On again, past the loveliest cottages, through farmyards and orchards within a few hundred yards of the sea, until we come in sight of *the* corner to my mind in the Isle of Wight. There is no spot like Shanklin. There is no cool green corner in the island like Shanklin. Its wonderful variety, its woods and streams, and brooks and picturesque houses, give it the prize unquestionably for beauty.

The great drawback to most seaside places is the glare of the sun. The Isle of Thanet and the South Sussex coast are charming enough, but the white blaze from the chalk is often terrible. There is no need of blue spectacles at Shanklin. It is soft green and soothing. You enter the village from the sea through a tunnel of green, and the famous Chine is all shady nook and babbling brook. Nor need it be said that Shanklin is dull or uninteresting. The girls do not dress to please, but please to dress. I find archery on the sands, and boat-building and bathing, and horses to ride, and croquet in the villa-gardens, and all over the village cool corners for reading and working. Who can call Shanklin dull, when sands, village, Chine, grass-promenade, and garden are happy with pleasant faces, and when a jocose house-owner has called his tenement " Grigg Villa ?" Shanklin, among those delightful trees, and facing that calm blue bay—Shanklin, with its box-covered cottages, and its ante-apartment and lodging-house air—Shanklin, with its rare beauty unadorned and its natural effects left to ripen—is, save in some corners of the island of Jersey, one of the most desirable seaside homes I have ever seen. To be within a walk of the Landslip, the nut-garden, and of Bonchurch is something, but to be a resident and to sleep in the romantic Shanklin village is better still. The journey alas ! is nearly done now. Blackgang and Niton, Ventnor and Sandrock, Bonchurch, and Shanklin have all been thoroughly explored. We have had a walk by the sea, a blow on the downs, a rest in a sweet-smelling garden, a meditation in a churchyard, a regret at leaving a place where we would summon all we love and have loved, a day most varied and picturesque ; but when, after the short railway journey, as the sun sets we get to town again, the charm of all freshness and nature is blotted out, for Ryde in silks and satins is still walking on the pier.

THE FALL OF THE LEAF.

"*Oh! le bon temps! J'étais bien malheureuse!*" The more you think over this pathetic inconsequence, the more you are convinced that Le Brun knew something of the world when he put the epigram into the mouth of Sophie Arnould. Every poet, from Horace downwards, has expressed the same thought in different language. "*Oh! le bon temps! J'étais bien malheureuse!*" And it is not only true of lovers and love-making. The intense meaning of this fanciful thought strikes us most keenly when the leaf falls. Is there not an exquisite strain of melancholy about the autumn weather; a fascination in the gloom which heralds the advancing November; an inclination to dissipate in grief, when the beauty of the year is dying out? I am not alluding now to the autumn of the country and the lanes; the autumn we see in the picture galleries, or listen to from the lips of poets. It will not be my task to take you down a long beech avenue, and teach you the sweetness of melancholy, as we rustle our feet through the dead leaves; we shall not see together the swallows gathering to depart, or the dead branches of the willow drop into the hurrying stream. Not down the leafless lanes, or through the bare wood, or across the clinging plough-land we shall enjoy our luxury of grief

In the town which man made, the leaf falls too. We have no beechen avenues in the mighty town, no carpet of dead leaves to trample on, but the passion-flower dies out in a golden fruit, and the Virginia creeper falls in a crimson shower.

We can scarcely believe that the end is so soon to come; that the summer is past, the autumn nearly over, and the winter hurrying on. Why, it only seemed yesterday that the pavement was scorching and blistering to the feet; that chariots and victorias were tearing past us; that the club windows were full; that Parliament was in full swing; that the opera was open, and all of us in a whirl of dinner-parties, dances, kettledrums, and excitement. Is this really the same London; was this desert in which we wander ever animated and noisy; are these streets, with their crawling cabs and omnibuses, those recently so gay and brilliant, with such carriages and horses as few capitals can boast; is this great building, covered up with hoardings and scaffold poles, splashed and smeared and untidy, the club at which we dined so well? What has happened to this London of ours since we left it? What magician's wand has caused such a marvellous transformation? A plague could not so effectually have decimated our great city. Where shall we begin? Say at Pall Mall, where the representatives of the London season are latest to linger and earliest to return. The leaf is falling, and the street as silent as the grave. Not a carriage is to be seen, save a doctor's brougham at the Athenæum, or the barouche of a senior War Office clerk. The Carlton is given over to a gang of contractors' men, and Irish labourers with hods blunder up the stone steps, on which we left the most aristocratic men in England lighting their afternoon cigars. The Travellers' is apparently deserted. You may walk up and down the "sweet shady side" all day long without finding a bishop, and the whole regiment of Guards is evidently on leave, for neither in the well-known bay-window, nor on the pavement, is an officer to be seen in uniform. Not a T cart stops the way at the Junior Carlton, and the commissionaire, with the memorandum-book, is relieved of the duty of saluting the jaunty little boys, who, in tightly-fitting gloves, and with button-hole bouquets half as big as their closely-shaved cannon-ball little heads, used a few weeks ago to be coming in and out all the afternoon for a cigarette and a stimulant of Angostura bitters. Such a pretty relief as a lady is not to be found. An occasional brougham, driven by a stable-help, and containing a child and a lady's-maid, now and then dashes up to Waterloo House for the execution of a hurried commission, and when it is getting dusk, a petticoat may be noticed passing from Pimlico a round-about way to Piccadilly. With this exception Pall Mall is innocent of female charms. At the clubs there is no one to fetch, and in the windows there are no eyes to stare at those who have no business there. The one sentry in the semicircle behind Lord Herbert's statue, makes his semicircuit with a depressed air ; and the two sentries who have been thrust shoulder to shoulder into the portico of Burlington House, hardly large enough for one man, to represent the ducal dignity of the Horse Guards, wish the Carlton contractors and their rubbish at Jericho, and envy the space and freedom awarded to the one military representative of the Secretary of State for War. The fall of the leaf is even represented by the Government clerk, who, for a few weeks, has discarded the inevitable frock coat, though he retains the beloved umbrella. He takes the opportunity of wearing out his old coat, he has discarded gloves, and his hat will not bear a close inspection. Some of his brethren are more independent still, and are not ashamed to desecrate the sanctity of Pall Mall with shooting-coats and billycock hats. They are cleaning up at the Carlton, and at the Rag ; perspiring soldiers, with excusable indolence, are helping to move the goods and chattels of the Horse Guards, Whitehall, out of spring-carts and vans, apparently hired from all the cheap greengrocers in Westminster, and the said goods and chattels, unable for want of space to pass the sentries in the narrow portico, are flung higgledy-piggledy into an open window. The well-known crowd of nursemaids, loafers, and milliners has vanished from the gates of Marlborough House ; not because the Prince of Wales is absent from home—for during certain months, whether the Prince is at home or not, the crowd is sure to be there, watching the black gates with terrible anxiety—but because Pall Mall is so intensely dull, that even a crowd does not take the trouble to collect.

We will turn our backs, therefore, upon Pall Mall, if you please, and pass under the arches of St. James's Palace to the Green Park. The clock, which always strikes when you pass under it, strikes now, of course; but there are no carriages at the Lord Chamberlain's Office, no messengers making stereotyped speeches about the forthcoming drawing-room to ladies who prove the truth of the saying that brains do not necessarily accompany beauty; no britzkas calling at Stafford House, given up, like the clubs, to contractors and scaffold poles; no signs of life, save when Pimlico still saunters to Piccadilly; and the Pall Mall clerks let loose like schoolboys, are hurrying to the Victoria train. A pall of pale blue fog hangs over the Green Park. The grass is wet and sodden, the same grass on which how recently ugly loafers were sprawling, over which children were scampering with their kites, escaping from the dress of nurse or hand of governess; where little lads played cricket with india-rubber balls against the stump of a tree; and here, where in a pretty hollow "hard by a fountain," many a "Damon sat complaining" the lateness of his love.

But what do we see now at the very hour—five o'clock—when the youth of fashion used to hurry along the gravel path, making a short cut to the other park, where the world was to be found? The turf, unsoiled with the doubtful garments of the half-drunken and sodden loafers, and untrampled by the little feet, is rich in colour. See even the sparrows appear afraid of getting their feet wet, and having touched the cold grass with their naked claws, fly off again with a chirrup of pain. No more is the newly-married clerk met half-way to his Brompton home by an affectionate wife. He ploughs through the wet gravel alone, hoping by chance to meet her among the gaudy Knightsbridge shops. The pretty garden of hawthorns on the slope is bare and desolate; that trysting place by the drinking fountain, hidden in summer time by a miniature forest, is exposed now, and is taken possession of by a melancholy policeman in a shiny cape. The children are playing with their toys after tea in the nursery, instead of taking their afternoon walk in the cool, and this fact will account for the total absence of redcoats strolling quite by accident from the barracks round by Buckingham Palace. Still, this change from mirth to melancholy is not unpleasant. "*Oh! le bon temps! J'étais bien malheureuse!*" An earthy smell, a scent of decaying leaves; the pressure of the foot on the sodden grass, or the gravel drenched with damp, and far away to the west, through the pale blue autumn fog, a broad band of crimson across the sky calls up a scene which cannot be resisted.

Let us shut our eyes for an instant, and as we hurry along we can picture another scene. The country cannot be kept back any longer. We have been shooting all day, and are doing the last mile through the lodge gates, along the carriage drive to the white house. The same damp gravel, the same dripping leaves, the same soaking grass, the same rich moisture arising from the ground, the same melancholy gloom of autumn, the same gorgeous reds and browns, the same band of crimson across the evening sky. The shades of evening are closing round with quite as much melancholy sweetness as in Mr. Fred Clay's delightful musical romance; and the ladies, weary of scandal and embroidery, bored with female society, and relieved from the after-disagreeables of an enormous feminine luncheon, are filing down the damp drive to see the men shoot rabbits. Here is colour in abundance. The petticoats of scarlet and violet, and brown and blue, the gleam of colour on the hat, the rose-colour fading off the pale cheeks which have been toasting at a boudoir fire, or printed with the pattern of a counterpane after a heavy afternoon sleep, the neutral tints of the male garments, and the colours of nature aforesaid. Suddenly the night closes in. The band of crimson in the sky fades into the pale blue mist. Couples fall out and wander apart. It is too dark to shoot rabbits, and the men and women take to whispering. On they wander till they come to the long white house, where the lights gleam through the heavy red curtains, where dressing is suggested, where dinner is promised, and where ends the brief romance. "Oh! le bon temps! J'étais bien malheureuse!"

But after this digression let us step across the road to Piccadilly, a task now easily accomplished, but not so a few weeks ago. What a marvellous change! Where are the broughams, the victorias, the traps, the drags, the dandies, the heavy yellow chariot from Cumberland Place, the ponies from Pimlico, the real swells, the seedy swells with a third day flower and boots vamped up with somebody's electric polish; the horsewomen in the blue habits and the tall hats; the walking court guides, who know everybody and long to be known; the nobodies learned in heraldry, the eccentricities of the park, the mysteries of the season, the gossip from the clubs? Where is the noise, the chatter, the drawl, the refinement, the carelessness, and the vulgarity of "afternoon park?" Vanished!—absolutely gone! A solitary mounted policeman walks his horse through the slush of which the Row is composed, waiting to arrest a phantom horseman for furious riding, and maliciously eyeing a wild enthusiast who has come up from the country, hired a worn-out nag, and thinks he is creating a sensation by galloping through the mud. Not a carriage is to be seen. A few suspicious broughams make their way down south, and go through the park, not because it is the shortest route, but because livery-stable broughams are privileged, and it is some gratification to take the change out of a hack-cab. The trim garden where the rhododendrons bloomed so well in June, and which all through the season was so admirably kept, looks utterly forlorn. The subtropical plants hang down their limp heads, and there are deep grave-like holes from which rare plants have been rescued and transformed to a more genial climate. The regiments of chairs have been stowed away in some horticultural pantechnicon, and only a few broken-backed and lame patients remain to accommodate damp beggars and the disreputable ghouls who prey about the park to feed apparently on nothing. The leaves have long ago got the mastery over the gardeners, and are tossed about hither and thither, crunched into the gravel-paths by the labourers who always choose "a bit of country" on their way home, and by the hundreds who are bound to the desk and forced to take a melancholy constitutional before they turn towards home and dinner.

Having done our autumn park let us pass up Piccadilly as we used to do the other day. Every house is closed. Servants on board-wages are calling on one another and pretending to be ladies and gentlemen. We hear no more the cheering horn of the Brighton coach just arriving at the White Horse Cellars. Not a ghost of a drag passes us. It is almost night. The gas is turned on full in the shop windows, making the goods look double the value they were before. We stroll for an instant in the Burlington Arcade, and see the same scene which has been enacted every autumn and winter these twenty years past. The same owners of hats and sealskin jackets gathered to meet and talk to Jack from Aldershot and Tom from Woolwich. The same baby faces sucking huge cigars or playing with perfumed cigarettes, the same wicked faces and wicked eyes, familiar to the observant Londoner, unsatiated after a lifetime of dissipation; the same weak women, the same unmanly men, making us so sick and weary that we make a bolt from the River Styx, fling an *obolus* to the horridly deformed Charon who ferries us over the muddy river of Piccadilly outside Hades, and make the best of our way to the large club fire, which strikes vastly pleasant now that the leaf has fallen.

PUTTING ON THE PAINT.

STRICTLY speaking, Christmas Eve is not held until this moment. We reserve until now the bowl of punch, the good wishes, and the cordiality which precede our domestic festival, but to all practical intents and purposes our Christmas Eve is past. Already the paint has been put on. It was near the holiday to begin with, and all the marketing had to be got over. Tradesmen insisted upon your ordering a supply of solid flesh, turkeys, bread, butter, dessert, and what not to last over the holidays and odd times antecedent to the Day of Boxing, when we are all out in the streets, lounging about, and not knowing whether we are at work or shirking. It became necessary to decorate the house at home, and festoon the font at the "little church round the corner," to make the pudding, and buy the annual present, to put up the holly, and artfully hide the mistletoe; to prepare and lay in stores to fortify the garrison, and to brush up, to sweep the hearth clean, and leave nothing undone; to prepare for a charge of hungry friends, and to be above suspicion on points of hospitality, to set our house in order, and to put on the paint.

But elsewhere than at home the paint was vigorously applied I can tell you. There was work, hard work, anxious, trying, and annoying work to be got over before many of our brothers and sisters closed their eyes. When the fumes of the potent Christmas punchbowl, or the back-aching work of decanting had wrapped us in a deep and lordly sleep, the paint was still being put on, solely for our Christmas pleasure and amusement. Others were at work that we might laugh. Some were sighing in order to extract a smile from our faces. Anxious women and determined men, children whose pale faces would have wrung another passionate stanza from Mrs. Barrett Browning, carpenters and labourers, painters and gas-men, authors and managers, scene-shifters and door-keepers, husbands waiting for their wives, and wives wearily watching for their lords, mothers hungering for their children, brothers lingering in the mud, like brave knights, to escort their pretty sisters home—all these were out and about, working and waiting, dozing and dreaming, longing and lingering, for it was the last time for rehearsing the Christmas pantomime, and night was turned into day. Even now as the Christmas bells are ringing the work may not be quite over; the daylight will possibly have conquered the artificial glare of the gas, and at the foot of the half-set Transformation Scene a dozen carpenters may be dozing. It appears to be an English rule to put off everything until the last minute, and then by sheer pluck and dogged determination to carry off the prize triumphantly. Contractors break their promises, scene-painters are obstinate, authors are not prepared with their telling couplet or the attractive song, part of the music is unscored, words are uncertain, the traps will not work, alas! the pretty fairy is pitched forward on her delicate nose, the magnesium light refuses to flash, the ballet breaks down, the clown is sulky, and the stage manager worn to death. But, somehow or other, it all comes right at night, and out of the insufficiency of the rehearsal arises the utmost care and watchfulness when the public rushes in.

At the risk of being considered cruel for disclosing the secrets of the prison house and destroying the illusion of pantomime night, I should like to give a faint idea of the astounding confusion attending the last pantomime rehearsal, that supreme moment when the weakest points in the armour are discovered, when there is no turning back, no half measures, no temporizing, no alteration, but when the thing must be carried through neck or nothing and made to succeed. What an hour for a general, for a commander of men; what a test for the temper, and what an opportunity for the exhibition of tremendous vigour and bull-dog pluck! There is no time to think. There is no chance for reconsideration. All must work together or all will fail. The sulky fairy must be snubbed, the impertinent comic gentleman must be slanged, the noisy children must be cuffed, the clumsy scene-shifters must be abused, satire must be flung into the teeth of the property man or all will go wrong. Argument must be deposed and a stern autocratic rule established.

Just come with me only to the stage-door to begin with. Here is an autocrat with a vengeance, and properly so, as he would have to answer for any freaks of good-nature which conceded anything and pandered to curiosity. The door-keeper is almost mad. His orders are strict and imperative. Though his heart bleeds he must carry out his instructions. The hall is filled with a miscellaneous, pushing, struggling mob; a mob which must be kept back, or confusion will be worse confounded. It is the art of the door-keeper to sift business from mere curiosity. He has to convey notes to Miss Millie de Vere, to say that a brougham and supper are waiting; and to console a lachrymose mother, who is waiting for one of her fairies, and who, as she thinks, good soul! ought to have been in bed hours ago. He has to keep back idlers, who would sneak into a theatre on some paltry excuse, and detect a falsehood in a moment. He must decide a hundred times if the manager is or is not to be interrupted to read a letter. He must chaff and growl, abuse and console, talk to friends, and check interference; detect a painter from a dresser, know the faces of charwomen and wardrobe assistants, study the peculiarities of all the new comers, neglect no notes, and refuse all bribes, preserving at the same time his supreme power, never yielding, and keeping all in good humour. Truly, the stage-doorkeeper's work was no sinecure on this occasion, and if he sleeps now he will deserve it, for his Christmas troubles are not yet over.

We will pass on, then, if you please, past unpacked and half-unpacked hampers, past huge crates and piles of straw, through avenues of properties, startled at one minute with a row of grinning and hideous masks, and stumbling at another over a dragon's scaly tail, or a cradle containing a property baby, or by a very armoury of spears and swords, and daggers and wands; on through banquet halls, and hopping over tables groaning with tinsel pies and wooden fruit; on again through larders of carrots and turnips, geese and turkeys, woolly puddings, and uneatable joints, until we come to the stage, or to its approaches. Was there ever such a bustle? The children are swarming everywhere, playing at leapfrog, chaffing the properties, dozing on the staircases, pully-hauling, as boys will do, and chattering as girls will chatter; for ever in the way, and utterly irrepressible. There is no doing anything with them. In vain is Mrs. Smith shouted at "to keep those children quiet;" in vain is the assistant-acting-deputy-stage manager implored to apply his cane. The racket ceases for an instant, but on it goes in a few minutes worse than before. The wings are all crowded. Mothers and patrons, brothers and friends, have somehow evaded the vigilant door-keeper; and what with imps and fairies, ladies of the ballet, supers, and subordinates, it is scarcely possible to move. It will be better for us to get right away from the crowd, and grope our way in the dark to some deserted private box, and having put aside the covering to watch the fun. A more amusing, varied, and extraordinary sight is rarely presented, and those who possess any sense of humour, will find in a pantomime rehearsal plenty of capital. The demi-toilette of the artists is remarkable to begin with. Here is a lovely maiden, the burlesque prince of Boxing night, who is shot up a trap clothed in a long, scarlet dressing gown to her heels, but when the trap is unruly, and plants the lovely creature in an ignominious position on the dusty stage, beyond the folds of the flannel drapery, are discovered pink silk tights and high-heeled satin boots of the approved burlesque pattern. The upper portions of the costume are not less curious. Her neck is swathed in a handkerchief of cream-coloured silk, and on her head is a Tyrolean hat, with a scarlet feather. The fairy who fascinates the prince, and goes down the opposite trap, is not *de rigueur*. She wears a pork pie hat and an astracan jacket, it is true, but her skirts are of spotless tarletan, *à la* ballet, with scarlet leggings, corresponding with the gaudy pantelettes, exhibited so freely when she suggests a pirouette. There are fairies, it is true, who disdain any theatre toilette, half or otherwise. They appear on the stage as they may be seen on the pavement, wrapped in fur and sealskin, swathed in mufflers, and evidently determined to fascinate rather than work. But how they work, those other fairy-sisters (you will see a wedding-ring on the orthodox finger if you notice carefully), the women with the brains, who earn the bread! They just tuck up their petticoats, to allow their limbs fair play in a suggested dance; they sing just enough to show they have caught the tune, and that the words are safe; they speak sufficient lines to exhibit the points they intend to make, and the cues are spoken clearly and distinctly. Such women as these are the joy of the harassed stage-manager. They look careworn, pale, and haggard, it is true, but their soul is in their work, and they will never fail. They are never caught flirting at the wings, or giggling in a corner. They mean business, and they want to get home to bed. But the industrious and hard-working must suffer for the thoughtless and stupid. The delays are irritating, the repetitions too tedious. A dozen times the ballet comes on carelessly, and out of time; a dozen times it is sent back. The active little stage-manager, in his prosaic coat and trousers, has to express the listening attitude of a fairy, and to trip on his toes across the stage—a feat he performs with ludicrous effect. Then the music gets wrong, and the leader of the orchestra tears his hair, till at last, by constant repetition, and after much vigorous language, the proper effect is secured, and the rehearsal is advanced another stage. One instructor succeeds another. When the musicians have had a turn from the conductor, and the children have been twisted about, on comes the ballet-mistress, with the white tarletan petticoats and scarlet pantelettes—a vigorous contrast—to lead the ballet scene. How hard some work, and how stupid are many, we need not add. After time has been lost over and over again, after the same faults have been almost obstinately committed, the dance is almost perfect, and on goes the pantomime.

At an early hour of the morning spirits flag, the girls are worn out, the children are dog-tired, the carpenters are simply stupid; it is then that the strongest and most patient of men are apt to lose their tempers. A simple incident may illustrate the painful sides of a pantomime rehearsal, and at the same time the merit they possess. Picture to yourself a pale and cadaverous comic man, wrapped in a threadbare coat and a seedy muffler. His strength is evidently gone. He is not stupid, he is simply dazed and very weak. The stage-manager has a heart, but rehearsals are not the places for hearts, and the little stage-manager has lost his temper with the pale, lean man. He bullies him and bawls at him, he makes him go over the business again and again. But the result is the same. The pale, thin man struggles like a lean horse tugging at a heavy coal-cart. He cannot get up the hill. The stage driver is fairly furious. He forgets himself, and abuses the poor wretch! "Confound you!" says he, "I never saw such a stupid idiot in the whole course of my life! There, go on with the rehearsal." There is a moment's pause, and then a voice, "monotonous and hollow as a ghost's," breaks the silence with these words, "And so would you be stupid if *you had not tasted meat for eleven weeks.*" Good friend! good friend, there are tears in your eyes; let us get home to bed. That plaint has hit you hard. But let us all hurry to the pantomime next week in order that the starving man may eat and bless with us the happy Christmas time!

A JOURNEY EN ZIGZAG.

HALF the pleasure of holiday travelling is lost if the traveller maps out a trip before he starts and holds to it with conservative severity. I like a vague and indefinite traveller, and a companion who does not care whither he goes or in what inn he sleeps so long as home is left behind and an inn is found somewhere. What is the use of plunging into the mysteries of *Bradshaw*, making up your mind to catch certain trains, giving yourself a fixed time to do so many miles, and worrying to carry out to the letter a predetermined programme? Frequently nothing but despair follows such an arrangement. You miss the train, and are out in your calculation, you quarrel with your best friend, and go to bed at the wrong place in a sulk. Let it be granted, then, that twice twenty-four hours can be stolen out of a busy week, that the brain requires rest, and that London dust is clogging up the pores of the skin. How can a blow of fresh air be best obtained in the shortest possible time and in the most agreeable manner? Well, here are the notes of a journey *en zigzag*, the results of an indefinite tour, and they may be taken for what they are worth.

Having provided ourselves with a pair of stout walking boots, a thick stick, a small bag or knapsack containing a little clean linen, and the ordinary brushes which cannot be dispensed with; a pipe, a tobacco pouch, and a box of lights, supposing we meet at London Bridge at ten o'clock. This will give time to knock off the remaining work, to answer the letters by the early post, and to get breakfast comfortably. London Bridge at ten o'clock is a suggestive rendezvous. The imaginative traveller meditates a journey to Ostend, and is at once carried on through the Belgian cathedral towns straight to Spa, or up the Rhine to Wiesbaden. Or the destination may be merely Boulogne, or possibly Edinburgh, or Hamburg, or Rotterdam. Come down the dirty, fish-smeared, disreputable steps which will lead us to wharfdom, and land us in the middle of an army of touts. Gaudily-dressed girls and flashy young men, dowdy matrons, and children all provided with a hunk of bread-and-butter or an enormous orange are scrambling towards a steamer. They do not look at all like Spa, or the Rhine, or Rotterdam, or even Edinburgh. Of course not. They are off to Margate—merely Margate—and so are we, in the A1 copper-bottomed, fast-steaming vessel, the *Prince of Wales*, property of the Steam Navigation Company, and provided, if not with a chaplain and surgeon, at least with a steward; and a stewardess too for that matter. The company is certainly jovial if not select. Though the vessel is full of eatables and drinkables at moderate prices, each passenger is provided with a bag full of mysterious food wrapped up in wet newspaper, and with more mysterious fluids in soda water bottles. An old woman who has brought a basket of fruit on board is sent to shore with an empty basket and a pocket full of money. And now the bell rings and we are off. It is to be hoped that the imaginative person who soared to Ostend or Rotterdam is not bruised after his tumbledown to Margate. For many miles it will be just the same thing.

We shall now as then travel seaward through the delightful shipping, pass the crazy old wharf where Quilp lived, and see the exact spot where the dog was chained and Tom Scott stood on his head; hold our noses as we pass the chemical works and the bone boilers; recall cosy dinners at Greenwich and Blackwall, hear the old tale about what would happen (as if anybody knew) if all the powder at Purfleet blew up; watch the little yachts off Erith getting ready for a race, and see the trees which overshadow the place whereat to spend a happy day. On a Margate boat, price four shillings all the way first-class, you have just the same pleasant feeling of leaving England and going out to sea as on the upper deck of the *Baron Osy* or the *Batavia*. This river-scene is perpetually bright and ever changing. No trip can be taken which contains so much variety. You may go up the river and enjoy the paddle vastly, but it is down the river you acquire a sudden change which nothing else appears to give. The boat is not over-crowded, for the regular Margate season has scarcely commenced, and it has been a terrible time as yet, so they say, for the Isle of Thanet.

By the time we have read a little and smoked a little, dined a great deal, and watched with some interest the extravagant flirtations of three yellow-haired damsels in book-muslin, who after dinner are by turns sleepy and affectionate, we find that the Reculvers and Herne Bay are passed, Birchington and the new colony of Westgate have disappeared, and the famous jetty is in sight. There is a sigh of despair when the sad intelligence that the Hall-by-the-Sea is not open is conveyed to the yellow-haired maidens. Without the Hall-by-the-Sea, and the dancing, and the comic songs, and the society of the man in the red tie, these yellow locks are surely useless, and the face so carefully made up will be smeared with tears of disappointment. It is evident that the boat will be half empty at Margate, and now occurs one of the great charms of an indefinite journey. "Supposing we do not stay at Margate at all," suggests Damon. "Quite so," answers Pythias. For us the yellow-haired girls have no charm, and see, they have actually been deserted by the very men they fancied they had ensnared; dancing is out of the question on a summer night, and fresh air is not secured or health obtained in an asphyxiating atmosphere, or by frequent potations of brandy and water. The jetty and the songs at night are all very well, but let us get on. A shriek in unison from the votaries of King Auricomus when they find that their lovers have not disembarked, and that they are left alone in Margate, is the sole excitement of the disembarkation. Margate chaff does not commence until August, so Circe is left on the Isle of Thanet, and Ulysses and his companions put to sea again, congratulating themselves on their freedom.

On we go, the wind freshening up, and blowing the cool spray into our faces, past Kingsgate and its castle, past Broadstairs and its Bleak House, past the leaf-covered estate of Sir Moses Montefiore, until Ramsgate is reached, and we must land, whether we like it or not. Ramsgate, like Margate, is also dull, and virtuously respectable. We land without so much as a whisper of chaff, and pursue our way unannoyed along the noble granite pier. Again comes up the inevitable question—where shall we go? The day is yet young. We are rested and have dined. We wish to stretch our legs, and surely it is a waste of time to settle down at Ramsgate at four o'clock. Let us trudge on towards the West Cliff, past Royal Crescent and its croquet ground; past laughing girls, fresh in their evening muslins, with never so much as a word for that blue-eyed maiden pretending to read a novel, and ready to flirt on the smallest provocation; past the blue-grey Catholic church and the quiet monastery, over the cliff and along a narrow path, where more girls linger, and we demand a toll, and so on to Pegwell Bay, if you please, where tea and shrimps are not amiss in the open air. Ah! this is peace. The sky is all blue, the sea comes rolling in at our feet; no jolly dogs are here to disturb the quiet of the delicious evening, the birds in the next estate are singing good night to one another; the tea is strong, the butter fresh, the bread new, and the shrimps newly caught. And again comes up the question where shall we go?

That is Sandwich over there at the bend of the semicircle, eight miles off; and yonder, at the extreme point is Deal, a good thirteen by the coach road. Well, anywhere you like, only let us get on as long as our legs are firm. Do not hint at a train or a carriage. So away we trudge again past the coast-guard station till we get on to the fine road which skirts the sea. A tumbledown and romantic inn attracts our notice at the village of Cliff End, and stopping for an instant to admire the house we are astonished to find the proprietress, one Madame Pyle, occupied with a double duty. She sells beer and makes feather bonnets. Over the sign-board of the inn the following announcement is emblazoned in letters of gold: "Madame Pyle, the inventor and maker of feather hats and bonnets." Madame Pyle is a character. There can be no question about her nationality. She is a Kentish woman from head to heel, but her feather hats and bonnets have got into society, and though she "thinks it all rubbish," she has yielded to the entreaties of her patrons and put Madame Pyle on her card and on her original shop-front. A more contented and quiet old lady we never met than Mrs. Pyle. Nothing pleases her more than to take any visitor into her *sanctum sanctorum* upstairs, where lie in state the happy results of her winter's toil. Bonnets composed entirely of sea birds' plumage, hats all wings and feathers, fans manufactured from quills picked up on the beach, boxes and work-baskets, reticules ingeniously contrived from sea shells and polished stones, patchwork mats, and cushions, and quilts. All these the worthy old lady exhibits with some pride, and owns without any affectation that hard work and a determination to keep up a cheerful disposition alone dissipate the bitter sorrow of a past life. Those who enjoy a chat with a quiet old body should not pass Cliff End without stopping for a glass of ale at the quiet inn, and an inspection of the magazine of curiosities collected by the milliner by the sea.

A good broad road skirted by the sea takes you in the shortest four miles straight into Sandwich. This is just the time for a walk. The sun is no longer hot. There is no dust. A cool breeze blows off the water inland, and, in company with women trudging homewards to Sandwich with their marketings, we arrive in good time at that venerable town. The desire to press on is still unabated. The light will hold good for some hours yet. Sandwich is clean, it is true, but dreadfully desolate. Even on Saturday night not half a dozen people are in the streets, and so, sitting in the old churchyard, looking up at the fine grey Kentish church, admirably restored, we determine to trust to our legs again, and press on for Deal. We might take the train, it is true, but neither of us are tired; we have got accustomed to our knapsacks, we are telling one another tales of adventures of long ago and old rambles, and, as we have got into a melancholy frame of mind, we have determined, by way of variety, to get to Deal over the sand hills.

If you have been thrown over by the girl of your idolatry, and wish to feed on melancholy—if, like Eugene Aram, you have committed an awful crime, and desire to wrestle with your conscience—if you are to be made bankrupt when you return to town and to be put in gaol on Monday morning—if you have lost a fortune or a dear friend, been cut out of your uncle's will, or made a reckless speculation, if you have gambled and lost, and desire the scenery to suit your frame of mind, take my advice and walk to Deal in the gloaming over the sand-hills. Of all desolate and melancholy walks it is the most desolate and most melancholy. Now you are Christian in the "Pilgrim's Progress," and now the "Wandering Jew." The wind howls over the dark, uncultivated land, and the peewit shrieks in the adjacent meadows. You do not meet a solitary soul, and you have to grope your way by the last remaining traces of a forgotten path. Every now and then a melancholy house is seen suggestive of ghosts and murders, but the windows are darkened, and not an inhabitant is to be found. The conversation takes a hideous turn, and your companion being well up in the "Newgate Calendar," and Mrs. Crowe's "Night Side of Nature," you look ahead to the miles and miles of dreary waste with fear and trembling. All at once you stand rooted before a white sepulchral stone, which the moon brings up in relief. For fifty yards around this spot vegetation has ceased; the grass will not grow, the flowers refuse to bloom. A few dark weeds struggle to appear through a surface of uncomfortable boulders. Let us kneel down in this awful spot, and read the inscription on the stone. Is it a mile stone or a boundary mark? Neither. It is a murder sign! Here, on this very spot, we are told poor Mary Bax was brutally murdered by one Martin Lash, a foreign seaman. She was only twenty-three, and, as if to console us, we are told that Lash was executed for the ghastly deed. Our blood curdles in our veins, and we picture the murder on such a dreary night as this, and the shrieks of Mary Bax being carried out to sea over the salt sand-hills; no help at hand, nothing to save her from the bludgeon of Martin Lash. But our companion, who is of a Mark Tapleian disposition, reminds us that the murder took place in 1792, so long ago, that possibly it was not true, and at any rate if Mary had lived, she would now be 102, so all sympathy is out of the question. So we pull ourselves together again, and laughing, we see in the distance the bright light of the South Foreland and the twinkling lamps of Deal. This is a freshening walk, indeed, after the lonely·sand-hills, to skirt the sea once more and hear the delicious roar of the waves upon the shingled beach; and, surely, after such a day, we well deserve an enjoyable supper, the last pipe, and the clean fresh bed which await us at the Royal Hotel.

When we wake in the morning to the pleasant music of the everlasting sea we can hardly believe that only a day and night have passed since London Bridge was left. What a sleep we have had; not one restless turn, and here is a tub full of water, just brought up from the beach, and an angry summons from Damon to say that the mackerel are at this moment being grilled. Breakfast over, and the prospect before us of a heavenly day, we are on the tramp again, purposing to make for Dover over and along the cliffs. No pleasanter walk than this can be found within an easy distance of London. Sometimes you are reminded of the coast line of Devonshire, frequently of the charms of the Isle of Wight, and occasionally of the grand rock effects of Cornwall. Pleasant, indeed, is Walmer and its castle, the trees of the park approaching almost to the water's edge. Charming will be found the rose-covered village of St. Margaret's, with its little church on the cliffs, and enviable the trim coast-guard cottages we pass on our way. Now we are under the cliffs, with their blinding white, watching the curlews as they make their way to the nests in the fissures of the rocks; now we are resting among the wild. flowers on the top, and are almost sleepy with the "murmur of innumerable bees." Now we are mounting break-neck steps, and traversing tiny paths within an inch of destruction; now we are looking from the Foreland Light at the coast of France and Cape Grisnez, which only seem a mile away; and so, with the blue sky above, and the blue sea to the left, and the flowers on the right, and the pure air everywhere, we arrive in good time at Dover, meeting Mary Jane with the inevitable soldier, and the Dover folk enjoying their Sunday afternoon stroll. There is little more to tell. Dinner must be eaten, and then with a cigar you can stroll about the Admiralty Pier, and make believe you are to cross to-night and find yourself in Paris to-morrow morning. It will be best though if Black Monday promises hard work and collar-toil again to go up to town by the last train—third class, if you like, for six shillings! and you will arrive on your doorstep long before midnight, with the variety of a fortnight compressed into barely two days. Your face will be burned and your brain freshened, and if Mr. Cook had to cater for you from end to end he would guarantee this journey en zigzag for a sum which, with Sybaritish extravagance, could not exceed thirty shillings!

AFTER DARK.

WE have unquestionably felt the first grip of winter. No one could have mistaken it. When the sun went slowly down surely a perceptible shudder went round the whole island, and for the first time this year we pooh-poohed balmy evenings and starlight nights, thinking only of a greatcoat on the back, and a cosy fire in the study at home. It came with terrible and dread significance, this first cruel, biting blast of winter, whirling the curled leaves and the blinding dust through the streets, bringing in its train miserable moanings of dear coals, twinges of rheumatism, sore throats, and influenza. There is no getting out of it. The warning has come. We felt it in the lonely and deserted club, where we went wandering about for a warm corner, and looked savagely at the highly-polished and cheerless grates. We all edged away from the open window, and peremptory orders were suddenly given to the waiters to close up the glass swing-doors. We experienced the chill touch in the dull grey streets, and on the top of the omnibus, lately so pleasant, we crouched down, and dreaded "a facer" at every street corner. At home most of us made a compromise with plenty of gas-burners, and the cheerful aspect which is the next best thing to warmth; but we shut out the day as quickly as we could, and turned our back indignantly on the shavings in the grate. But if that first sad warning of the decay of the year, if the " lisp of leaves and ripple of rain," if the melancholy prophecy of darkness with its Banshee cry and miserable moan—penetrated into the heart of London; if here where there is gas and noise, we were suddenly conscious of the death of beautiful summer, and the advent of a season of dark, mourning, and despair—how much more was it felt by those away from home still holiday-making, how much more will it be dreaded by the thousands who had postponed their outing for September, their sentiment for the "hunter's moon," their activity for the turnips, and their pictures for the tints of autumn!

It was felt—that first ice-blast, that first cutting, penetrating breath of winter blown from the cruel East—everywhere among the hearts of holiday-makers. At the seaside, when dinner was over and chilliness is a sign of digestion, they all shuddered at the pier, though the band was playing at the extreme end, and there were glass protectors from the wind. No child ventured on the sands after tea. Sealskin jackets and cloaks of sable, velvet mantles with trimmings of fur, heavy shawls of wonderful colours, soft woollen wrappers for the neck, in which the prettiest of faces nestle like comfortable birds, appeared as if by magic. When the shooting was over at country or farm house, and the athletes' meal was at an end, no one suggested a cigar on the croquet lawn, or a ramble in the wilderness. The grass was damp and sodden. The gravel was cold and sticky. The day had ended without any interlude of warmth or colour, and the dead leaves fell from the moist branches in paddock and orchard. No moon was worth the misery of the landscape; no stars repaid one for the sorrow of the scene. Better the lighted billiard room or the comfortable study, or a chat over the wood fire in the drawing-room, than any more wet feet and damp jackets. If, then, it may be granted that suddenly the light of the summer time has gone out, if it is not extravagant to state that the after dinner hour all over England is not quite so pleasant as it was, if there is everywhere an inclination to shut out the day rather than retain it, to draw the curtains, to put up the shutters, to light the candles, to come home and not stay out of doors, to get inside some room or to hide in some corner or another —and if at the same time it may be taken for granted that a good half of us have not taken our holiday at all—then the position of most holiday-makers in England at the close of the day is most miserable and unenviable.

Let us take the case of residents at English watering places in September, and a September like this, when the chill has come too soon. No difference is felt in the morning. We can enjoy our bathe and pick our matutinal shrimp at an open window. We can dig the sands or promenade the Spa and hear the band, or read our book, or walk or drive or ride or picnic as before. The sun still shines, the water still sparkles, the atmosphere is still delicious, the seaweed is still exhilarating, and all is as before until the sun goes down. At that moment, according to the almost prevalent English fashion, utter misery and depression take the place of gaiety and amusement. We cannot all go to bed like children at nine o'clock, and, if we did, we probably should not sleep. It is too cold to have anything more to do with the sea. An evening at one of these uncomfortable company hotels, with their business-like coffee rooms, their miserable smoking-rooms, and their billiards monopolized by the shopkeepers of the town, is too appalling to contemplate. No one but a millionaire can occupy a private apartment, and even then the comfort is comparatively limited. An ordinary resident at a seaside hotel these autumn evnings, is in despair for occupation and amusement. The conjuror or the perambulating entertainer is not yet due at the town hall. The circus has departed. The annual regatta is over. There is nothing between a chilly walk on the esplanade, and a sulky silence in a lonely bed room. The conversation in the public smoking-room is a bore; the talk in the public billiard-room is offensive. We go to the door, and light a cigar on the steps. We put on a greatcoat, and attack the breezes. A walk without an object is ridiculous, and the cold once more drives us indoors. But where can we see life, and be amused? Where are the *cafés*, the ball-rooms, the music, and the dance? Is there nothing to be done but listen to the irritating discussions on the Tichborne case in the smoking-room, or to the counter-jumper braggadocio over a game at pool? At Dieppe there would be dancing and amusements at the casino; there would be reading rooms, and conversation rooms, and excitement everywhere. At Ostend we should be dancing in the rooms by the sea, or hearing the band in the other hall by the side of the esplanade, or hurried away in the crowd to the glorious large dancing-room in the town—either dancing ourselves, or watching the amusements of others. At Boulogne we should be at the "Etablissement," hearing good music, or enjoying ourselves at the Tintelleries Gardens. All round the coast, from Schevening in Holland, to Trouville in France, some public rooms, called either casino or "Etablissement des Bains," are found, wherein the evening of our holiday is made as pleasant as the day.

Turn from this gaiety, this merry rendezvous, this important event of the day—apart from all theatres and entertainments with which the town may be favoured, to the melancholy lodging, the deserted beach, the cheerless hotel, and the deadly-lively streets of an English watering-place. The construction of public rooms, or the establishment of public dances, the existence of a public seaside club, with innumerable attractions, is unheard of and unknown in England. For instance, at Scarborough, on the Spa, where of all places in the world there should be an establishment answering to the Continental casino, there is not a room in which a newspaper can be read night or day, and not a room devoted to a public dance. The rooms on the Spa are given up to a nightly entertainment and to public drinking. The evening's amusement at Scarborough is not provided by the town, or the proprietors of the Spa, but distinctly by the various hotels, who get up dances for the amusement of the visitors, now at the Grand, now at the Crown, now at the Royal, and now at the Prince of Wales Hotel. If it were not for the energy and enterprise of hotel proprietors and visitors, the evenings at Scarborough would be as dull and pointless as at Hastings, St. Leonard's, Folkestone, or Worthing. There never was a better place for an establishment or casino than Scarborough. To the rooms on the Spa should be added public reading rooms and a public ball-room. At Ems, at Spa, at Wiesbaden, at all the foreign watering-places, the visitors assemble in the evening and enjoy themselves. We look round all England, and only at the Assembly Rooms, Margate, do we find anything approaching the Continental fashion of a preliminary concert, ending in a pretty dance. We are not talking now of special festivities at regatta time, or of the energy and good sense shown at various popular hotels; but we maintain that the town or municipality at the seaside does not consult its own interest, when it refuses to run up parallel with the seaside, and opposite the sea, some such establishment as is found the centre of all attraction at Dieppe, Ostend, Boulogne, Blankenberge, St. Malo, Trouville, and Biarritz. A suite of public rooms, a public band, good management, and a subscription, and the whole thing is done.

Why is it, we would ask, that the Margate season commences so early and ends so late? Because Margate looks after her visitors. At the Assembly Rooms there is a concert—and an admirable high-art concert—and a dance in rooms as noble as could be found at Bath, Cheltenham, or Tunbridge Wells. At the Hall-by-the-Sea, there is also an excellent concert and a merry dance. When we do get away for our holiday we like our fill of amusement, and a seaside place, where life is kept up until the last moment, is naturally more acceptable than the limited existence between sunrise and sunset. Blankenberge, in Belgium, is considered by the Ostend folks a dull hole. Bognor is, no doubt, snubbed considerably by Brighton. But compare an evening at Blankenberge with an evening at Bognor! It is ridiculous; there is no comparison. Blankenberge, with its lighted *cafés*, its promenades, its casino, its dances, and its elasticity, lives until midnight. Bognor goes to bed immediately after dinner. The Aquarium is kept lighted until a late hour, and various amusements relieve Brighton from the charge of dulness; but after all, Brighton has only just saved her bacon in this respect, and should be ashamed to live another day without scattering *cafés* with little tables along the sea-front, and increasing the activity of that glorious parade. But the answer in England is, "Thank you very much, but we do very well as we are." Brighton and Scarborough, Folkestone and Hastings, Ramsgate and Margate, could not very well be much fuller if they tried. "We are very much obliged, but we can get on very well without any casinos or establishments." This is all very well. We are penned up in an island, and are forced to make the best of a bad job. But there is another way of looking at it. Is it just or unjust, kind or cruel, considerate or foolish, to tell us that at the ordinary seaside place we shall not read the paper, enjoy society, dance, sing, or make merry—after dark?

THE SORROWS OF SARK.

"Well, then, old fellow, I suppose that we perfectly understand the arrangement. If you wake up on Wednesday morning at sunrise, and find the sea decently calm, you are to come off to St. Helier's, and leave for a few hours the delightful solitude of Gorey. Franz and I will be ready for you on the pier punctually at eight o'clock; and if old Jones isn't ready with his yacht, woe betide old Jones!"

These were my parting instructions as I left Bellevue Cottage, deliciously situated among the trees on the hill-side, midway between St. Helier's and St. Aubin's, in the charming island of Jersey, before preparing to walk home from there to Gorey in the moonlight. Ah! what a moonlight it was, and how refreshing came the cool breeze which was blown towards me from the bay, after the weary heat of a long summer day which had just sunk composedly to sleep! But as there may be many people who will not care particularly about my rhapsodies, and to whom my thoughts, as I trudged on my solitary way to Gorey, may not prove in the least interesting, I may just as well "hark back!" here a little, and relate how I came to be acquainted with Carl and Franz, and the two young ladies, from all of whom I had just parted, and how it was that I was lucky enough ever to put my foot inside the hospitable portals of Bellevue Cottage; all of which circumstances must of course be explained before introducing my faithful companions, who shared with me the forever-memorable "sorrows of Sark."

I took Jersey on my way to Normandy and Brittany during a summer ramble in the year, no matter when, and having left some extremely pleasant companions on board the steamer which landed me at St. Helier's at ten o'clock one morning, towards evening I felt I was getting mopish and dull. I was travelling alone. The lonely traveller finds the daytime pass pleasantly enough, and will be sure to fall in with many and many a jolly fellow; but it is not altogether enjoyable to be by yourself in a strange place after sunset. To tell the truth, I found St. Helier's unbearable after I had been in it half an hour. There is an intolerable Cockney air about the place; and some estimable folks who happily are enabled to visit Jersey and its delightful scenery at a ridiculously small expense unfortunately think little of the enjoyments of the surrounding country, but make St. Helier's obnoxious by their music-hall ditties and unenviable swagger. They "do" the island, as they call it, in an excursion car, for two shillings between breakfast and dinner-time, and at night make St. Helier's and its environs hideous with their senseless screaming and overwhelming confraternities of snobs. On this account I took no bed at St. Helier's, but sent my traps on by omnibus to a cosy little inn situated under Mont Orgueil, in the seaside village of Gorey, of whose delights and enviable repose I had received many pleasant experiences. The chief cares of a traveller's existence—his portmanteau and hat-box—having been thus satisfactorily disposed of, I proceeded to take a pleasant stroll along the sands towards St. Aubin's, where I knew that some artist-friends of mine were located, busy on sea-pieces—sea-gulls, rocks, and quiet bay scenery. But the day was too hot for walking on the open stretch of sands intervening between St. Helier's and St. Aubin's; and, glad of the pleasant shelter of the trees in a quiet secluded lane, I wandered on up the hill-side, smoking a cigar and meditating, until the sounds of a piano and the ring of a clear soprano voice made me halt before a pretty rose-covered cottage on the brow of the hill overlooking the bay. It was Bellevue Cottage; at least, so it was called on the gate-post. The afternoon sun was streaming against the cottage, whose windows were open; the green jalousies were unfortunately closed. The sound of a piano was refreshing; the voice was singularly sweet and sympathetic, and the song was familiar to me. So vividly is the whole scene impressed on my mind now as I write, that I even remember the name of the song. It was "White Daisy:"

"Singing all nature loves thee,
 Queen White Daisy."

This was the refrain that fell upon my ear; and, in spite of myself, I stood in the road before the cottage, smoking, and certainly meditating in a strange fashion. The song being a new one—it had only been published in London that season—was, I suppose, sufficient reason for its being repeated by the sympathetic songstress. At any rate, much to my delight, I heard the piano commence the first notes of a very charming pastoral prelude; and, as if the ballad had been encored for my special edification, the first of its melodious words,

> " O, happy forest glades,
> O, murmurous green arcades,"

were warbled forth once more. My acquaintance with the song gave me courage; so, choosing my seat on a low wall just under the window from which the music proceeded, I took the occasion of "putting in a second" every now and then; not boisterously, but in a low, subdued voice; sufficiently loud, however, as I well knew, to be heard by the fair singer, whoever she might be. "White Daisy" was succeeded by another melody equally pretty; and again I joined in. There were evidently two people in the room, for every now and then I saw curious eyes peeping at me through the folds of the jalousies. I suppose I am of an inquisitive disposition. Anyhow, a strange desire came across me of becoming acquainted with the interior of Bellevue Cottage, and obtaining some more intimate knowledge of its inhabitants. You see, one cannot live for ever upon fancy; and sitting on a wall picturing to oneself an imaginary Beatrice is apt, like most other things, to get tedious. A chord of sympathy had somehow or other been struck between the owner of the soprano voice and myself; and I had worked myself up to such a fever-pitch of imaginative excitement, and those closed jalousies were so particularly irritating, that I felt it would be despair, if not death, to leave Bellevue Cottage "so unsatisfied." As Juliet once whispered to Romeo, so whispered I most unhappily to myself,

"What satisfaction can you have to-night?"

The remedy for my disconsolate condition was nearer than I for a moment had dared to imagine. I cast my eyes up to the cottage, and there read the following words, not of warning but happily of invitation :

"*Apartments to Let, Furnished.*"

My mind was soon made up. My luggage was gone on to Gorey, it is true; and if I did not require "Apartments to Let, Furnished," there was no knowing what I *might* want at some future time. At any rate, I was a *bonâ-fide* traveller, and was as free as any other inquisitive fellow to look at the apartments. I had certainly an object in view. One glimpse of the owner of the soprano voice would be even worth the forfeiture of a deposit.

Inspired with an honest feeling of chivalry and romance, and emboldened by the reperusal of that tempting notice-board, I opened the little wicket-gate, walked up to the portico, and, with my heart literally in my mouth, like a philosopher rang the bell. I was shown the vacant apartments by the Abigail of the establishment, and this form damped my ardour. But once under the peaceful roof of Bellevue Cottage, I was not to be disappointed or put down. I played my cards so well, talked so adroitly, and somehow put my case so forcibly, that the trusting Chloe, jumping at the conclusion that I was at once a probable and in every way an eligible lodger, went downstairs to consult her mistress.

"You can board with the family, if you prefer it, sir," she remarked.

"Delightful," I inwardly responded.

My head swam with visions of impossibly beautiful sirens, and my ears rang with melodies sung to me tenderly by the impossibly-beautiful sirens aforesaid. "Board with the family? Ah! that would be extremely convenient," I said artfully; and then I waited in the deserted apartments, dreaming a long day-dream of expectation, and waiting the return of the trusting handmaid.

"Will you please to walk downstairs, sir? Mistress will be delighted to see you."

I leaped rather than walked downstairs, and preparing an orthodox smile, entered the room. A pleasant-looking, silver-haired widow lady; a golden-haired, pre-Raffaelite daughter; and, confusion! a little fair, gentlemanly man. My rival, of course. But I had still some hope left. Had I thought otherwise, I certainly should not have made myself as pleasant as I did. However, I will not spin out the details of this pseudo-romance, for the romantic part of the story comes to an end in a very short space of time. Be this as it may, my new friends were certainly most charming people, and welcomed the solitary traveller in the most confiding and affable manner possible. We began talking; and my powers of conversation being braced up, I was asked to take a seat after my "fatiguing walk." I wondered if they really knew anything about the dusty tenor on the garden-wall? I rather think they did, but were too polite to allude to it. This courtesy of the chair was extended to a refreshing cup of tea; the welcome beverage was succeeded by songs, reminiscences, sketches, and impromptu composings, in which I joined. As I sat there in Bellevue Cottage, some hours afterwards, at the open window—it was starlight now, and we were watching the moon playing upon the still waters of the bay, which sparkled in the distance—I summed-up mentally the little party by which I had been so hospitably, and in such a genial and friendly manner, entertained. As it turned out, I was correct in almost every one of my conjectures. Mrs. Delacroix was the widow of an Indian officer, who had died some few years previously, leaving this gentle and kind-hearted lady only sufficient capital to live in Jersey, and not even there without obliging her to let off some portion of Bellevue Cottage to travellers in search of scenery and society. Isaline Delacroix, the owner of the sympathetic voice and the sunny hair, was, of course, Mrs. Delacroix's daughter, and —*heu! miserande puer nimium ne crede colori*— evidently the *fiancée* of Carl Oppenheim, the gentlemanly man of whom previous mention has been made. However, in all honour let it be said that Carl was an uncommonly good fellow—good at conversation, anecdote, and jest; good at music, and, as far as I could see, quite proficient in the art of making love. But who would not have been in love with Isaline? But there, we will let that pass; it looks like jealousy, and, in the face of Carl's many excellences, it is most decidedly mean. There was one more yet in the little drawing-room of Bellevue Cottage—Franz Wolfgang, a German, of course, like Carl Oppenheim, and who had accompanied the latter from London to Jersey. The one had come across the sea on a pleasant mission of love, the other on an equally pleasant trip of pleasure.

So far so good. With this preface, it does not require much imagination to guess how we three young men, eager-hearted and excited like boys let loose from school, after discussing the various sights of the island and its adjacent sisters, hit upon the notion of exploring the island of Sark. The fact that it was extremely difficult to get there made us all the more eager to put our plan into execution. We were told by the ladies that the island was most inaccessible, and warned that its inhabitants and sailors had the character of being inhospitable, uncourteous, and greedy.

"Well, I think we can take care of ourselves sufficiently, and so far rely upon one another, as to risk all that," said I; "but how are we to get there?"

"You will have to go to Guernsey first of all," said Mrs. Delacroix, "and then take your chance of a small steamer that runs occasionally, or of one of the market-boats, whose owners may most probably object to taking you at all."

We all looked at one another and gave a low whistle of despair.

"Do you mean to say it is impossible to get to Sark straight from here without the intervention of Guernsey, its casual steamers, and grumpy market-boats?" said I, determined not to be done out of my expedition.

Hereupon came a chorus of objections from the ladies. I did not know what I was proposing, they said, and was evidently ignorant of the danger of the rocky coast of Jersey, and the terrors of the sea, to say nothing of its under-currents between Jersey and Sark. Some yachts attempted the journey occasionally; but it was generally thought, even by the most experienced sailors, to be an exceedingly dangerous one.

My digression here must be to state that all three of us had made up our minds for a good long sail. We were all of us pale-faced and overworked, and wanted a thorough good pickling. We had had enough of screw-steamers, stewards, cabins, and other horrors, and pined for "the sea, the sea, the open sea," with a good old weather-beaten tar, and the wind and salt waves full in our teeth.

"Well, I vote we try to make Sark in an open boat," said I. "If it has ever been done before, why should it not be done again? And you may be pretty sure that no sailors will risk their lives on the expedition if it is really the hazardous and madcap scheme that it is—with all respect to the ladies—represented to be."

My speech was applauded to the echo by Carl and Franz; but Isaline crept up to the former in a cosy, half-pleading manner, and Mrs. Delacroix shook her head at me in a warning manner.

"But how are we to get a boat and a man?"

Carl Oppenheim solved the difficulty. He had been out that morning for "a shilling-an-hour sail" from the harbour of St. Helier's, and in the course of the voyage, the salted owner of the vessel had been expatiating strongly on the merits of his pet craft. He had confided to Carl Oppenheim his opinion—with a view, no doubt, to ulterior beer, baccy, and shillings—that his boat would go anywhere, and live in any sea.

"I don't mind finding out," said Carl, "whether old Jones is as good as his word. It is quite certain that if the thing can be done he will do it; and I believe he has the character of being a plucky sailor and trustworthy man."

And so it was arranged. If I heard nothing to the contrary, and if the weather was decently fine, I was to be on the pier at St. Helier's punctually at eight o'clock on the following Wednesday morning; meanwhile, Carl Oppenheim was to sound old Jones, and take upon his good-natured shoulders the management of our impromptu expedition. The ladies saw that it was no use objecting any more, and so with many farewells I left the merry little party at Bellevue Cottage and walked out into the moonlight, this being the first step towards my solitary journey to Gorey.

There were "white horses" on the sea when I awoke on the Wednesday morning. There is no need to say that it was uncommonly early in the morning when I drew aside the blind and looked out; and the pleasant and cosy associations of the very comfortable bed I had just left prompted me to "turn in" again and leave my new-made friends in the lurch. Inclination kept whispering, "It is sure to be stormy at St. Helier's;" and Reason kept answering, "Supposing it is all right, and Carl and Franz are waiting for you on the pier?" and between the two, as I stood in a state of *déshabille*, I must own I was in a sad quandary.

However, Reason gained the day, and with the first splash of water in my tub I wondered how I could ever have doubted which was the right course to take. A mere snatch of a breakfast over, and the rather dismal walk between Gorey and St. Helier's happily accomplished, I found myself, with my pockets well loaded with ammunition in the shape of wooden pipes and tobacco, saluting my friends on the pier at St. Helier's.

"What does Jones say about the day?" was my first question; for the proprietor of the vessel in which we were to embark had promised to report faithfully on the state of the wind and tide before we entrusted our lives to his keeping.

"Oh, it's all right," answered Carl. "Jones reports all well, and promises us a delightful trip."

Here the worthy Jones appeared on the scene, laden with sundry packages which looked uncommonly as if they contained the items of a sumptuous luncheon—a surmise which turned out to be correct; for, as I discovered afterwards, the ladies at Bellevue Cottage, with a generous, womanly instinct, had made up their minds that, notwithstanding our rashness and obstinacy, at least we should not starve by the way.

We were not, happily, to trust ourselves entirely to the tender mercies of Mr. Jones. He told us just before we started that he had taken the liberty of asking a brother-sailor to accompany us, who had the management of a gentleman's yacht that lay in the harbour, and who, as his master was in England, had nothing to do, and would be glad of a day's outing.

"He's been to Sark often and often in the *Blue Belle*, his master's yacht," remarked Jones, in a tone which certainly implied that the aforesaid Jones had never before attempted the journey in the tiny vessel in which we were just about to embark. I did not like the notion of this altogether, and I began to doubt the saneness of our project; but there was no going back now, and I was determined that whatever happened I would not show the "white feather," knowing that I suggested the expedition originally.

We had embarked, and all the bottles and packages had been comfortably stowed away, when I asked—

"What do you call your vessel, Captain Jones?"

"The *Reform*, sir," he answered.

I did not like the word, and at that time I took this much-debated name as a bad omen for our expedition.

The *Reform* was a four-ton pleasure yacht, open-decked, and with a tiny cupboard of a cabin under the bows. We sat in a kind of well, cut out in the centre of the vessel, which was surrounded by a foot-platform and a circular bench. The sun just stole out of the heavens as the *Reform*—containing Carl Oppenheim, Franz Wolfgang, Jones, his friend "Bill," the head sailor of the *Blue Belle*, and myself

—tacked out of the harbour of St. Helier's at exactly nine o'clock in the morning, bound for Sark.

Carl Oppenheim and his young German friend I have already described. Jones was a sturdy, red-faced, jovial-looking, and talkative sailor, a direct contrast to his friend "Bill," who was lean, black, and uncommonly taciturn. Jones bustled about from the first, arranged us all in our seats, tidied up the deck, and put everything ship-shape; while "Bill" took the helm, chewed a quid, and said nothing.

It was easy-going enough when we were sheltered by the island; and the sun being now well out, and the wind not too boisterous, we were full of spirits, talkative and jolly. A quarter of an hour makes a great difference at sea. Past the Corbière rocks, and with no shore to protect us, a noticeable change took place.

"We shall get it pretty fresh to-day," quoth Jones to his companion, when we experienced the rough-going consequent on a rocky bottom, and when the fresh sea dashed into our faces, every now and then sweeping over the bows and rushing in and out of the *Reform*, as if to see of what stuff she was made. I must confess that this part of the journey I enjoyed amazingly. Jones had invested me with one of those yellow waterproof garments, all stiff and salt with repeated duckings; and so far from resisting the encroachment of the waves, I allowed them to smother my face with spray, knowing that the sun was drying the water on my skin, and so preparing it for that healthy, ruddy-brown colour, the delight of tallow-faced and pasty Londoners.

I cannot say that my companions either were or looked as jolly as I was. Franz was really ill in the cabin under the bows, and Carl, with one hand on the rigging and the other holding an unfinished cigar, looked unutterably bored and uncomfortable. He had no tarpaulin jacket to cover him, and every seventh wave must have wetted him to the skin.

According to Jones's calculations we were to arrive at Sark at mid-day. The dark island appeared in sight long before that time, but I suppose it must have been long past two when, famished to death—Mrs. Delacroix's luncheon had very quickly disappeared—wet, weary, and rather cross, we got under shelter of the island of Sark, and prepared to anchor within a hundred yards of what they pleased to call the harbour, but which was in reality a tiny bay of rough shingle at the base of huge, formidable-looking rocks.

Anxious to free himself as much as possible from all cares and impediments, Jones had decided not to bring with us the little boat which belonged to the yacht. Under these circumstances, our only chance of landing was to attract the attention of some kindly soul on shore.

It was like arriving at some uninhabited island. Not a soul on the shingle, not a soul on the cliff, not a house in sight; nothing in the way of life or animation to be seen anywhere. We had to shout. It is not very lively work, screaming on an empty stomach; but it was either a case of scream or despair. And so we called loud and long, till at last, after exercising our lungs for twenty minutes, to our delight we brought a solitary individual in his shirt-sleeves to the edge of the cliff. This was one step nearer landing, but we were not so near it as we imagined. This solitary individual was "cute," and knowing that in the matter of landing we were entirely at his mercy, we had to enter into a business transaction at the top of our voices. He stuck out for a good round price for the trouble of putting out in a boat some eighty or a hundred yards; and we, too hungry and weary to object to anything, easily consented to be robbed. Meanwhile, Jones lost one of his anchors, and it ruffled his temper considerably.

It was quite three o'clock before we landed at Sark, and the sun was now out in its full fury. The man in the shirt-sleeves, who had just robbed us, pointed out a rough path up the cliff by which we should ultimately arrive at civilization, and we were all preparing to make for Sark's solitary inn, when Jones stopped us.

"I say, gentlemen," said he, "if we are to go back to-night, I must get you to promise that you will be down here punctual at five o'clock. I don't quite like the looks of the weather; and if we don't sail past the Corbières before the tide turns, it will be as much as we can do to get past them at all. I don't like the looks of the weather."

"We mustn't meet the tide in that boat," said Bill, laconically, and with this remark he looked significantly at Jones.

We promised faithfully that we would be down at the shore punctually at five; and as we wended our way among the rabbits that swarm in this uninhabited island, we consulted one another as to what Jones and Bill were up to.

Carl's idea was that they wanted to frighten us into staying at Sark all night, and were most probably in league with the proprietress of Sark's solitary inn; but this I did not altogether believe, for the worthy Bill was bound to be with his master's yacht the first thing in the morning. I hardly dared to say what I thought were the real facts of the case, namely, that Bill was the only soul of us that knew Sark, its shore, currents, winds and waves, and that neither Jones, nor his pet child the *Reform*, had ever been seen so far from the comfortable harbour of St. Helier's.

We walked on for quite a mile before we saw a sign of a human habitation. As to inhabitants, we did not meet a soul. There were rabbits, nothing but rabbits. Ankle-deep in the heather we plodded on, till at last, emerging from a shady lane, we came across three cottages. But still not a soul, and not a sound of life. Again we screamed, and the wind, blowing every moment fresher and fresher, took the echo of our voices out to sea. Eventually the inhabitants of Sark woke up, and a little child directed us to the farthest cottage, which rejoiced in the high-sounding title of "Hotel."

This mansion we entered, and represented our forlorn and famished condition.

Another difficulty now stared us in the face. There was only one piece of meat in Sark, and that was to be devoured by a small party who had come over from Guernsey, to stay a few days at Sark's solitary hotel.

I happened to peep into the *salle à manger*, and there I saw the tempting beef, with its accompaniments of salad, bread, beer, &c., calmly waiting on the table, to be devoured eventually by the Guernsey people, who, as good luck would have it, had taken themselves off for a stroll.

This was too much for the endurance of hungry men. We implored the landlady to allow us to have a turn at the beef; and she at last, thinking, no doubt, of her pocket, opened the door and let us in. We were a very short time at it, for we were not at all anxious to be surprised by the Guernseyites; but I am bound to say, that while we were there we did our duty. We hurried away after this repast, to smoke on the cliff till it was time to go; and I have often wondered since how the forlorn visitors at Sark managed for dinner that day.

There were more "white horses" than ever on the sea, as we lay among the heather smoking, and we could see that the wind was freshening up every moment. To stay at Sark all night looked like giving in, and was altogether out of the question. But I thought of meeting that tide at the Corbière rocks, being now fully persuaded that this was the *Reform's* trial-trip in a heavy sea, and that neither of the sailors knew what she could or what she could not do.

We were down on the shingle punctually at five, and there we found Jones looking at the wind, and evidently anxious to be off. Bill had promised to follow in a minute, with a sailor who would take us out to the *Reform*. Report had told us of the incivility and rapacity of the sailors at Sark, but we were not quite prepared for Bill's tidings. Not a sailor would put off with us to the yacht. They were waiting to be bribed. And still the time was going on, more "white horses" were coming on the sea, and the wind still freshening up. Half-an-hour we waited, but still no sailor came. At last we got desperate. Beyond was the yacht flapping its sails a hundred yards off, and here were the boats at our feet on the shingle, ready to be unmoored.

"Let's frighten them," said I, " and put off in one of their boats. If they don't come and fetch it, we'll send it adrift."

The first part of my proposition was accepted, and we put off, but Jones and Bill hesitated about adopting the latter portion. We got to the yacht, and then commenced a weary time of tacking, in order to get the boat back to its moorings.

It was half-past six before full sails were set, and the *Reform*, shaking herself in the wind, plunged forward on her journey home. It was all right for the first hour, though the waves seemed to get larger and larger, and we went deeper and deeper into the trough of the sea. At last, however, we were fairly open to the sweep of water which comes without a break from the Atlantic, unsheltered by the land, and in the teeth of the tide, which was dashing along towards the fatal rocks.

I had never been in such a heavy sea before, and certainly not in such a cockleshell of a boat. Bill, the taciturn sailor, sat at the helm, and soon it came to be a question of steering for every wave. Every few minutes the decks were swept from end to end with a furious wave, and we were up to our waists in water; and again and again the plucky little boat righted itself, and expelled the water ignominiously which had dashed in.

There came a change in the aspect of all aboard. Jones sat up by the helm, and looked anxiously at the sheet, which was nearly torn into ribbons by the wind. Franz Wolfgang, worn out with the snubbings he had received from all of us for attempting to give advice to the sailors, had coiled himself up in the little cabin, afraid to look at the sea any more. Carl sat by my side, clutching nervously at my arm, and whispering every now and then, " Mein Gott, this is awful !"

Still taciturn Bill, with his teeth clenched, sat quietly with the helm in his hand, and waited for every wave.

Matters got worse instead of better, and to my

horror I heard Jones say, "We had better put on the pump; she wont stand this much longer."

Bill silently nodded, and the pump was worked. The waves now looked so awful, and so deep did we sink every moment into the hungry and pitiless sea; so helpless seemed the little vessel; so black looked the sky, for the sun had now disappeared; so despairing paled the faces of the sailors and my friends, that I could bear the sight no longer, and burying my face in my hands, I thought of England and my friends at home; and then I prayed.

The thought suddenly struck me, it might never be discovered that I was drowned. My people at home did not know in the least where I was. I was travelling alone; the landlady at Gorey was not aware I was meditating this trip. Would they ever hear in England that I had been lost? In such a sea, not a vestige would be left of the boat or its crew.

"Will the horrible end never come?" I thought; again and again the water came up to our necks, and again and again the *Reform* sprang up to the top of the waves, and refused to be beaten by any sea.

This frightful anticipation of death lasted for about half-an-hour. At the expiration of that time, the laconic Bill broke the silence.

"We are all right now. You've got a splendid boat, Mr. Jones."

Immediately we all woke from our lethargy. It puzzled me to know how Bill could tell in an instant that all danger was past; but so it was. The sea was still furious, but the tide had turned, and the

Reform, after its plucky feats that day, could battle on to harbour. Uncovering my face from my hands, I watched the sea dashing over the Corbière rocks. It was a noble sight; and the white crests of the waves stood out like silver against the ink-black mantle of the clouds. The danger had passed, but we were not home yet. With wind and tide dead against us, we battled and tacked and dodged round all the bays; but at last, at half-past eleven o'clock, with a hearty " Thank God!" on all our lips, we passed under the lights on the pier-head at St. Helier's, and were safe in the "haven where we would be." Jones owned that night that we had had a narrow shave of it, and that, had he known what would have happened, he would never have started from Sark.

"That boat is one in a thousand, sir," he said, returning to his old conceit. "I don't believe there's another yacht in the harbour that could have lived in such a sea."

I believe Jones spoke the truth; but he had no right to allow us to risk our lives, or to risk his own, in an untried boat. It ended well, as it turned out; but suppose the *Reform* had proved cantankerous? Well, I'm afraid none of us would have landed any more at Jersey.

Wet to the skin, stiff, worn-out, hungry, and thirsty, we stood on the pier of St. Helier's in the moonlight. We had spirit enough left to give a joyful shout as our feet touched the land.

They would not hear of my returning to Gorey that night. We all jumped into a fly and drove off at once to Bellevue Cottage. Poor ladies, how they had suffered! There was quite a dramatic little scene when we got home, and perhaps it is true that we were all crying. But soon came the luxury of a change of clothing, and thanks to the attentions of the ladies and the many home comforts we strove to forget the sorrows of Sark.

BEFORE THE BATTLE.

A QUIET, clean, small provincial English town, the time mid-day, the season spring, the period present.

A lazy train, puffing leisurely from London, has deposited a scant handful of passengers at the modest railway station of the aforesaid provincial town, hardly disturbing the equanimity of the short, grey-haired little station-master, and quite incapable of giving work to the half-dozen or so dreamy porters. There are some carpenters erecting extraordinary deal barricades outside the station door, apparently with the view of resisting an imaginary invasion, but this is the only sign round and about the station of honest work. I proceed on my way, disturbing a couple of schoolboys playing at pitch and toss on the steps opposite the station-door, and make my way along a miniature avenue of flowering shrubs to the open square of the pleasant sunny provincial town. It is the same as other provincial towns, except that if anything it is cleaner and more respectable. A handsome clock-tower with a *bonâ fide* clock, sound and warranted to go, adorns the market-place, and at a glance it is easy to take in the ordinary provincial properties—the butchers, cleaned up and sold out by this time ; the chemist, extremely neat and respectable—evidently a candidate for the Mayoralty next November; the solicitor and doctor, each with a polished brass door plate; the station, with papers a fortnight old and religious photographs; the rival inns—everywhere and in every corner rival inns—the King's Arms sneering at the White Hart, and the White Hart frowning at the Spread Eagle. Apparently nothing is doing at the small and clean provincial town. The butcher is nodding to a passing acquaintance; the chemist is standing at his own door, and gazing admiringly at the clock-tower and the clock; the young ladies at the stationer's are hopelessly struggling with reams of paper flung about higgledy-piggledy; and the first female assistant at the best linendraper's comes to the door to show off her maroon dress, to take stock of the sunshine, and to wish it were Sunday afternoon.

There never was such a dreamy and delightful provincial town—not even a passing commercial traveller to prove by his presence that once upon a time something was purchased here. The clergyman passes nodding up the street; a parochial authority stops under the tower and sets his watch, defying all Greenwich and a host of observatories to produce better time than this; a county gentleman drives through in a mail phaeton, with a wife, a couple of children, and an old Scotch deerhound limping behind the happy family; but in spite of the smiles of the first assistant at the best linendraper's in a maroon dress, the county family drives on, and does not purchase so much as a button or a yard of tape. Look where you will, up the street or down the street, the only sign of life consists in the extensive importation of ginger beer, soda water, and lemonade. The carts of Mr. Ray are as plentiful as blackberries in a fine autumn. Mr. Ray is represented at every inn, and it would appear as if the inhabitants of the peaceful town "went in" for gazo-genous water to an alarming extent. At the top of the town three empty waggons from Messrs. Ray's establishment are standing to bait, but it is quite clear that the White Hart does not intend to be outdone in soda or seltzer by the Spread Eagle. As the hours go by more long waggons come and unload mineral waters at the doors of the rival establishments, planted opposite to one another at the rival corners of an important street, leading through villadom to a mighty stretch of open down.

There is really no use my remaining any longer in the sunny market-place, or in the clean streets, watching the solitary chemist, the dull butcher, the smart milliner, the perplexed girl at the stationer's shop, or the general unloading of the mineral waters. There is nothing to be done here but stare and be stared at, and as it will be some hours before the Dorking coach comes through on its way to London, the only real excitement of the day, perhaps it would be advisable to stroll out through the little colony of villas on the high road to a pleasant Down.

People of an observant mind cannot fail to notice that an impulse has taken possession of the villa-holders in the immediate neighbourhood of the town. Apparently in concert, and with some ulterior object in view, each villa abutting on the road is having its garden done up. In every garden a gardener is to be found, and the general scraping, cutting, pruning, mowing, and planting is extraordinary to behold.

The croquet lawns are being shaved with the sharpest of scythes or the most expeditious of machines, the brightest of geraniums are being bedded out; every weed in every path is in the course of being excommunicated, and the passing traveller's sense of smell is gratified by a sharp sweet smell of grass newly tossed from the scythe or mowing machine, mixed with the scent of laburnum and almond. There is clearly an existing craze for tidying up. The rural police station is particularly spick and span, and the parish authorities have hired a gang of labourers to widen the road leading to the down, and to protect the young wheat with stout fences. The quiet cemetery half way up the hill marks the apparent limit of civilization. There are no more gardeners, no more croquet-lawns, no more labourers on the highway; nothing is seen but an Indian file of gipsy carts toiling up the slope; nothing is heard but the note of a cherry cuckoo in the grand, green plantation over the way.

It is just one of those days when Nature comes to the front, and, backed up by the sun, resents the insult of recent bad weather. Like a young lady who, owning a handsome wardrobe, and of necessity kept in-doors during a period of mourning, is nevertheless free to deck herself at last in gorgeous array, so does Miss Nature on this occasion almost outrage the orderly decorum of colour. There is no stopping her eccentricity and extravagance. There never surely was such fresh green before. Never before was seen such an outburst of bloom. The chestnut trees, with their spires of white blossom methodically arranged, look like Christmas trees with white candles rapidly changed by Robert Houdin or Wiljalba Frikell. A graceful poet has observed, "the faint sweet smell of lilac pierces me," and I can only say that a stroll through spring lanes hedged with blossoming hawthorn makes me feel faint with its never-ending almond odour. There is no stopping the mad extravagance of the blossom. The gardeners cannot keep down the daisies on the lawn, and in the hayfield the buttercups assume Brobdingnagian proportions. I have spoken of the chestnuts white and pink, of the may-trees pink and white, of the gold of the buttercups in the meadows, and everywhere of the soothing green; but under every hedgerow, if you search, you will find flowers of bright blue and flowerets of mauve, just to add to the colour picture, assisted by the afternoon sun, such a rare assistant to effect.

But is it not sad to think how, in a few hours, the scene will have changed as rapidly as a dissolving view in a magic lantern! The quiet railway station will be battered in, stormed, and carried by a howling, surging, jovial, devil-me-care army. Hence the barricades of white deal—a precaution to save life when it is held so cheaply. The sunny market-place will be filled with a motley gang of sharpers, touts, beggars, cadgers, sight-seers, and pedestrians. The butcher will have to put up his shutters, and the chemist will be dispensing " pick me ups ;" the pretty modest milliner will be driven upstairs to her attic, and the clock on the clock-tower will calmly look down on a scene which has no parallel. No wonder, indeed, that the White Hart and the Spread Eagle laid in a stock of cooling drinks, for there will be no limit to the demand for them. Instead of serving as to-day one traveller and a weary gipsy, there will be fights over the counter for a "split-soda" and heartrending appeals for burning brandy. Round the corner guarded by these two hostelries will come such a procession of vehicles as can be seen only on one day in the year—in one country in the world. Drags and traps, cabs and carts, barrows and omnibuses, horsemen and policemen, blue veils flying and voices tuned to the loudest pitch—on will come this quaint cavalcade, mightier than the army of Xerxes, and powdering the fresh, green country with clouds of almost impenetrable dust. In a few hours more, green and gold, blue and mauve, green tree, and coloured flower, wheat and hay-field, croquet-lawn and geranium-bed will be reduced to one dead level of dust—nothing but dust. There must be a truce now to this allegory. It is little use trying to keep the secret any longer. Rub your eyes, then, and see where you are. Do you see the white-painted stand, and the long booths at the top of the hill, the black-tarred enclosure for horses in the rear, the posts and chains, the solitary public house, and the paddock protected from view by a park palisade? Of course this is Epsom just before the races.

Is it possible that before a few suns have set this desolate down will be swarming with human beings, and that here where I stand, in the centre of the course, one solitary speck on a desert of turf, in a few days more I shall not be able to move? Some ragged children are scampering up and down the benches on Langland's booth, and a gipsy family is pic-nicing on the grass in front of Barnard's stands. In the centre of the course a nursemaid is sprawling on the fresh smooth turf, making a daisy chain for the laughing children gathered round her. There is the sound of one solitary hammer echoing from the deserted Grand Stand; not a soul is in the betting ring, not a face is seen on any balcony, the thieves' alley is deserted, and the silent, dreadful bell looks ridiculously out of place.

Away on the hill are a few labourers mending the road, and dotted about here and there a caravan and a miniature encampment. Away beyond the Grand Stand, away at the corner and the furze bushes, there is not a sign of life. Civilization has not proceeded so far. Whatever animation there is centres about the winning post, and on to the solitary public house over against the paddock. Here two of the very vilest blackguards it is possible to conceive are cursing one another across the course. One of the villains is uttering hideous oaths and blasphemies because he cannot find the few feet of ground he has purchased for a pitch, and the opposite rascal hints with bursting sarcasm that what "he didn't buy he is sure to steal," so it does not much matter. This stinging remark brings out a fresh volley of revolting curses, and the sarcastic ruffian is threatened with the awful fist of one "Chummy," a pock-marked, shambling, down-at-heel villain, who follows at the heels of his blasphemous master, to be set at and tear down any one who insults him. The curses gain strength, and the first rascal, irritated almost to madness, partly because he cannot find his pitch, and partly because of the home-truths of his enemy, devoutly prays he may live again in such good old days as those wherein his enemy would have been caught in a corner when drunk on a Saturday night, gagged in a sack, and beaten to a jelly by the sticks of half a dozen enemies! So utterly revolting is the badinage that the nursemaid with her children drop the daisy-chain, sneak away, and hide behind the Grand Stand; the gipsies stop their play; and dark women issue from the tents of mysterious caravans attempting to stop the fury of the storm.

The note of the cuckoo in the wood and the tinkle of the sheep-bell on the down, the murmur of the wood pigeon in the trees fringing the paddock, the cheerful babble of the gipsy children, the ring of the solitary hammer at the Grand Stand, the occasional thud of knocking up booths and shows—are drowned by the abominable din of these most foul and abominable men. These two wretches, shrieking and cursing at one another across the course, attended by villains almost more obnoxious than themselves, on the top of the careless down and under the pleasant sun, may be taken as the overture to the extraordinary drama to be played here next week. Just as the dust will soil the green leaves and flowers on the highway, so will the silence of yesterday be once more broken and the curses gather strength. The Derby must be run, the small provincial town must be shamed out of its propriety, the countryside must, of course, be powdered with dust; and, on the whole, it was not altogether uninteresting to journey to Epsom, and see the scene "just before the battle."

LONDON IN THE DARK.

WE have heard dreadful tales of what might have happened if the gas-stokers' dismal plan of a strike had been carried out to the bitter end, and if the forbearance of consumers, coupled with the superhuman energy of the managers of the various companies, had not averted a serious catastrophe. It was bad enough as it was, but not quite so bad as it might have been. Armies of ruffians did not sally forth from Short's Gardens; and Whitechapel courteously stayed away from Whitehall. The horse-patrols, though in readiness were not seen in the street, and the suburbs were not exercised with any alarm, additional to that created by the exceptional gloom of the long winter evenings. The omnibuses and cabs could get along; there were no torches necessary, as is the case in a heavy fog; and, apparently, the most severe disappointment caused by the strike was the sudden and unavoidable closing of one of the theatres, owing to a total failure of the gas supply.

We were warned in our suburban homes that something was amiss, and the old theory that the gas always is out of order on a Sunday did not somehow satisfy paterfamilias, who went fidgeting round his little domain, trying this effect and that, suggesting a Hart's burner here, and the attention of the gasfitter there; grumbling about the appalling gloom of the hall; nervously asking, as he attempted to read his Sunday paper after dinner, if his eyes were getting bad, and finally flying for refuge to the blessed light of the delightful and neglected candle. Poor paterfamilias! all those experiments with copper wire and a hair-pin—those introductions of pipe-cleaners down the gas-tube, those hideous imprecations against gasfitters in general, and the suppliers of suburban gas in particular, though well-intentioned, were not to the point, for towards dusk one winter evening, there ran round London a hideous rumour that the gas-stokers had struck, and that the gas supply of London was likely to fall dreadfully short.

The report spread like lightning, and persons of imaginative tendencies set to work in good earnest. Good heavens! how dreadful! The streets will be occupied by the scum of London! Shops must close, and the inhabitants of houses, having exhausted their supply of candles, must grope upstairs disconsolately to bed, and stay there. Popular plays must be put on the shelf, every theatre must close their doors, there will be no getting home by any conveyance, and progression on the Metropolitan Railway will be impossible. London did not like the notion of "darkness that might be felt;" and the agents of the various companies who went round to theatres, shops, institutions, clubs, music halls, and the like, warning their proprietors of the dreadful consequences ensuing upon a waste of gas, and imploring their aid to avoid the worst, were looked upon with the same melancholy awe as would be awarded to those who went stealthily about the streets and marked houses with a scarlet cross in plague time. It was no laughing matter, and the faces of the gas company messengers assumed the necessary gravity and importance.

Only one set of gentlemen well used to cosiness, and understanding many of the good things of this world, treated the matter as a supreme joke, and surveyed the melancholy streets from their bow-window with a chuckle of satisfaction. They laughed merrily while they surveyed over the way an illuminated clock flickering with half the power of a damp rushlight; while they saw the piazza at Charing Cross as dull and gloomy as Salisbury Plain after nightfall; while they picked out a bead of light here, and a miserable twinkle there, and then put down the blind again with a sigh of satisfaction. For why? Because, happily, they belonged to the celebrated club which prides itself on its ostracism of gas and its faithful adherence to wax candles. But where shall we go to see the effect of the gas-strike as it stands? Shall we begin with the streets? Well, upon my word, I honestly like them better as they are. You notice, of course, how that conscientious curiosity dealer fills his Dresden china sconces and candlesticks with the best Ozokerit, partly with a view to aiding the companies in their distress, and partly, no doubt, with an idea of showing off his articles of refined taste.

You will see again and again shop windows illuminated with dips and composites stuck into odd corners; but, joking apart, the effect in the Strand is far more cheering than usual. I like that noble stream of light sweeping the Strand from the top of the Gaiety Theatre to Charing Cross, meeting a bright Vaudeville illumination half-way, and joining forces with Mr. Gardner's illumination at the end of the journey. It sends along its course the same spray as is seen when a ray of light breaks through a half-closed shutter. It is a pure clear blaze, that from the masthead at the Gaiety; and, contrary to expectation, it is so well toned that you can look it full in the face without blinking. The Strand has once more the strange, weird appearance of an illumination night, and those who from one circumstance or other do not wish to be noticed, would have done well to avoid the Strand or Regent Street during these days of darkness. Regent Street so dead and dingy, when the gas-stokers are at work, so bitter a contrast to the streets of Paris, even when the shops are in "full swing," is, thanks to the Polytechnic illumination, in festive garb; and, as we pursue the course of its broad pavement in extra spirits on account of the extra gas, we ask ourselves if we have made peace with some hostile nation, won a battle, married a prince, or obtained a double dose of Lord Mayor's day?

S

But there is a reverse to the gay picture of the illuminated Strand and the festive Regent Street. If any one required a truly melancholy spot, wherein to meditate, we would recommend him to the corner of Spring Gardens, cold, damp, disconsolate, and wretched. To change from the corner of Spring Gardens to the inside of an omnibus was as welcome as the ballet scene after the ogre's den at the opening of a pantomime; and, to tell the truth, during the gas-strike it was not an enviable task to be compelled to dine out in a lonely road in St. John's Wood, and, in addition to the misery of short sight, to be horrified with the reflection that the guest was in happy ignorance of house and number some few minutes before the dinner hour. St. John's Wood is a mystery at the best of times, and it is not seen at its best during a fog or a gas-strike. What more horrible situation can be conceived than that of a punctual man, who knows the dinner hour has arrived, who feels the driver of his Hansom cab is in happy ignorance of the precise locality of the mansion, who is perpetually compelled to dash open the doors of the vehicle, and pursue a passing postman, or is finally tempted severely to chastise the stupidest of boys, who is groping his way in the dark, and making a pretence of delivering bundles of firewood to various customers? Why is it—we ask—why is it that firewood is always delivered at dinner-time in the suburbs, except for the benefit of diners-out who have lost their way?

But, on the other hand, how is it that the deliverers of firewood never know the geography of the suburb they inhabit?

We will politely draw a veil over the depressing scene of the interior of the house when it is reached, the late arrival adding one more sorrow to the accumulated cup of the household. In the hall a murky yellow flame is making a ridiculous attempt to show a light to the over-burdened hat-stand; and as the supply of candlesticks is limited, and a dip in a bottle does not look genteel, the poor hall is left to itself. It would have been far better, if the hostess only knew it, to extinguish the gas chandelier altogether in the drawing-room, and to have trusted boldly to the illuminating power of the piano candles, and a pair of tall, new wax lights on the mantelpiece. Dinner guests received by the illumination of the pointed top of a composite candle must necessarily be depressed. Why, the candle itself has not learned its business sufficiently to give you a welcome, and it is all very well to chaff about the days when snuffers were brought in on a silver tray; but where is the modern and genteel candle who does not want his hair cut in that juvenile period of his existence, before his pointed head has grown into shape? So on, in due time, to the dining-room, where the never-failing supply of gas has prohibited the use of lamps, moderator or otherwise. They have lamps of course, but they are not trimmed; they are dirty and dusty from not being used; there is no oil, the wicks are out of order, the lamp scissors are lost, and, to tell the truth, the failure of gas was so sudden and there were so many other things to attend to (the dinner party for instance), that the hostess falls once more back upon candles, and commits the old fatal error of keeping the gas on in the chandelier to do its best—or its worst.

It is its worst in this instance, for the attention is perpetually directed from the steady, even and respectable light of the candles to the dissipated, hiccoughing, jerky, half-drunken flicker of the four inevitable burners. Can anything more irritating be conceived than burners perpetually squirting up a jet of light, grumbling, groaning, and eventually lapsing into a dogged and obstinate darkness? It is far better to put the disagreeable light out altogether than to leave it there promising to be agreeable one minute and then subsiding into sulk again. There is nothing like a good, even, cheerful light, and a warm room to promote jollity; while, on the other hand, can depression be better suggested than by flickering candles and a jerky gas chandelier?

The whole dinner is, of course, a failure. The after-dinner smoke in the little sanctum is *triste;* and as the hats and coats are once more groped for in the Stygian hall it is almost cruel to think of the poor woman who has cooked the haunch of mutton by a scullery naphtha lamp, and is mournfully endeavouring to wash up the dishes by the aid of a tallow dip stuck into the last empty champagne bottle. This is an appalling picture. As we accept the comfortable hospitality of the Underground Railway on our way home to the Temple, we notice that the company has laid in a stock of costermongers' naphtha lamps—those queer lamps with a reservoir at the top seen in the New Cut and the Vinegar Yard—which are hung from the ordinary gas lamps now extinguished, and flare boldly, but vulgarly, like the lights in the butchers' shops on Saturday night in Clare Market. The effect was not strictly refined, but for once an air of gaiety pervaded the Temple Station, which, with its thick pillars and gloomy tone, always remind me of the crypt of an old abbey, or the heart of the catacombs. Penal servitude at Pentonville must be preferable to a porter's life at the Temple Station; and, strange to say, this gloomy spot is saddest of all on a burning summer afternoon when all else but the neglected attendants are in the fields or on the river. Happily, theatrical fears in the matter of the gas-strike were groundless, and the bold threat of lighting the houses by limelight was not carried out. The corridors and approaches of the theatres which were worst supplied were tastefully decorated with lamps and candles; and the poor theatre in King Street, which suffered most from the disaster, cheerfully announced next day a "Feast of Lanterns" outside and in. But in all stations of life—in the suburbs, in the shop, in the club, in the singing hall, in the theatre, and in the street—we must rejoice without ceasing that it was no worse.

Most of all those will rejoice who have lost for so many days the welcome glare of the bright gas-lamp wherewith to decipher illegible manuscript, to set up diminutive type, to read awkward proofs, and to prepare our morning news so punctually and so accurately. Few have suffered more from the recent annoyance than those who pored over candles and lamps to prepare the newspaper literature, which was never missing, though our dinner parties failed, our streets were desolate, our shops were dingy, our managers were frightened, and London was in the dark.

THE "AFTERNOON DORKING."

"Go call a coach, and let a coach be called; and let the man that calleth be the caller; and in his calling let him nothing call but 'coach, coach, coach!' Oh, for a coach, ye gods!" But there was no need on May Day for this peremptory injunction of Chrononhotonthologos. The difficulty was not to find a coach, but to get out of the way of them. The parcel vans and the railway carts could not get up to the White Horse Cellar. The Hammersmith and Brompton omnibus drivers were irritated to madness as they vainly endeavoured to cut their way through an idle collection of gigs, dog-carts, broughams, and victorias. There were ladies on the steps of the hotel, and enthusiastic ostlers hanging to the railings opposite. Traffic and locomotion were virtually stopped; Piccadilly was gay with ribbons and rosettes, and everywhere about— down Hay Hill, round by Dover Street, along Arlington Street, and over by St. James's—was heard the orthodox coaching chant on the guards' silver horn. It was just as if the clock of time had been put back thirty years or more. Smart coachmen and neat grooms, old gentlemen with bottle-green coats, and young dandies in spruce white gaiters, top jackets, and mufflers, great bunches of roses, and thick driving gloves—all came back once more to the White Horse Cellar.

The mail guard came back also, with his scarlet coat; the names of Tim Carter and Cracknell, Edwin Fownes and Moon, Captain Cooper and Chandos Pole, Angell and "Charley" Ward were passed about from lip to lip; "swells" stopped here on the way to the park, and business men halted, though bound for the City, to see the "turn out" of the coaches on as bright a May morning as ever gladdened a Londoner. There was no end to the coaches. The Tunbridge Wells drove off with young Selby handling the ribbons, and Cracknell vigorously blowing the horn. The new Westerham coach, with its neat uniform of olive green and buff waistcoat, started for the first time under the personal direction of Sir Henry de Bathe, and Moon behind looking after the music. Mr. Sedgwick drove the morning Watford into Piccadilly at half-past ten to the minute. The morning "Dorking," our old primrose friend, whose proprietor and courteous secretary gave the first impetus to the wonderful coaching revival, started away for the first journey this year along a road which cannot be matched for loveliness in all England. Mr. Eden drove round with his Wycombe coach from the Scotch Stores, in Oxford Street, to pick up passengers at the Cellar, and add one more to the list of gallant teams. Colonel Twyrhitt, accomplished whip, and most amiable gentleman, with a pretty child beside him, started off to Reigate with plenty of friends and enthusiasts behind. Portmanteaus and parcels, rugs and bonnet boxes having been packed into the "boot," a merry party of ladies and gentlemen clambered up on the Brighton stage, and was taken out of London in first-rate style by Mr. Tiffany, the American coaching enthusiast, and the pupil of Mr. Charles Ward. And last came the Sunbury and Hampton Court coach, whose owners are so devoted to the amusement that they wear the driver's badge required by the police regulations for all coachmen of public conveyances within the metropolitan district. Meanwhile, during all this clatter and excitement, when the coach-horns are blowing, and the blue bonnets are seen upon the drags; when the sun shines so merrily, and the country carts come rumbling along Piccadilly, decorated with flowers, and adorned with bunches of may; when, for a few shillings, we might be driving through the cherry gardens of Kent, or the glorious vales of Surrey—why do I stand here in this "long, unlovely street," watching the coaches go, and not stirring a finger to beg for a place? Listen, and I will tell you the reason. A rumour has gone abroad that this year we can combine business with pleasure, and the report is confirmed by consulting the coach list at the White Horse Cellar. Clever men have put their heads together, and given us a coach for working men.

They have started an "Afternoon Dorking," and it

promises to be the most popular coach on the road. For, to tell the truth, we like to be virtuous, although we enjoy our toasts of pleasure. We are not averse to the reputation of being hard worked. A day without business is a day lost, and many a man who only rushes into his office in the morning to open his letters feels that his official conscience has been relieved of a dead weight.

For the toilers and the hard worked; for the business man, who cannot give up a whole day; for the Government clerks, who do not care to "lose a day's leave;" for the club men, who cannot stir until they have read all the papers; for the ladies, who cannot and will not start out until the day is warm, this "Afternoon Dorking" has been started, and to such as these it will prove an inestimable boon. How pleasant to think, when grinding away on an official stool, that the Surrey lanes are awaiting one when our work is over! How merry the thought that the din of Capel Court and the chatter at Lloyd's will be silenced by the waving of green trees round Box Hill! How delightful the reward of a rush through the air, over Epsom Common, to shake off the dust collected from briefs, and to dissipate the fog from our muddled brains!

Come away, then, from counting-house and stool, from chambers and dirty courts, from minuting and docketing, from ledgers and from law, and try to be at the White Horse Cellar by four o'clock in the afternoon! We do not envy the fashionable ladies in their *réséda* bonnets, or their robes of *eau de Nile*, hurrying along in those diminutive victorias to the park. We are not jealous of the young swells labouring along Piccadilly, in patent leather boots, and casting a look of admiration at their button-hole bouquets, which we know have cost exactly half-a-crown at Solomon's or Warren's, in Duke Street. We have no desire to go shopping in Bond Street, or to hang about the gates of the new Burlington House to see the aristocratic people paying a visit to the private view of the Royal Academy. Not a bit of it! The primrose coach is in sight, and we are off for an evening in the Surrey lanes. Here comes the drag, driven in by Edwin Fownes, and the Secretary is on the box to start his new toy, and see every one is made comfortable. The morning was beautiful enough; the afternoon is lovelier still. Piccadilly is radiant, and once more the appearance of Captain Cooper's team, with bunches of primroses in their ears, attracts to the White Horse Cellar a crowd of enthusiastic admirers. The horses are patted, the coach is complimented, seats for another day are booked at once, ladies come in their carriages to see the start, and for the second time to-day Piccadilly is quite blocked. But there must be no shilly-shallying or dawdling on the pavement. If we see a dozen friends we must treat them with scant ceremony. For our driver, Captain Cooper—true coachman—is the soul of punctuality, and he will start at 4.15 to the second by the Horse Guards' clock. The

Secretary has long ago got his party complete, so up we get. Fownes blows up with the horn, the word, "All right, sir!" is given by the guard, the cloths are off in a second, and the new "Afternoon Dorking" with—yes, an actual cheer from the crowd—starts on its first journey.

This is something like travelling, and already round Waterloo Place, coming up from the park, the soft spring air blows about our hair, and promises us an invigorating evening. Down Parliament Street we go, musty and dusty with the law, and with a glance at the crowd congregated round Westminster Hall to cheer the Claimant when the day's sitting is over, we are soon over Westminster Bridge, and looking at the grandest picture in all London. Round Stangate we go—where Polly Eccles lived with her sister and her drunken father—in order to avoid the tram, and here there are breezes from the delightful river. Away round a colony of villas, over Clapham Common, where we find the old red brick mansion of the old London citizen, hidden in a garden of blossoming trees. Still away, the team going beautifully, along the pretty road to Balham, arriving at Nightingale's stables for the first change at five o'clock to the minute. All is regular and in order, not an instant's delay, and, with another pretty team, we are off again for the real country. The evening is so beautiful, and the scenery so varied, that we have honestly little time to talk. We drop our cigars, for they seem to poison the air, heavy with the scent of almond bloom and may; we are cheered and pelted with flowers by school children at Malden, and pass boys playing their first cricket in the grounds of Morden College. Through villages, and past old country churches, on we go, and then we see Cheam Church in the distance, and if anything, before our time arrive for another change at the gates of North Cheam Park Farm. "But the other coach ought to be here," says the active Secretary, "they are not up to time, Captain, they should have changed and been off before we arrived." However, we have hardly started again before the returning Dorking comes in sight, and as we pass we interchange a cheer, and even Captain Cooper makes allowance for the geniality and champagne toasts of the first day of coaching.

But did any one ever experience so delicious an evening? The twilight gives the colour; the greens and the golds are intense. What romantic old houses, what meadows of cowslips, and what a still, peaceful promise of the calm of the oncoming night! Labourers coming home from their work give us welcome, handkerchiefs are waved from cottage windows, and every half mile we travel an artist might fill his note-book with pictures. Never mind the facts. Let us give up ourselves to the fancy. Who cares a brass button that Lord Nelson lived in that old abbey, and built those stables; or that in the old house over yonder Queen Elizabeth smacked the face of Lord Essex, because Her Majesty was caught in curl-papers by her handsome favourite? You will find all this in *Murray* when you get home; but never more for some time will you see such spring fields, or such hedges, or such a promise of a sunset. But here is Ewell, cleanest and prettiest of towns, and five minutes before the clock strikes six we have sighted the Grand Stand on the Downs, have passed the clock-tower in the centre of the market-place, and have drawn up at the hospitable doors of the Marquis of Granby. This is indeed a welcome, and shows that the good folks of Epsom take interest in our welfare. Here, at the door of the Marquis of Granby, there are wreaths, and flags, and triumphal arches, festoons round the old stump of a tree, and all the "oldest inhabitants" have congregated round the inn door to cheer the coach. But notice how artfully provident is that sensible secretary. He expects the ladies down by the "Afternoon Dorking," you may be sure, for he has warned the good hostess of the inn to prepare a "kettle-drum," and we can honestly say that better tea, cream, and farmhouse bread-and-butter were never tasted. It is worth going down to Epsom—but only by the coach—to take a dish of tea (with a dash of brandy in it if you like) at the Marquis of Granby.

But there is no time to lose, and Captain Cooper will not wait, though you scald your gullet. Off we go again, mightily refreshed with that cup of tea, enjoying to the full the breeze blowing pleasantly to us over the golden gorse of Epsom Common. The scenery increases in beauty. Here is Ashtead Park, with its old walk and palings, with its noble trees and herds of deer. We might be hundreds of miles away from London. How still and exquisite is the evening, and how the sinking sun casts long shadows on the pleasant turf! Cheered and congratulated at every turn, we arrive all too soon at the romantic Leatherhead, and here—if only for a minute, Captain Cooper—we must pull up, for the Leatherhead people have prepared us a welcome. The village school children, with may garlands and nosegays, are drawn up on the pavement, and they cheer enthusiastically, excited thereto by the tone and encouragement of a rosy beadle with a wand decorated with flowers. "Welcome to the Coaches" is written on the inn wall, and all Leatherhead is here to give us joy. Would we could linger here! but we may not, because of the time refusing to wait for any man. And remember there are more beauties in store. We have passed over the plains and commons, down the lanes, and through the villages. We come now to the hills and the valleys. It is ridiculous here to eulogize once more the glory of Box Hill, that garden in the heart of Surrey. Here are our old friends Mickleham and the mansion of Mr. Grissell, streams rushing at the foot of the hill, Mr. Cubitt's estate in the distance, Box Hill, with its steep ascent and its groves on the summit, and in the distance that treasure-house of art—Deepdene, in Surrey. Who has not dined at the Burford Bridge Hotel or smoked in its lovely garden? Who has not envied those cosy houses, with their lawns and croquet grounds, on either side of the English roadway, and spent a Saturday to Monday occupied with exercise, and envy, and delight? Why is it that Captain Cooper hurries us along when we have not time to take in all the beauty at one gasp, when fair-haired girls run out upon lawns to wave to us, and dear old ladies in amber silk nod us a welcome from the kitchen garden? It is like all pleasure—too soon over.

But Captain Cooper is right, for he knows we shall come again, and at one minute past seven he draws rein at the Red Lion, Dorking. And of the rest what need be said? The pleasure is over; and now for the repose. Some silly folks hurry through their dinner, and catch one of the late trains for London. But we, who have come to do the whole thing in an orthodox manner, enjoy at leisure the excellent fare of mine host, Wallace, and wander off with a cigar at nightfall to hear the nightingales in an adjacent wood before we turn into the lavender-scented, clean country sheets of the good old inn. And what more? A rest unbroken, a country breakfast, a bathe if you like it, a morning drive, a morning pipe, more country, more trees, more fields, and we arrive at the Clock Tower, Westminster, at 10.30 to the second, when—confound it!—we find the

Tichborne enthusiasts once more collecting about Westminster Hall. It is all over! The dream is past! We have awakened to life again and the Tichborne trial. But, joking apart, there are worse things to be done between four and ten, than travelling down with Captain Cooper by the "Afternoon Dorking."

THE ROUND OF THE CLOCK.

BURIED here in London, with only an occasional glimpse of a green field, and seldom the refreshment of a bird's song; with no signs of the changing seasons save as shown by the leaves on the London plane trees, or the coat on the back of an omnibus driver, we mark the year's progress by the advent or departure of steadily-recurring excitements. We have no hay-time or ripening corn to guide us. When we see our roses they are cut from the trees. No pleasant sound of the plough turning over the earth; no clash of flails in threshing-barns; no hedge-making, or sowing, or reaping, or stacking warns us of the year's advance, without the necessity of an appeal to the almanack. We are deephidden here in London, surrounded and enclosed. The lark is caged in Great St. Andrew's Street, and the nightingale is almost driven from the Old Hampstead Gardens. But, for all that, we know surely enough when the "golden year" is hurrying to a close. Looking out from our London window it might be any weather—April or September. It always rains, and never now is it quite comfortable. Still, we have arrived at the blank, dead interval which settles down upon us before the end. This is the old age of the year. It is feeble, and worn out, and spent. There is no energy for amusement left, and the year is calmly and resignedly waiting for the end.

How well we remember the birth of the year—the congratulations, the hand-shakings, the presents, and the good fellowship when the new stranger was introduced. In London how delightfully are these early months associated with children and innocence. Pantomimes and fairy tales, Christmas books and Christmas trees, Twelfth-night parties and crackers, the old English game of characters and King and Queen, snapdragon, and hunt the slipper, toys everywhere, and journeys to the Lowther Arcade or the Soho Bazaar. Admirably is our London life suited to the conceits of the new year, and cleverly suggestive of the geniality and merriment inseparable from the time. Some maintain that there is an affectation in that season of presents and innocence, and argue, with that terrible want of enthusiasm so peculiar to the age, that we can spend our money as well in August as in January, and that it is folly to reserve our charity for any time or season. But such arguments are as affected as the enthusiasm they condemn. Those who can walk through a toy-shop without thinking of a nursery, or can stand round a Christmas tree without kissing a child, are as hopeless as the old grave-digger Gabriel Grubb, in one of Dickens's stories, who went to his horrible work on Christmas Eve, and hit a lad on the head with a spade because he whistled and was merry, in unison with the harmony of the times.

In a few weeks the innocence and childlike nature of the year changes suddenly and completely. The shops are full of Valentines and love-verses. The innocent year is becoming a little worldly, and some one has whispered into her ear the fatal secret of love. This second conceit is ever present and inevitable. It is apparent everywhere. In the handsome Regent Street shops there are guinea boxes of satin devices and artificial flowers, Cupids and silver cord, and perfumed sachets—all adding to the general whisper of love. In the small streets, and courts, and alleys, the fat-coloured cook is flirting with the blue-coloured policeman, and you can purchase the doggrel marriage ode for a penny. Once more we advance, and when we see the first sun we feel the first strength and manliness of the year. The "winter's rain and ruin are over," and we have felt the first tingle of an oncoming joy. The fires are out in the domestic grates. The streets are not innocent of cries concerning "ornaments for the fire-stoves," horrible abominations, showing the extravagant vulgarity of paper. Early plants are sold in the markets, and colour is coming into the cheeks of the year. The first yellow crocus springs up in the garden. The lilac bushes are bursting in the London squares. The pavement is becoming white and pleasant, and the exhilaration of a new life is seen on the face of all the passers-by. This youth, this excitement, this joy, and this advancing colour, the first promise of the garden, the first bud and blossom in the square, the sense of sun and satisfaction, is well illustrated by the Oxford and Cambridge Boat Race—London's very first mad holiday. It is all in harmony. Youth and manhood, and muscle and pluck, a race for honour and nothing more, the marvellous endurance of sixteen athletes making tens of thousands glad. These things suit well the health and vigour of the year at Easter time. But the innocence and hope of the infant year are fading silently, but gradually away. As each week passes the youth mixes more and more with the world, and is more and more contaminated with it. The gentlemanly and well-conducted lad is becoming a little rowdy and coarse. He thinks it clever to make a noise and be heard.

We soon arrive at the Derby; the Derby with its drink, and dust, and dissipation; the Derby hoarse, and feverish, and wickedly exciting; the Derby, with its old tale of the road and the rail, the trap and the tax-cart, the first suggestion of gambling and horseracing, the first introduction of the young year to life—a life as new, strange, and excitable as that enjoyed by Corinthian Tom and Jerry. The Derby once over, the year is fairly launched. He has fleshed his sword, and though the poor mother sighs, he must have his latchkey;

he must take care of himself now, and remembering that he has had the advice of affectionate parents, and the education of a gentleman he must do the best for himself. Excitement and extravagance begin in good earnest now. The early flower shows at the Botanical Gardens and the Crystal Palace give back the old notes of innocence. The Oxford and Cambridge Cricket Match at Lord's reminds the young man of the world that there was once youth and principle, but the whirl and turmoil of the London season drown all good resolutions and deaden all determinations. It is wild, reckless, extravagant life now. There are Circes in Rotten Row and Siren voices at Ascot Races. Dress, and dinners, and dissipation, fight and scramble for the year. There is no end to them. The Shah comes and is *fêted* by Royalty, by civic magnates, and by private enterprise. We are at Dover, at Spithead, at Sydenham, or at the Mansion House. The roses have bloomed and the strawberries are ripe. The gardens are in flower, and ices and coffee are pleasant on the lawn. Society goes out of its way to *fête* and feast the still handsome and stalwart year. Entertainments at Greenwich, Richmond, and Gravesend; polo matches and croquet, pigeon-shooting and club dinners—there is no rest in society, and no end to the amusements of the year.

The Eton and Harrow Match, with its tinge of innocence and affectation of forced life, makes the middle-aged year conscious that it was once a lad, and suddenly becomes sick of the follies and frivolities of the time. This is the wind-up and breaking-up day of all the reckless gaiety. It is the fullest festival of the year. All the champagne and raised pies left from the season are devoured, and the tired year begins to think it is time to break up. Some, fevered and *blasé* with dissipation, repair to Goodwood for more excitement, more gambling, more dresses. Others longing for quiet, seek comfort by the sea, and are found cruising round the Isle of Wight. It is clear that the pace has been too fast, the excitement has been overdone, there must be an end to gaiety, and a moment's rest. The seaside, the Spas of Germany, the highlands of Scotland, and the mountains of Switzerland receive the shattered year as willingly as a humble penitent. And with their exquisite ozone and rest they grant him absolution. Invigorated, hopeful, and strong, back comes the London year, back to his own fireside to reflect on the past, and pray for the future. There are temptations still, even to the last moment of existence. Barnet Fair is the last bait for the rough. Doncaster St. Leger is the latest fall for the faded gentleman.

But soon they are all over. We have lived our life. The last rough has come home from Barnet; the latest gambler has returned from Doncaster; Switzerland and Scarborough, Malvern and Margate have yielded up their holiday makers or their invalids. We have a time to rest, and reflect and look forward to the end. A few months ago we smelt the rose above the grave, but now we smell the grave above the rose. We have come to that cold, shuddering period when night and morning meet, when the tide turns, and when sitting up with the sick year, we must put on some more coals or a top coat. It is not a sudden, but a very peaceful decline. The Virginia creeper on the London houses turns red, then purple, and then falls into a damp decay. The landscape becomes wet, and chill, and miserable. We can do no more for the year. He is wearing out, and a strange film is coming over the eyes that have sparkled, the eyes we have loved. The tick of the pendulum of life is fainter and fainter, weaker and weaker still. At last, after the flash of Christmas gaiety, we look at one another strangely, gazing over the death-bed, and say in the silence that it is the end. Yes; this is the *Tour de Cadran :* this is the Round of the Clock.

AMONG THE ROSES.

WITHOUT State ceremonial, but with complete success, was one day thrown open to the public the Alexandra Palace on Muswell Hill. To the public was presented another palace of art, one more treasure house, one more focus for pleasure hunters. Here, in the north of London, was one more centre of amusements; here, we said, among the buttercup meadows, away on hill and in delightful air the free foresters can dance, lads can play cricket, horses can race, dogs, cats, and horses can be exhibited; flowers can bloom, and the art of music can be cultivated. Here on fine Saturday afternoons the young ladies of the north can show their pretty bonnets and sweep the boards with their rich silks; here there are courts, and pictures, and show-cases, scents by Rimmel and silks from Japan, a theatre and a concert hall, paint and gilding, galleries and domes, arcades of pleasure, polychromed walls, painted windows and baskets of flowers—every opportunity, in fact, for a holiday outing, and the very place where can be concentrated the amusement or the folly of the hour. The sturdy Palace, with its brick walls and its coloured windows will surely stand. The surrounding scenery, the trees and the fields and the meadows, the buttercups in the grass and the may in the hedges, the peep at Barnet, the glimpse of Crouch Hill, the spires and patches of suburb and park, the belts of wood, the glorious panorama of English scenery will remain, so long as builders are merciful and nature is bountiful. Hither, then, will come to the palace on the hill Sir Michael Costa, with his trained musicians, the music of the future and the ballad of the past, the song and symphony, the drama and the dance, the rose-growers and the naturalists, the zoologists and the athletes, the racing men and the cricketers; for inside and out the Alexandra Palace on all sides has quickly stamped itself on an enormous public as a success, and a place to be in every way encouraged.

But let us begin at the beginning. First, then, where is the Alexandra Palace, and how is it possible to discover Muswell Hill? The public has a vague notion that the north of London is very beautiful, though very unexplored; that, judging by Hampstead and Highgate, it is possible to get to green fields quicker in this direction than any other; that the Alexandra Palace is a promising rival to the Crystal Palace at Sydenham, charmingly situated on a hill-top—but that is all. There is an indefinite idea abroad that the new Palace is somehow connected with the Metropolitan Railway, and that recently a new line has been opened up to the very doors, preventing any tramp over grass or gravel path, and providing successfully against the ills of the most uncertain climate. There are several methods of arriving at the Alexandra Palace.

The most pleasant plan is to drive there through woods and real country lanes—an easy matter of six miles from the metropolis, and a delightful excursion. The ordinary plan would be to take any metropolitan train to King's Cross, and then to cross over the road to King's Cross Station. It is a mistake to suppose there is a direct communication between the Metropolitan line and the Great Northern Railway. It is necessary to deliver up your ticket and to cross the road, when, at the Great Northern Station, will be discovered an organization so complete and admirable that it looks as if it had been in working order for years. "Palace Train! Palace Train! The way to the Palace!" We rub our eyes with astonishment, and believe that the porters at the Victoria Station have been specially engaged to give the peculiar ring of intonation so well known to the Pimlico district. The arrangements at King's Cross really are admirable, and without the slightest trouble in the world a return ticket to the doors of the Alexandra Palace is secured at a convenient wicket. They were correct who declared we soon get into the country by the northern lines. There are no housetops to pass, or miles of squalor to shudder at. Here we have no boneboilers or makers of indigo blue, no knackers or manufactories for patent candles. All is prosperous, clean, and sound. The towns of Camden and Kentish are left behind. Holloway disappears with its trams; Finsbury Park, bare and treeless, struggles into notice; and long before we get to Crouch End and Highgate our eyes are delighted with meadows of rich green grass, avenues of old trees and golden buttercups in such profusion that they quite conquer the green, and give the landscape a rich and noble effect.

Soon the passengers in the carriage detect a compact building on an eminence, covered with flags, and looking gay enough on Her Majesty's Birthday; and winding round about it, ever through the noble old trees and the fields of grass and buttercups, we are landed at last at the very foot of the staircase of the new Palace. How gay and merry it all looks!

The terrace is crowded with strollers, waiting to see us arrive; carriages are rolling up to the grand entrance, boys and girls are playing on the grass slopes, flags are flying, geraniums are beginning to bloom, the sun is shining over everything, and it promises to be a delightful day. It is of no use. The comparison will come. We know comparisons are odious, and in bad taste, but the comparison here with the Sydenham father of Palaces is unavoidable. It strikes us directly the train draws up at the clean tiled platform. "The way to the Palace! The Palace! The Palace! Programme for the Palace!

Sixpence for the book of words for the Palace! The Concert at the Palace!"

Why, it is the old thing in a different place. The comparison is more obvious when we enter the building. We forget the gigantic proportions of the Sydenham glass house, when we enter the gaily-decorated miniature building. We forget the loftiness, the expanse, the grandeur of Sydenham, when we are so thoroughly struck with, and surprised at, the bold child rearing its head upon Muswell Hill, and having an entertainment all to itself. We forget the fountains and the rich flowers at Norwood, when we see these baskets hanging down with false fern, imitated nasturtium, and sham geranium. However, it looks gay and bright enough. There are courts here, and cases of china; there are set scenes, with figures illustrating the costumes of all nations; there are toy shops and scent fountains, refreshment bars with coloured bottles—it is all on the old model, or delightful miniature. Here is a centre transept, and a noble organ, built by Mr. Willis, glorious in tone, and radiant with polychrome pipes; here are the old bedroom chairs, ticketed as reserved seats, and fastened with official tape; here is a theatre, set with a woodland scene, and everywhere groups of statuary, by Brucciani, and a beautiful sunlight streaming through the round star of painted glass upon the well-dressed crowd, increasing in avenue and transept each instant. No one can fail to admire the symmetry of the cruciform building, the good taste of the mural decorations, or the bold effect of light produced by the arrangement of windows in the fine dome. Everything is pleasant on which the eye rests, and, at mid-day, the sight in the interior is almost perfection. For, at mid-day, is added to the colour of frescoes, and the colour of glass—to the robes and costumes in cases of Japan, to the brilliancy of china and the dazzle of glass—a flower show, which, in point of arrangement and effect, is admirable.

Hitherto, when flowers have been exhibited, it has been necessary to take a turn round a stuffy tent, through whose sides the most brilliant sun in the world can never penetrate. Hitherto the azaleas have been dimmed, and the bloom of the roses deadened. The glory of the cactus, and the waxiness of the heath, are never apparent without the sun. But here, with no velarium under the dome, with no curtains at the sides, with no suggestion of tent or covering, the glorious flowers received the full embrace of the May sunlight, and the effect was simply superb. Raised sufficiently high above the heads of the promenaders to make a noble bank of bloom, but not so high but that a passing maiden might smell a rose, or brush the young fern with her fair hair, the first Alexandra flower show was one of the most beautiful sights that can be well imagined. Lucky, indeed, those who caught the roses of Mr. Paull, with the full glory of the sun full upon them. They were not rose bushes as we know them, but banks and pyramids of flowers. There was more blossom than leaf. The exquisite crimson of Madame Victor Verdier, a noble rose, stood next to the lovely red of the Duke of Edinburgh ; and then, in bold contrast, was the cream yellow of Madame Margotin, the crisp, choice, biscuity effect of the pale Miss Ingram, and the still unequalled glory of Celine Forestier. This splendid bank of flowers, perfect in shape, noble in blossom, and exquisite in scent, naturally caused a block in its immediate neighbourhood, and many an artist might have obtained a hint, or a society poet an inspiration, as girl after girl, passing the rose bushes, buried her face deep in the grand blossom of some remarkable flower.

When the sun had done with the roses it attacked the azaleas, pink and crimson, and cream white pyramids of blossom ; and when it had sufficiently kissed these lovely flowers, off darted the fickle sun to coquette with the heath, or flirt with the exotics, or play pranks among the wide-spreading branches of some tree fern or Eastern palm. Few can have seen a flower show arranged with better effect, or in greater taste. But time must be found—when the flowers are seen, and the pictures admired, the effect of the building appreciated, the bold concentration of colour noticed, the dazzle of glass, statuary, showcase, and fresco marked—to stroll out upon the glorious terraces of the new art palace on the hill. This is a relief, after all, from the blues, and golds, and reds, and purples; from the chromotrope glow of those round painted windows, from the theatre, the scenery, and the polychromed balconies, to let the eye rest upon this superb panorama.

Up comes the comparison again with the Crystal Palace. Well, suppose the grounds are larger, the gardens more undulating, the terrace views more vast, this glorious circle of landscape is not to be despised. At Sydenham you get a slice of landscape. Here you get a circle. It is like going round St. Paul's or the Round Tower at Windsor. There is landscape everywhere, and apparently no horizon. How clean, well-fed, and well-brushed it all looks. The trees appear to have been washed, the fields to have been painted, every house and suburb has been employing the whitewashers. Round and round the terrace we go, and we have not an idea where we are. We are told this is Highgate, and that is Barnet, and the other is Crouch Hill, and over there, if it was only fine, you could see the Crystal Palace; and yonder is the Cattle Market; and in the dim distance is the smoke of London. But it does not very much matter; we see a racecourse, and a cricket ground, and flower garden in the immediate foreground; we see villas and railways and church spires beyond, and over that is a delicious haze, telling of distances and country sides miles and miles away.

But the Alexandra Palace would never have been inaugurated at all if the well-dressed crowds after luncheon remained on the delightful sunny terrace, pluming themselves like beautiful peacocks, showing off the latest dress of Madame White and Rosalie, the newest bonnet from Paris, and the last most daring contrast of colour. This landscape is very pleasant no doubt, the flirtation is acceptable, away here from the crowd and the noise and the pushing, and so is the quiet cigar, smoked as we rest on the grass slope, lost in amazement at the landscape, and looking far away to the horizon and the blue mist. But the Alexandra Palace has to be inaugurated. The Princess of Wales is not here to see the first of the noble building named after her. We see no scarlet liveries in the Palace, or royal carriages on the terrace. There is not a prince apparently, or even a royal duke; but there will be a throb of excitement for all that, and some sign that the Alexandra Palace has been formally handed over to the people. With no documents, or parchments, or inaugural addresses; with no red carpet and no *daïs;* with no "May it please you," or "This is to give notice;" with no "With your leave," or "By your leave;" but with a simple, honest, downright "God save the Queen!" heartily sung, and all standing, the Alexandra Palace was given to the people. It is a fine sight at this moment—three o'clock. Colour to the right and left, north, south, east, and west. Colour in the windows, colour among those banks of flowers, colours everywhere on the walls, colour on the organ pipes, colour in orchestra

U

and auditorium. It is imposing when Sir Michael Costa lifts his wand and prepares for the first note of our National Anthem. Here is M. Sainton and the leader of the best orchestra in the metropolis; on the right hand the contraltos, on the left the sopranos; and now, all at once, with a full swell, bursts out the prayer, "God save the Queen." The sopranos take up the melody, the deeper voices echo it, and partly with rattle of drums and full orchestral effect the song is answered, and the short opening ceremony is complete.

AMONG THE RUINS.

I MUST own that I was not prepared quite for such a sudden shock as, when looking out from the train just arriving at the Wood Green Station, I saw for the first time the Alexandra Palace in ruins. I expected the object would be very dreadful and depressing, but I did not anticipate such a thorough wreck and smash as that. The Palace as seen from the railway is not even a shell. It is the barest outline of a suggested design. You see a few arches, a few pillars, some rent and torn girders, and nothing more. The whole idea of the original building is not even conveyed. If ivy could only be induced suddenly to grow, and the moonlight could be turned on, the directors might reap a fortune by exhibiting the remains of the Alexandra Palace as a picturesque ruin.

I can see a great success here, and the hint should not be lost upon the board of management, now that our evenings are so pleasant, and the park is so divinely still. If the moon were not quite successful the limelight might be turned on, and with a judicious expenditure of fireworks the effect would be altogether admirable. It is an astonishing wreck, and as the train whizzes into the Wood Green Station it is impossible to avoid a contrast between this quiet June summer afternoon and that recent May morning, when the gates were flung open, and the Alexandra Palace was opened to the world and all comers. What a difference! The buttercups are not yet dead in the green fields of Hornsey and round about Finsbury Park. The rhododendrons are still in bloom in the garden skirting the New River. But where is the Palace in the pretty new garden—the Palace with its shining dome and gay show of bunting—the Palace with its wealth of flags, its polychromed decorations, its terraces of well-dressed women, its bands of music, its summer air, and promise of indefinite amusement? Why, there it is, contained in those few standing walls, those tottering arches, those blackened façades, the faint suggestion of coloured walls, and the ironwork either tumbled flat, or swinging here and there neglected in the summer air. There is something very terrible in a ruin, particularly when you have known and appreciated the original building. I may be peculiar, but I cannot bear to see a house pulled down, or a house in the course of demolition. A house half pulled down in London is a distressing sight, with its papered walls exposed to the view of omnibuses and cabs, with its suggestion of a piece of staircase, with all its homeliness and comfort cruelly exposed to view. But no ruin was ever so completely distressing as that of the Alexandra Palace, particularly to those who assisted at the opening ceremony, who saw the flower show, who heard the first notes of the ruined organ, who were impressed by the chorus shouting "God save the Queen," and who felt an earnest wish for the success of a really noble undertaking.

Let us go in at the Wood Green Station entrance, and commence our melancholy pilgrimage. Here are the ticket places and the turnstiles, arranged for the admittance of thousands to see the rhododendron show by the Messrs. Waterer, of Bagshot, but only a few stragglers wind their way up the charming hill. The country is in perfection. There is a smell of hay making, the bees are in the flowers, the slopes and lawn are pleasant to rest upon, and sounds of music and festivity come from the banqueting hall, but the eye will rest upon the charred ruin on the summit of the delightful hill. The ruin fascinates us. We cannot go down and examine the preparations for the forthcoming horse show; we cannot wander among the long grass on the pretty racecourse; we cannot scrutinize the excellent "wicket" prepared for the great cricket match next week; we cannot linger where the band plays in the banqueting hall, nor yet trust ourselves to the admiration of the tent of rhododendrons. We must press on to the great ruin, to the remains of the beautiful house, where so many treasures were kept, to all that is left of the Alexandra Palace. As we make our way through the grass our feet kick aside innumerable relics of the disaster—splinters of charred wood, pieces of burnt plaster, scraps of paper scattered here during the fire. The nearer we approach the building the more terrible appears the ruin. Very judiciously a fence has been erected below the great terrace, to prevent the public approaching the walls, which are tottering and dangerous; but a privileged few may stand on the original terrace, which always was and always must be, the glory and the success of the undertaking. It was this view from the terrace that on the opening day first persuaded the public that there were more views than one to be obtained within an easy distance of the metropolis.

Here, gazing at the glorious landscape, the trees, the gold-starred meadows, houses and spires, churches and factories, looking down upon the park, and beholding the view in the distance, we were first impressed with the beauty of the place, and were convinced of its ultimate popularity. There was no need to go inside and enjoy the concert provided for the fashionable world; there was no necessity to hear the organ, or see the loan collection, or admire the decorations, or stand under the dome, or smell the flowers, or wander about the newly-painted, gay, fresh-smelling building. The view from the terrace was quite sufficient to make the fortune of the Alexandra Palace. The view and the situation no fire in the world can destroy; and here we emphatically applaud the decision of the directors in wishing to rebuild the palace at once on the old site, amidst the old charms, when the scene is fresh in the memory of thousands, and where any such building must ultimately succeed.

Here is the view, here is the park; here are the grass slopes, the cricket-ground, the racecourse, the banqueting hall, the garden paths, the flower beds, the pretty wood at the back where the lovers wander. Why not another Palace? Our spirits return as we turn our backs on the ruin and look at the view. We have had enough of the ruin. There it stands, a mass of iron bars and pillars and lath and plaster, an indescribable chaos and confusion. But we feel sure that a lovely house will arise out of the ruins, and that almost before we are back from our summer holiday the design of the clever architect, will have assumed excellent proportions.

How curious are the freaks of fortune, and how much depends upon the quarter of the wind! Here was a gigantic structure levelled with the ground in a few minutes; not a room, not an apartment, not a section, or a subsection left, with hardly one stone left standing on the other; with the gardens strewed with charred splinters right down to the Wood Green Station, with documents discovered in an adjacent county; and yet within a dozen yards of the building still stands the simple tent of rhododendrons, which might have been destroyed with one spark. On the tent there is not the trace of a scorch. The flowers are as fresh and beautiful as when they were first brought from Bagshot. Not even in the best days of the Botanical Gardens have flowers been seen in such exquisite perfection. The variety of colour, the perfection of form, the new tricks of growing the plants, and the general arrangement for effect, tempted the handful of visitors on a visit to the rhododendron tent, irrespective of the other beauties still visible in the Alexandra Park. In spite of the dreadful depression caused by such a terrible accident to so favourite a scheme; in spite of the additional vexation of failure coming after so happy an inauguration; in spite of the paralysing effect of gazing upon so much wasted capital, the directors of the Alexandra Palace soon pluckily determined to rebuild and to re-endow. Not a moment will be lost. Directly the surveyors have done their work, and the insurance companies have settled their accounts, down will come the remaining walls; the ground will be cleared, and the building will recommence. That the scheme will be ultimately prosperous there cannot be a moment's question, for it is commenced with pluck and spitit. The staff of the Alexandra Palace, who managed to secure almost every work of art at the risk of their lives, do not sit idly in sight of their sorrow. Those who suffered most from the calamity are the officials connected with loan exhibitions. Possessors of art treasures have long been chary of lending, and most anxious for their property. After this shock they will readily find an excuse. As a matter of fact, however, it will be remembered that the Turner pictures were every night taken from their place by the attentive secretary and deposited in a strong box — fire-proof — in which was preserved intact, through all the fury of the fire, a hat in an ordinary hat-box. If the fire spared the silk hat, it would have probably spared the Turner pictures every night in the same safety place. All about the fallen pleasure-house there was hope, and cheerful talk about the future. But it was better to sit at the pavilion looking upon the summer landscape, than to wander with old recollections among the ruins.

A GRUMBLE ABOUT INNS.

It is disagreeable to quarrel with a poet who thoroughly enjoys the romance of travelling; it is almost unkind to cavil at the enthusiastic record of one who scratched with a diamond on the window-pane of an old-fashioned hostelry his supreme satisfaction at the calm and contentment of a traveller's life; but I will cross swords with that kindly gentleman who, having "travelled life's dull road," irrespective of all his troubles, still found "the warmest comfort at an inn." Unhappily, it is all changed now. If we travel with a lac of rupees in our purse, if our portmanteaus are stuffed with sovereigns, if we have unlimited credit at our banker's, we can no longer find that cheery ease and gentlemanly comfort which were once upon a time the privilege of travellers.

There was a time when those driven from home did not miss home comforts so dreadfully as now. There was a day when the cheery landlord and the buxom hostess went out of their way to distribute that perfection of hospitality which comes so gracefully from strangers. I have still memories of such an inn. I can see the rigidly polished wainscot in the old coffee-room; the strong, roomy, and old-fashioned furniture; the broad, square sofa inviting one to a snooze; the slippers carefully prepared and awaiting that luxurious moment when the weary, dust-covered boots are withdrawn. I can remember the careful and courteous attendant who had ever a plump chicken or a fat duck, some wholesome meat, and a brave country cheese awaiting the first comer in the glass pantry hard by the neat and comfortable bar. I can still recollect the old china dishes distributed about the room, the rare specimens of delf in the oak corner cupboard, the silver tankards and wine coolers engraved with crests and coats of arms, and purchased at the sale when the old squire's place was broken up, or when the property of the lord of the manor was divided.

Gratefully I remember the honest old four-poster, the white dimity curtains, striped with red flowers; the splendid coarse linen sheets, scented with lavender, and redolent of an oak linen press; the chest of drawers, with brass handles; the bold, huge looking-glass, with a drawer to it for shirt studs and watch-keys; the vast ewer, with a plentiful supply of water ice-cool from the well; the great canopied four-post bed, into which the weary man sinks once, and never moves till morning. And the same sense of comfort and peace was found outside. An archway led to a courtyard where the ostlers groom the horses; the stalls were roomy, well-ventilated, and adequate; and at the back there was a long, old-fashioned garden, full of carnations and foxgloves, bound with hedges of privet—a garden with a broken sundial and tumbledown seats; a garden made musical with the cooing of doves in a cot over the stable yard; a garden where the poaching cat sneaked under the laurel hedge, and the hens broke through an opening at the back, and grubbed about the weed-covered paths. It was a comfort and a delight to rest in such a place. It was a joy to doze here for an hour over the local paper; to chat with the intelligent traveller or bluff farmer; to rest pleasantly until the servants spread the table with snowy white linen; to watch carefully the preparation with honest glass and undeniable silver; to dine sufficiently and well; to drink good ale or wholesome wine; to smoke a pipe; to take a nightcap; to sleep soundly, and to be wakened next morning with the scythe of the grass-mower, the song of birds in the wood close handy, or the hum of the early bees in the garden. Such joys as these, such a change as this, gave both rest and pleasure. The bill, brought in on an old silver salver, was paid with pleasure, and the thanks were expressed as warmly on the one side as the other. The good landlady gave her thanks for your custom; the traveller generously expressed his obligation for the cheery reception.

But these good inn days have disappeared, alas! for ever.

A journey of some weeks through the leading towns of England permits me emphatically to state that the traditional courtesy of innkeepers and hotel proprietors is gone for ever. They do not care one brass farthing for your custom, and pointedly show that the obligation is not on your part, but on theirs. Their implied tone is—" Well, if you do not like it you may lump it. We do not care if you never come near us again. It is a matter of profound indifference to us if you grumble or smile when you pay your bill. It is the travelling season : we are near the hotel or pier, and the sovereign of John Smith is just as valuable to us as the sovereign of Tom Brown." You come in tired and fagged from a journey, and expect to be a little petted and considered. But you are treated as a nuisance and an abominable interloper. "What can I have for dinner ?" "Anything you like, sir." "What is anything ?" "Cutlets, sir; very nice cutlets." This is the invariable answer. "Have you any joint ?" "No, sir." "Have you any cold meat and salad ?" "No, sir." "What have you got, then ?" "Cutlets, sir;" which eventually come up warmed from a dinner in the private room; and at the seaside for a dry, undecorated, loathsome cutlet, supplemented by a tiny sole, which costs on the beach the tenth part of a farthing, the traveller is charged "Dinner, six shillings." The same abominable imposition is forced upon you throughout the day. A plain breakfast—that is, a cup of tea and a slice of bread—is 2s. A breakfast with a couple of eggs is 2s. 6d. A breakfast with an ordinary fish at the seaside is 3s. 6d. Eighteenpence is charged for attendance each day, which, added to the three-shilling bed, makes the nightly charge four shillings and sixpence;

and if the town is full, or any event of importance is coming off, an innkeeper has no hesitation in running up your bed to half a sovereign. On one occasion lately I telegraphed for a bed to an hotel, and was informed the house was full, but I could have one out. The answer to the telegram was charged to my account. The bed out cost five shillings, the attendance in the hotel cost one shilling and sixpence a day, and each night there was a charge at the rooms of one shilling for boot-cleaning, one shilling for gas, and one shilling more for attendance, so that a night's lodging cost nine shillings and sixpence.

The worst of it is, there is no remedy for the miserable traveller. He is never allowed to ride the high horse. The hotel proprietor, or his servants, do so continually. The mistake is always on your side, and never on theirs. There is no idea of making an inn a convenience and a Bohemian home. If you dine at an abnormal hour you are snubbed. If you come home late you are grumbled at. If you rise at an early hour to catch a train, you find nothing ready, and as much inconvenience as if you were disturbing the routine of a friend's house. To drink wine at a modern hotel is an impossibility; at the club you can get a decent pint of claret for tenpence or a shilling. There is no dinner claret sold at any hotel I have entered under four or five shillings a bottle. No champagne is on any card under ten shillings. Every bottle of sherry—and very bad sherry—costs five shillings. If you ask for a sponge bath in the morning, and the water tap is outside the door, the cost is sixpence a morning. Why charge for cold baths at all? A bath is as necessary for daily existence as sheets, soap, or towels. Why not make everything an extra? A luncheon of bread and cheese and butter is three shillings, and sixpence a pint for the ale. And all these monstrous prices are charged with the worst possible grace. There is no one to talk to or consult. The landlord no longer comes in himself with the principal course, asks you if you are comfortable, and adds courtesy to the score. The landlady never appears and shows you to your room. In the old days all the house came out to welcome you in courtly style. Now you are stared at as an intruder when you enter, and considered a good riddance when you depart. In these days there is no such thing as ease in any inn within the range of tourists or seaside visitors. It is difficult to see a remedy. We must have meat, we must have bread, we must have coals, we must sleep somewhere. We may growl, but we must pay; and this fact is sufficiently appreciated by butchers, bakers, coal owners, and hotel keepers.

AT THE ACADEMY.

"Hang it all, my dear, I wish they'd have five-shilling days!" These rich-sounding words were wrung, at the hottest part of the day, from the mouth of a cheery old gentleman who, once upon a time, discovered he had chosen the wrong time for a visit to the Royal Academy Exhibition. Four o'clock is a fatal hour every day, but four o'clock on a hot summer day is the perfection of misery in sight-seeing. The Exhibition rooms are literally crowded to suffocation; crowds ten deep surround the principal pictures; the doorways and approaches are blocked. Perspiring matrons are dragged about by grumbling children. Weary women watch for a seat, and dart at it like a cat on a mouse. Parties are separated into minute fragments; laughing girls escape the watchful eyes of their chaperones; lovers escape and are found, after anxious hunts, flirting behind some gigantic specimen of sculpture; the worst features of bad breeding are exhibited on the part of either sex; dresses are trampled on; rudeness is triumphant; and to the full is shown the occasional pain of pleasure.

But these are the occasions for noticing how little the ordinary Academy visitor knows about art; how utterly unsympathetic and unappreciative is the ordinary lady; how arrogant is the ordinary gentleman in expressing an opinion before he knows whether he possesses one or not; and how thoroughly, as a rule, the Academy is visited because it is a thing to do and must be done, because without it ballroom conversation would be at a discount, and dinner-table talk a bore. Four o'clock on a Saturday afternoon is the hour for the Academy Philistines. The real picture lovers, the true enthusiasts, the artists in sentiment, if ignorant of the technicalities of art, the refined, the educated, and the intelligent, choose other times for their pleasure. They will be here the very first thing in the morning before the day is warm, or will manage to steal an hour these long, light summer evenings, before the Exhibition finally closes its doors for the day. According to all appearances the Academy on Saturday afternoon is the trysting place for lovers, the meeting spot for families, the opportunity given to women for showing off their fine clothes, and a chance not thrown away upon the youths in stiff collars, whose buttonhole flowers are marvellous, and conversation limited. It would be a good study at this moment for a clever caricaturist. Richard Doyle should have given us such a picture as this. The tired old dowager, being dragged about; the energetic people struggling to peep at some celebrated picture through a dozen backs, and attempting to get a view when they are blocked by some tall hat or preposterous bonnet; the pain endured by the unfortunate man with one catalogue between six, and who has to answer the questions put all together by the combined half dozen; the curate endeavouring to keep up his stereotyped smile, though he is being pushed about, and some reckless fellow thrusts himself between the picture and the curate just as that divine is waxing eloquent on the subject he has mastered; the bishop, altogether out of his element, and forced to become an item in a turbulent, irritating crowd; the goodnatured folk who, giving up pictures "on the line" in despair, study, with apparent interest, from the centre of the room, with an opera-glass, such works of small interest as have been hopelessly skyed; the cross papas and mammas, who want their dinner, and begin to feel they have literally wasted a shilling; the clever children, who *will* ask questions on history and heathen mythology their parents are utterly unable to answer; the careless, vacant faces seen in every room; the questions, the answers; the bold criticism, and the hopeless mistakes—these are opportunities for the caricaturist as well as for the cynical essayist.

But, to begin at the beginning, we are bound to confess that the Academy authorities in many minor arrangements are still utterly unable to cope with a large crowd, or to study the convenience of the public. We should have thought, after the repeated remonstrances year after year—after the hints, demands, and entreaties — that dreadfully-shaped article, a catalogue of the Academy, might have been altered to a convenient form, and to some decent proportion. It is quite painful to see the fruitless efforts made to do anything with this ill-looking tome. It refuses to double up; it will not go into a pocket or a muff; it persists in curling round and becoming utterly unmanageable; doubled in two it is awkward; stretched out it is impossible; and the good-natured person who has offered to act as Chorus to his party soon discovers that he has undertaken a very unenviable task. But the misery of the Academy catalogue does not end with the effort to find out the places quickly, or deftly use the inevitable pencil. Let any one walk along Piccadilly any afternoon, and then watch the struggles of the public with their catalogues. Curled round, unless they are gripped with fingers of iron or strangled with a bit of string, they will bulge out and annoy the ladies, already overladen with parcels and parasols. They are so much in the way in an omnibus that a four-wheeled cab has frequently to be taken in order to repress the energy of the most lively volume. Ladies take it in turn to carry the book, or it is handed over to some poor child whose life is made a burden by it. Men who do not usually carry parcels, and who naturally hate anything in their hands but stick or umbrella, are even in a worse plight. The possession of this uninviting light-green magazine tells the whole of Piccadilly and Regent

Street where they have been; and they either take a shilling ride to the club, and add the book to a large collection made by the door porter, or indignantly they fling it down the first convenient area. Students and art-lovers, who would bind these books, and so preserve a useful record of the progress of English art and the history of our painters, are in quite as bad a plight, for bound Academy catalogues will fit into no shelf ever devised in any ordinary library in the kingdom. When the authorities of the Royal Academy discover it is time to print, or to allow the printing of a pocket and convenient catalogue, they will be conferring a benefit on mankind. So much for the catalogues.

We now come to the old-standing nuisance of the sticks and umbrellas. The palatial splendour of Burlington House, the opening of the new quadrangle, the possession of a fine gallery, and the increased and increasing popularity of the Exhibition have not yet suggested an alteration of a difficulty which has existed ever since the Exhibitions were started. No matter how many visitors arrive; no matter how expedient it is to encourage order, system, and smartness, the same three hard-worked, perspiring men are employed on a work which would well occupy a dozen. It takes on an average a quarter of an hour to leave a stick, and longer to regain it. In the heat of the day the scandal of the sticks becomes so obvious, and the annoyance so great, that an extra official is told off to start a temporary stall on the opposite side; but very soon the numbers run out, or the officials become too tediously slow, and the public is compelled to wait in the *queue* with hundreds of angry men and women. We presume, in the interests of the artists whose pictures are in the custody of the Academy, this rule about sticks and umbrellas is a wise and salutary one; but the old trick of feigning lameness is widely adopted, and it is curious how rapidly attacks of gout, rheumatism, and sprains recover when those who have hobbled through the turnstile mix with the crowd in the various galleries. Besides, in the present state of the rooms it would be absolutely impossible to raise an arm, much less a stick; and if umbrellas and parasols are prohibited, why not the enormous catalogues so extensively used for pointing by the energetic public? We saw Mr. Poynter's dragon distinctly wiped with the leaves of a catalogue, and More, of More Hall, rudely pushed with the same weapon in the hands of a gentleman who acted as an amateur lecturer—he was a clergyman—to a crowd of enthusiastic young ladies.

The authorities at Burlington House have so long neglected to listen to the cries of the public on these matters of catalogues and sticks; the books become so much more unmanageable, and the sticks are left and regained with such extreme difficulty, that we feel bound to throw out a hint to some enterprising tradesman in the immediate vicinity of the Academy. A convenient shop where you could leave a stick for a penny, or borrow a catalogue for a few pence, would be an absolute boon to Academy visitors. There is, too, much temper lost and time wasted over these visits to the Academy.

It is curious to observe how, as a rule, the portraits are much more appreciated by the Philistine public than landscape or subject. There appears to be an idea that when once the picture of one of the aristocracy has been seen the subject of it can be reckoned among the acquaintance of the sightseer. "Ah! that is Lady W——. I am so very glad I've seen Lady W——!" is said not once, but a dozen times in as many minutes, and the greatest delight is expressed when the features of duke, country gentleman, or divine have been mastered, not for art's sake, but for some curious and inexplicable curiosity. And this is literally a true story, bearing out my assertion. "My dear," says a lady to her daughter, intent on the catalogue, "my dear, here's a picture I want to see—Lady Teazle. Ah! there she is; well, Lady Teazle is very pretty. I wonder *what family she belongs to?* She looks aristocratic!" "But, mamma dear, I fancy she's a character in a play!" adds the daughter. "A play! What play? She looks like a portrait." And so they go on to find out Lady Somebody Else.—And the "School for Scandal" has been played at the Vaudeville for, who shall say, how many hundred nights? Of course Mr. Poynter's picture is called everywhere " St. George and the Dragon," and when that intelligent child corrects the assertion, and declares it to be " More, of More Hall, and the Dragon of Wantley," her question, " But who, papa, *is* More, of More Hall ?" is closed with the curt, " My dear, I wish you would not ask so many questions." Mr. Alma Tadema's noble picture comes in for extravagant abuse. King Pharaoh is called an old nurse, and the kindest criticism is, " Well, it's a very curious style, *but I suppose it's very beautiful.*" There is a long discussion about Mr. Topham's " Destruction of Pompeii," which is declared to be "all wrong," because, of course, every one knows Pompeii was destroyed by an earthquake! and a Philistine lady standing before Mr. Albert Moore's imaginative and poetical picture, dressed in the most barbarous costume, with every colour badly mixed and out of tune, says, " What ridiculous nonsense !" and whisks indignantly away. " Those Tissots are very curious indeed," is on the whole a safe criticism ; but the ladies find fault with the high heel boots of the " Captain's Daughter," and a stout mother declares. " that if she was a daughter of mine she should not loll about, showing her feet, in that ungraceful attitude." But, curiously enough, the scandal is most prominent and the meaning most misunderstood when the Philistines stand before " Le Lever de Monseigneur," by Claude Calthrop. The Monseigneur is supposed to be the Cardinal, who has just got out of bed, and come in a hurry out of his dressing-room ; but the impropriety of a cardinal having a son as old as that boy in the chair is widely and indignantly discussed. It never struck any one that the lad was the Monseigneur and the Cardinal his adviser! And so it went on until dinner time really came; until the truant lovers were found, until the catalogue had been well scored (for what reason it is impossible to say), and one of the duties to society had been satisfactorily accomplished.

"DOWN AMONG THE COALS."

[A Letter from Paterfamilias.]

IN attempting to avoid Charybdis I have fallen into Scylla. I have jumped from the frying-pan into the fire. A week ago no happier man existed, no fonder husband, no more affectionate father, no more respected master. I left my home each morning with smiling face, well clothed, well fed, and warm. I returned to it each evening with temper not possibly so serene—for the pangs of hunger are hard to bear—but soon consoled with the soothing influences of a clear fire, the welcome enjoyment of an honest, plain dinner, and the grateful addition of toasted slippers. Unhappily for me, all is changed now. My domestic paradise is a ruin. My wife is a scold. My children are in bed with croup and bronchitis. My servants persist in ruining the respectability of my villa by opening the door with their faces swathed in dirty flannel. It is not difficult to arrive at the immediate cause of all my domestic misery. Indirectly it is due to the strike in South Wales; it is more closely united to the fact that coals are fifty shillings a ton; but the more immediate reason is that I have sacrificed my principles and my comfort to the "national" obligation urged upon me by leading articles in influential journals.

I have ever had a passion for a coal fire. As a child I persistently crept nearer and nearer to my idol, until some grim maiden aunt, or conscientious parent, warned me off the rug, and impressed upon me the obvious fallacy that little boys could warm themselves far better at a distance. I did not believe them; but I obeyed blindly. Later on, and in advancing years, instead of studying my "Gulliver's Travels" or "Arabian Nights" at the proper time, and with the assistance of the family candles, I was in the habit of flinging myself down on a level with the fender, and scorching my eyes out to decipher the pages by my favourite light. At school—happily for me—I was prevented from sacrificing myself at the altar of my affection, for had not stronger and more influential minds compelled my rushing out into the frosty air for a kick at the football, a game "at fives," or a constitutional along the hard road, I should have wasted my half-holiday, and my constitution, dreaming over a yellow novel, and baking out my life over a fire large enough to roast an ox. In my cosy old chambers as a bachelor, I can recall no object so dear to me as this same treasured and idolized fire. For here, at least, it was all my own. No one would disturb me; no one dared to turn me out. Here I could draw my worn arm-chair right up to the grate, and, if I cared to do so, rest my feet upon the very bars.

There was no warning me off the rug; no taking me off to rough games in order to promote the circulation. The pleasure—the intense pleasure and companionship—of this bachelor fire of mine saved me from more expensive enjoyments; for here, when the day's toil was over, with a pipe in my mouth, I could hug my old friend, and dream for hours together.

Looking in between the bars, deep into the cavern of burning coal, I could see all the follies of my youth; and upon those red-hot mountains I built, of course, the castles of ambition time was destined to topple over. Here the verses were written and the plans formed, the fair faces idolized. Then, of course, in time the firelight fancies were realized, and when the plunge was taken the fires multiplied, and I was in the proud position of having a coal merchant of my own, to whom periodical cheques were sent for so many tons of the best Wallsend. It was not so poetical, but still not unpleasant. A few shillings over a pound would make my little house happy for a time, and it always seemed to me the money spent most pleasantly was that which procured the delightful luxury of a coal fire. How we used to hug ourselves like true Englishmen with a sense of our superiority when we returned in late autumn from the stoves and waterpipes of the Continent, and found at home our pleasant hearth, found the firelight flickering on the walls, lighting up the pictures, and throwing a red glow over the carpet! How thoroughly we felt this was indeed home, and with reckless extravagance dashed on more coals, and poked up an extra blaze in virtue of our proud position as householder and the possessor of a coal-cellar!

There was no end to the dissipation of warmth in those days, and all the fires seemed to me to possess a distinct influence. The breakfast-room fire, warming the morning paper and the well-blackened boots, was nothing like the dinner fire, throwing such a pleasant light over the white cloth and the silver on the prepared dinner-table. The drawing-room fire, which I approached only on sufferance, and in danger, as in the old child days, of being once more warned off the rug, was nothing like that best of all fires, the study fire, shining upon the backs of the favourite books, asking one to come and smoke at it, baking the favourite arm-chair, and making one, with friends and books and pipes and letters and papers, a bachelor once more, even in married life. And then there were still more dissipated and luxurious fires to be mentioned almost in secret. The fire in the bedroom, after dinner party or ball, some excuse of cold or stress of weather being urged for its existence—the fire that lighted up the room so cheerily when the candles were extinguished, burning upon the glass in the wardrobe, flickering on the ceiling, playing such games with the china ornaments on the dressing-table, picking out every scrap of colour in the room, and intensifying it until at last one became tired of watching the weird gambols of the flames, and dozed dreamily as the coals sunk and the ashes fell with melancholy into the quiet grate.

Then, too, though on rarest occasions, induced by frost or snow, there was the dressing-room fire, and the cold bath beside it; the nursery fire throwing a glory about the fair heads of the children, and the tall fender striping the room with bars in those delightful hours between daylight and darkness; the kitchen fire, when all the house was still at night, making the electro dish-covers look like shields of silver, warming the white deal table, and making the old cat purr beside it as it died a splendid death.

These were the thoughts suggested to me, and the pleasures within my grasp, until the moment when the colliers struck, and the price of Wallsend was quoted at fifty shillings. I need hardly say I was out of coals at the very moment. My wife brought me the alarming intelligence with a long face, and asked me what we were to do. My obvious reply was to order more; and I believe I would have sacrificed much to continue in the old routine, or pretty much the old routine, had not those fatal words, "a national obligation," compelled me to look at the matter in a serious light. This question of coals was no longer a personal matter. If I burned more coals than were absolutely necessary; if I worked in the study when it was possible to work in the dining-room; if I did not descend into the kitchen and lecture the cook on the necessity of economizing the fuel and using the winch persistently so as to screw up the grate into the smallest possible dimensions; if I did not turn my better half into an inspector of coal-scuttles, and urge the locking-up of the cellar, I should not only be a careless spendthrift, but should be contributing to the failure of the coal supply, to the encouragement of strikes, and to the general decay of the nation. Those leading articles did for me. My moral sense was twitted, and I resolved to do what I could in my humble way to assist in the diminution of my coal bill because it was "a national obligation."

Anxious not to be too rash, I attempted a compromise. I tried logs of wood—double in price, of course, because the coals are double—and set fire to the study chimney. I attempted peat, and asphyxiated myself in attempting to light it. I bought coke, and found that so much gas was extracted beforehand, that it would be as useful to heat a brick. At last severer measures were taken. I thought if some of the household remained in bed "until the day was warm" I might manage to breakfast without a fire. I boldly sacrificed myself for the public good. I ate my toast with blue fingers, and attempted vainly to warm my hands by the sides of a hot cup of tea. It was a miserable failure. I went out cross to my work, pinched and crabbed. My labour was unsatisfactory, and I returned to a cold home and a handful of uncongenial cinders in the desolate grate. The kitchen fire had been screwed so tight that the dinner was spoiled, and the things that should have been in the oven might just as well have been warmed on Primrose Hill. Unable to light a study fire, and forbidden to smoke a cigar in the chill dining-room because of the curtains which " smell so in the morning," I made an excuse, and pretending to go to the theatre, turned into a music-hall, got disgusted, and finished the evening at the club. This course was not appreciated. I was cold and lost my temper, and subsequently read in " Middlemarch," apropos of Lydgate and Rosamond, " It is a terrible moment in young lives when the closeness of love's bonds has turned to the power of galling."

My wife tried the experiment of warming the nursery merely by gas, and in less than a week the family doctor was in the house twice a day, and the whole house reeked of embrocation. The servants complained of sore throats and pains in the back, looked sullen and disagreeable, dragged their footsteps heavily, coughed the whole evening downstairs in an irritating manner, and as if they intended to be heard, finally offending my particular eye, the one by wearing a muffler of flannel round her throat, and the other by swathing her swollen face with an offensive bandage, and complaining of toothache, like a drudge in an ill-kept lodging-house. At last the mistress of the house has broken down, for last night she woke me up with a sudden clutch, declaring she was choking, implored me to venture down and instantaneously manufacture a mustard plaster. During the operation in the cold kitchen I myself brought on an old attack of rheumatism, and the household is at this moment absolutely disturbed and demoralized.

I have just this instant returned from consulting my friend, the family doctor, partly on account of my own ailment, but chiefly to get an honest opinion concerning my disordered household. He says I must be very careful—safe and sound advice—that my wife must keep to her room, and have a fire in it night and day; that the little boy will always be subject to bronchitis, that the girl has had a nasty attack of croup, and that both must be kept in a room with a fire, and a thermometer marking never lower than 60; that it would be well if I could send the cook to the hospital, where she would be better looked after. So you see, sir, owing to my desire to obey the maxim that " economy in the consumption of coal represents a national obligation," I am compelled to burn more coal than ever, disturb the peace of my household, ruin my health and that of my family, quarrel with my wife, and pay a long doctor's bill into the bargain. This, sir, is my sad and bitter experience, and as a warning to others I communicate it to you.

THE LAST MAN IN LONDON.

So much has been said and written about the sorrows of the man left in town when Parliament is up and the world away; such distressing pictures are drawn of the neglected clerk and the indefatigable partner; such grievances are made out of some sudden emergency which prevents a trigger being drawn on the 12th of August, or a breech-loader fired on the Feast of St. Partridge; such heartrending pictures are drawn of the hard-worked man deprived of his Margate, of the private secretary cut off his annual Homburg or Baden-Baden, and of the man of fashion at his deserted club, that I would ask leave to show the reverse of the medal, and honestly own that though I am left alone in London, I manage to spend a very jolly life, and to enjoy myself not a little in this magnificent desert.

Let it be remembered that I am no Mark Tapley. On the contrary, I like my growl when I can get one, but, honestly, they make so much of one in London at this moment that I should be ungenerous not to pride myself on my unusual and distinguished position. Now, I own that I love being made much of. It may be an idiosyncrasy, but I like to be petted, and, to tell the truth, the favours extended to me are not fitful, but constant. From the moment that I rise in the morning till the instant that I repose my head on the pillow at night, I feel that I am recognised, and am consequently proud. Under ordinary circumstances I am merely tolerated, but as matters now stand I am noticed. A good friend of mine, who boasted that his position was unfortunately so subordinate that he had never yet tasted the liver wing of a chicken or the first cut out of a leg of mutton, and that his means or the accidents of his life were so peculiar that he had never yet eaten sufficient asparagus at a sitting, consumed so many strawberries that he was enabled to refuse more, or had ever been helped in a ducal or princely manner to iced pudding—would, I take it, envy the position of the last man left in London. Under ordinary circumstances, at the club I pass muster, I believe, but I am not a remarkable representative of the community. On the whole I am a minnow among the lordly fishes, and though, like the small fry at the Crystal Palace Aquarium, I swim contentedly in and out, round and about, under the nose, through the feelers and claws of lords and honourables, and bankers and millionaires, and owners of Scotch moors, enjoying myself peaceably in the same water with such distinguished people—still I have to accept the penalties of my position. They can be rude; I cannot. Very rich men, or titled old fellows, can do things which, were I to attempt them, I should lose my gentle and insignificant importance, and become a public nuisance and a club scandal. Were I very old or very rich, or a member of Parliament, or something very distinguished in the City, I might act in a manner which, according to my modest light, is—well, never mind! I might gather together at four o'clock a copy of every evening paper published, and, knowing the room was full of brother club men thirsty for intelligence, I might sit upon a hoarded pile, and devour it bit by bit like a glutton. I might give out indirectly and by constant occupation that a particular corner, or a fixed seat at a certain writing-table, at a given hour belonged to me; and if by accident I found the chair or seat occupied I might flounce and pet, and make an irritating noise, and toss myself about, and make an undefined grievance for which a spoiled child in the nursery would receive a good whipping. I might talk loud or snore, or lay down the law, or bully the waiter, or abuse the committee, or blackball every candidate, and having done all these objectionable things I might receive the courteous attention of the members and the studied and abject servility of the attendants. But in my ordinary season position I am socially unable to do anything of the kind. Now, however, for once, I am an autocrat and a power. When I enter the door of the hall a boy rushes up to relieve me of my hat and cane. In the reading-room a footman in knee-breeches presents me as if by magic with the latest edition of all the evening papers ready turned down at the "Latest Intelligence." The bow window, with the cosiest of chairs, is ready to receive me.

In the billiard-room I need not wait my turn, but play right hand against left in three rooms at once. I have no longer to rush off to some deserted room at the top of the house for peace and quiet to enable me to compose an important letter. The drawing-room floor is as silent as the catacombs. The three volumes, all together, of all the latest novels, are on the occasional table, and I have no longer to hide "Middlemarch" when I go down to dinner. When I enter the dining-room I can obtain any table I choose, and am waited on with an alacrity which is quite embarrassing, necessitating the perusal of a paper or novel, with a fork or knife waving in the air to show that I have not finished. And the best of it is, now that it is a dull season, they have taken in the members of the only other club I ever wanted to join, so that I and my friend have the jolliest of dinners, and the cosiest of smokes afterwards—just as if we all belonged to the same society.

But they say the streets are so dull. I cannot see it; for liveliness means noise, and I have a strong objection to being run down by carriages, or waiting with a crowd of nursemaids and perambulators till I can cross Regent Street. As matters stand I can walk in the roadway, and the hansom cabmen are so dreamily pleasant that they check their horses for me in order that I may move along. Pall Mall was up the other day, and as silent as the grave. It was possible to pass by all the clubs without being stopped for small talk, and to-day they are amusing me with a steam roller in the busiest part of Bond Street. I can wear any costume I choose. I am not stared at if I wear a billycock hat; indeed, I am rather envied as passing through town to get my gun for the First. I have long since discarded gloves, and St. James's Square is so deserted that this morning I saw a gallant and distinguished officer sitting on a rout seat smoking a short pipe under the portico of the Rag. Apart from the steam roller in Bond Street, which alone distracts my attention from an interrupted view of the shop windows, they are carrying on several improvements of interest apparently for my special edification. I love tar and the Strand—two extraordinary combinations, perhaps, but I am now enabled to enjoy my favourite thoroughfare and boast of an additional smell. To the scent of M. Rimmel, to the invigorating vinegar of Mr. Burgess's pickle shop, to the appetizing odour of roast mutton and grouse from Simpson's kitchen, must now be added the invigorating tarry essence exuding from the new wood pavement round St. Mary's Church. Let it be known that they have widened the thoroughfare at this point, and pulled down the old railings round the churchyard; and I have occupied myself diligently with watching the deposition of the creosoted tesseræ in the roadway with as much interest, as peaceably, and as much advantage to my olfactory nerves as if I were dawdling about a lonely beach, where an old man was tarring the bottom of a ship. When I dine out at restaurants, instead of being snubbed and postponed, and waited upon on sufferance, the waiters trip up one another to be first at my side, the manager talks to me confidentially, and I cannot help thinking I am generally suspected of being a good-natured correspondent, bent upon writing to the *Times* to advertise a good dining place, to make the fortune of some speculator, and to rob the public of some reasonable and quiet little dining place. My experience tells me there never yet was a good, cheap, clean dining house which did not become dear and bad with popularity. Restaurants lose their heads, and become conceited when they are puffed.

But even a journey to the suburbs, now that I am alone and purposeless, is by no means uninteresting, not to find friends, of course, but to meditate on the melancholy of a deserted scene. The trim villa gardens are choked with weeds. You can scarcely distinguish the yellow from the green in the garden paths; a rich growth of wandering nasturtiums has choked the geranium beds, the lobelia has become spindle-shanked, the clinging ivy has obtained such wonderful strength that it has found its way down the gate-posts and hidden both the servants' and the visitors' bells. As to the

Virginia creeper left the other day in pretty curls about the porch, it has fallen down over the doorway a grand screen of green, and given the villa the appearance of a deserted home, all overgrown and romantic, all greenery and insectiferous, where the prince in the fairy tale found his lady love and awoke her with a kiss. I wonder sometimes to myself as I pass these suburb roadways, filled with deserted villas, all green, and overgrown, and sleepy, what would happen if I cut away the ivy-growth on the gate-post, and discovered the visitors' bell; if I trampled my way over the weed-grown garden path, and removed from my legs the tendrils of the clinging nasturtium; if I braved the insects and dashed through the screen of Virginia creeper to the cobweb-covered door—should I find a pretty housemaid in a trance; a maid-of-all-work writing to her baker lover at the master's desk, on the family note paper; or merely a broken-down old charwoman, dozing away in the company of two cats, by the hissing kettle at the kitchen fire? On the whole, I don't think I will make the attempt.

But the experience derived from many a walk among the deserted and grass-grown paths of the suburbs these autumn evenings, persuades me that the servant in charge is by no manner of means to be pitied, and that the householder who has his house done up and painted during his absence from town does a very rash thing, and exposes himself to an exorbitant amount of "men's time." All the suburbs are having their houses done up at this moment; that is to say, there are ladders up against all the roofs, and turned up trucks and pails outside the villa gate. But I never yet saw any man at work at any house. Whether the labour of house painting requires constant refreshers of tea downstairs I cannot say, but certain it is that the intervals of toil to the London labourer are not few or far between. And I notice, also, that the houses which are not enjoying the luxuries of a "clean" have innumerable kitchen visitors. At dark every evening all the suburban gateways are decorated with a neat figure, but I will leave it to others to say if these nocturnal appearances are alone to be accounted for by a desire to take the air. If the young butcher or the grocer's assistant does happen to pass by that way Mary Ann can at least plead she is dreadfully dull.

You cannot imagine how peaceful and quiet we are, how undisturbed are the streets, how arcadian the parks, how easily life passes, how pleasant are the walks, how cosy the little dinners, what amusement and instruction are to be found by those who take their holiday early and come back to the deserted metropolis. Instead of being hipped and *triste*, and disconsolate and melancholy, there are right hands of fellowship held out, river gardens at Twickenham offered, attention, petting, spoiling, and consideration in store for that luckiest of all individuals, the last man left in London.

IN THE HEART OF THE EARTH.

I THINK we created some excitement at Falmouth. Unconventional in our attire, merry in our deportment, excited in our demeanour, and altogether imbued with that excellent Mark Tapleian philosophy of being "jolly under any circumstances," it is small wonder if we did create some excitement at Falmouth. We have none of us a word to say against Falmouth—a charming, health-giving, and delightful spot, in the most beautiful of all English counties, Cornwall,—indeed, we are all of us inclined to mark with a white stone the day that the Falmouth expedition was proposed in a certain smoking room, of which history knoweth not, but certain individuals a very great deal. The little army that invaded the place of which I am speaking, where the sea is of the bluest and the harbour of the grandest description, was mixed in its tastes, talent, and temper. In this consisted our jollity. We gave and took; concealed our absurdities; exploited our excellences, offended no one, and seldom laid ourselves open to giving offence. I am not egotistical, for I am speaking of the party in its collective form. We behaved prettily on all occasions. It was too hot to put ourselves out of temper, and the society too pleasant to suggest boredom. If young Cecil, the budding poet, chose to read Tennyson's Idylls—encouraged most strongly by Isaline Langworthy, with the fair hair and blue eyes—on the pleasant cliff underneath the castle, we raised no objection. Those who cared to hear Cecil's melodious voice listened, and those who detested poetry went to sleep. If the famous Farquarharson, briefless barrister, orator, and suckling politician, chose to discuss Mr. John Stuart Mill and the female franchise, women's rights, and the rest of it—supported vigorously by Maude Carruthers, with the raven hair and olive complexion—we allowed the orator to rap his knuckles on the table, and talk us into a semi-idiotic state of stupor. If Harry Armstrong found delight in bringing his London manners into Cornwall, and preferred the society of a certain soft-eyed little divinity, who sold newspapers and gum-arabic in the town to our happy company, we allowed him to make excuses for deserting us, and, with the exception of a little innocent and unavoidable "chaff," he was free to "make love" all day in the stationer's shop for aught we cared. We excused Lilian Corner's scales and morning exercises, for the sake of her Heller, Hiller, Schubert, and Chopin; her tarantellas, moonlight sonatas, and reveries, with which we were favoured in the evening, if we behaved ourselves very prettily. The "irrepressible Edgar," as we used to call the youngest male member of our community, was allowed to give full vent to his overflowing spirits all day long, provided he woke us betimes in the morning, to get our matutinal plunge in the blue waters, that curled themselves refreshingly into "Summer Cove." And what of our host and hostess? Theirs, indeed, was a rule of love; and as they allowed us to do exactly as we liked, we were the more considerate in meeting their wishes and pulling well together.

We had vainly imagined that we had seen everything worth seeing in the environs of Falmouth, and enjoyed ourselves as much as is consistent with human nature, when our party received a valuable addition. A certain sweet songstress, of whom the world has heard, and of whom the world will, ere long, hear a great deal more, came down amongst us to breathe her native air, and get new inspirations and health from the woods and caverns, and rocks and sea-music, with which we were surrounded.

But the songstress did not come alone. She brought her sweet voice and all our old pet songs; the songs set to words which were poetry, and the words wedded to music which, breathing of love, was therefore quite unsaleable; she brought her cheery manner and indomitable pluck, and she brought her brother.

Her brother was such a good fellow that I must really introduce him with a little bit of a preface. He was, if I may make use of an expression most puzzling at school, and most useful in after life—a walking oxymoron. He was an Englishman, and not an Englishman. An Englishman he was in heart, and speech, and bearing; but destiny had stolen him away from his native land years ago, to shed his cheeriness on other climes.

So much, however, did he love the old country, that once in every three or four years he wended his way back again—the lucky swallow!—his pockets full of gold, and his heart full of love, to spend a holiday in England and a little fortune in generosity.

During these holiday trips he never left his sister or his parents; and as his sister and his parents had chosen to run down to Falmouth, like a dutiful fellow, Washington followed them thither.

We were at breakfast when Washington burst in upon us at Falmouth; and breakfast at Falmouth was not such an early meal as it might have been. With that generosity and unselfishness which is characteristic of Englishmen, I will at once exculpate the whole male portion of our party.

The irrepressible Edgar was bound to wake us in the morning; and we were always on our backs in the sea by eight o'clock. But the women! oh, those dear women! Well, generally speaking, we had but little to complain of. They were cheerful, and bore the fatigue which strong-legged men not unfrequently impose upon fragile women without a murmur; but they were not proof against the nightly exercise of that highly necessary, but eminently female organ, the human tongue! At ten o'clock deceptive yawns were chorused forth, to take us off our guard, and persuade us to allow them to go to bed. Not an objection was urged. The poet perhaps looked somewhat more lachrymose than usual, and the orator came to a dead stop in an able harangue on the " Female Franchise ;" but Isaline's hand was squeezed by the poet, and Maude's eyes followed by the orator, without another murmur at ten o'clock.

I am bound to confess that I don't altogether consider that the poet or the orator was quite fairly treated. Ten minutes after Isaline and Maud had disappeared in a bevy of beauty, the strangest, wildest, and most discordant noises proceeded from the upper regions.

That strange freemasonry of women which exists solely and entirely in the upper regions, at a time which should be devoted to sleep and rest, puts aside all thoughts of weariness previously assumed. Then commence the monkey-tricks of women. They wrestle and they plunge, they dance fandangoes in limited attire, they vie with one another in feats of agility and fancy; they talk, they do one another's hair, they do anything but that for which they left the sweet society of males—go to sleep !

The consequence is that, having devoted the freshest part of the night to folly, they have to devote the smallest part of the night to sleep. And when the morning comes, the great hungry men, ravenous from fresh air and salt water, have to fling pebbles and sand and gravel up at the windows in the upper regions, from which the tantalizing sirens will never emerge.

And so it came about that Washington found us at breakfast at an unorthodox hour, and we all got outrageously chaffed. We very soon saw that there were to be no half-measures with Washington. He did not intend allowing the grass to grow under his feet. His stay in England was limited, and that which had to be done was evidently to be "done quickly."

I must say that, up to the time of Washington's arrival, we had not made the most of our time. In the little smoking-room in which the expedition had been arranged, all sorts of excursions and drives and picnics and sails had been mapped out.

But once at Falmouth, we dreamed away our time. It was very pleasant. We bathed till breakfast, and basked till lunch, and lounged till dinner, and sang and strolled till tea, and talked till bed-time; and so day after day slipped away, and Washington found us at breakfast prepared for another day's dawdle.

I suppose we wanted a leader. Energy—that is to say, personal energy—was out of the question. Washington assumed the vacant directorate, and led us. It was a case of

"Ibimus! Ibimus! utcumque precedes Washington."

To tell the truth, it was Washington who persuaded me to go into the heart of the earth.

He did not begin rashly or impetuously. He did not frighten me with an accurate description of the "man-engine," and the "bucket," and the interminable ladders; but in a light and airy way—before all the girls, by-the-bye—he led the conversation gently up to mines and mining adventures. He told us how the Princess of Wales and a talented contributor to *Punch* had been down the Botallack; and then taking stock of me, after a preliminary examination of my biceps, and a general examination of other muscular developments, he asked me how I should like to be introduced to the Wheal Isabel.

"Of all things in the world," I said, "provided she be young and good-looking. But why Wheal? Is it a sign of endearment, or a token of respect? Am I to understand from the mysterious word Wheal that Isabel is a Cornish Countess, or a Gipsy Queen? Introduce me to the Wheal Isabel? Certainly! Wheal or woe Isabel, could anything unfortunate be synonymous with such a charming appellation?"

"Hold hard!" he said; "this Cornish air of ours has filled you too full of ozone. Restrain your ardour. Isabel is not an enchanting maiden, fashioned by your poetical imagination. She is no gardener's daughter, no maid of Tregedna, no coast mermaiden, no Cornish beauty. She is black, deep, dirty, and terrible. She will cause you a ten-mile ride, trouble, fatigue, and some little expense; but the Wheal Isabel is worth knowing."

"In Heaven's name, then," said I, "who or what is she?"

"The Wheal Isabel," said he, "is one of the largest mines in this magnificent district; and if you would like to be introduced to her you shall."

"Coal?" said I, shuddering.

"Or tin?" echoed the amatory Armstrong.

"Gold, no doubt," whispered Isaline in my ear.

"Nonsense," said Washington; "copper."

I very soon saw that at this very early period of the entertainment there was no getting out of an introduction to Wheal Isabel.

The curiosity of the women was fairly aroused. And that was quite enough.

In an instant the programme was mapped out entirely to the satisfaction of the girls. We were all to ride over to the Wheal Isabel under the mentorship of Washington, and I was to be the unhappy victim sacrificed on the copper altar.

Friend Washington, who at one time had been all cockahoop about the dangers and daring of the expedition, got out of it, or rather of the fatiguing part of it, with that irritating air of indifference peculiar to leaders of expeditions.

"You know, my dear fellow, I have seen these kind of things so often before, that it is really hardly worth while the trouble of changing one's clothes for it," said he, with that charming tone of superiority which is so comforting to the man who knows that he is about to make a fool of himself for the benefit of his fellow-creatures. " But I would advise you to go down," he added, suspicious that I would back out of it at the last moment. "You will never regret it."

And then he cleverly magnified me into a hero, whereat the girls said graceful and complimentary things, and the expedition was finally arranged. Our cavalcade was not altogether pretty to look at, but I think it may be safely termed a good one to go. Falmouth was not great in saddle-horses.

We had a 'bus-horse, a hearse-horse, a fly-horse, a wall-eyed horse, and a broken pummel. With these excellent assistants to a ten-mile ride along the Cornish roads, we started, amidst much laughter of parents, and cheering of neighbouring butcher boys, on our journey to the Wheal Isabel.

Very black and barren grew the land as we neared the Queen of Copperdom. The trees somehow or other left off growing; the fields seemed sown with ashes instead of grass; tall chimneys emitted huge volumes of smoke, and deserted shafts, broken wheels, and grimy-looking monsters met us at every turn.

When four cross roads met amidst a labyrinth of shafts and outhouses in the centre of a blackened heath we drew rein.

"I think this must be the place," said Washington. He was right. A stalwart Cornishman came out to meet us, and to him we presented our credentials, addressed to the Captain of the Mine.

The Captain was somewhat disappointed, I think, when he found that we were not all to be introduced to the mysteries of mining. Miners are after all but men, and the laughing merriment of our joyous girls had already won over the rough heart of the honest miner.

"No, it is only this gentleman," said the treacherous Washington, with the old tone of superiority again. "I have been down mines scores of times."

This was all very well of Washington vaunting his superiority in this way, but why should he, by implication, assert that I was a fool because I was a novice, and because I had *not* been down a mine?

I was quite prepared to go through all the dirty work, but I wanted to be thought a hero, not a jackass.

The girls stood by me bravely. Their sympathy relieved me from some of the humiliation I felt, and they seemed determined, at all events, that I should not go down into the earth without a cheer.

I was handed over to the tender mercies of a sub-captain, who hinted that it would be as well if two other miners were told off as a private escort, to guard me through the lower regions.

"It's as well to have two or three with you," said he; "they treat you with more respect down below, and they're a rough lot, I can tell you."

I assented, of course. At such a time it would,

by no manner of means, be politic to dissent from anything or anybody.

For the next hour or so my life was in the hands of the slaves of the Wheal Isabel.

The sub-captain led me into a little outhouse, where he personally superintended my toilette. I had imagined that it would merely be necessary to put a rough canvas suit over my ordinary clothes. But I was very soon disabused of this notion.

"We must have everything off, sir," said my guide, in a soothing medical tone, as if he were about to operate on me. "It's an awfully dirty place down there."

The costume will bear description. I was first encased in flannel—clean, of course—and over this came an old clay-stained, muddy, stiff miner's suit. My feet were wrapped in two flannel dusters, and then thrust into a pair of old miner's shoes, miles too big for me. On my head was placed a very stiff billycock hat, literally as hard as iron, smeared with tallow grease. On the brim in front the Captain dabbed a lump of clay, and into this he stuck a farthing rushlight. About half-a-dozen more rush-lights were suspended to my waist, and I was then pronounced ready for action.

On our way across the open to the hut in which our party was resting, my attendant asked me which way I intended to go down. Asked me, indeed! as if I knew what the good fellow was talking about. I was only anxious not to look a fool, and to do exactly what I was told. I must own that I felt a perfect child in his hands.

"Will you go down," said he, "by the ladders, or by the bucket, or by the man-engine?"

He might just as well have asked me the Hindostanee for Wheal Isabel.

"The ladders," said he, by way of explanation, "are the most tiring and the most tedious. You will take a good hour to get down by the ladders. The bucket is a dirty way of going down; besides, in this mine, it is used also for bringing up the rubble and the ore, and any interference with this arrangement stops the working of the mine. Now the man-engine is the quickest way, and it is the way all the men here go down. Would you like to try it?" and then he added, looking at me, "but you must be very careful."

This was the first suggestion that had been made to me that there was any danger in my undertaking. Now the principle of the bucket and the ladders I naturally understood, but I had no more idea what a man-engine was than the man in the moon. My mentor, for some mysterious reason of his own, kept on quietly pressing the superior advantage of the man-engine. And so I consented. If I had only known then, at that quiet moment, away from the laughing girls and the heroic Washington, what I was undertaking, and the mortal agony I was about to endure, my prudence would most certainly have got the better of my pride, and I should have been whizzed quietly down in the dirty bucket.

But as it was, in my ignorance and in the innocence of my heart, I decided for the man-engine; and in a minute more I was ushered into the hut.

My quaint appearance was the signal for a loud burst of laughter. Some would "never have known me, would you?" others pronounced me a fright; but one little soft persuasive voice declared me to be "a respectable young miner."

"You're sure you are all right?" said the same little confiding voice. "Have you had some brandy?"

"All right," said I, feeling very pale. "I should think so. Particularly now."

"But how are you going down?" said the sweet voice; "the Captain has been telling us all about it."

"By the man-engine."

"For mercy's sake, don't! it's very dangerous if you're not accustomed to it. He told me so."

That tone of entreaty persuaded me more than ever that I would take the most dangerous route. It was very brutal, I know, but at such a time I would sooner have died than shown the white feather.

They escorted me towards the infernal machine like a criminal on his road to execution.

"Set it a going, Bill," said the sub-captain; and then in a few terse sentences he explained the principle of the engine.

Two parallel horizontal bars provided with iron steps at intervals about ten yards were for ever working up and down—up and down. The method of getting down the shaft was by passing from bar to bar and from step to step, the very instant the word "Change" was given. It was essentially requisite to change the moment the word of command was given, and to make no bungle or shuffle about the operation. The engine waited for no man. There was no possibility of calling a halt, and no saving hand to catch one if a miss were made. All one's safety depended on nerve. One false step or false clutch at the next rung, and it would have been all over with me. Now this fun was all very well with the daylight shining down the shaft, when one could see the iron steps and feel the handles, but in the pitch darkness it was simply awful. The rushlight in one's hat gave little or no light; and it was ten chances to one if the water dashing off the sides of the shaft did not extinguish it.

They practised me at first for a turn or two about a hundred yards up and down the shaft, and even in the daylight I bungled a little.

"You must change quicker, sir," said my guide; "if the iron steps knock against you it will be all up with you."

I was very pale, I know, after the first short practice. I felt that I was doing a madcap act; I know that the man ought to have stopped me; the little voice now quite trembling begged me not to go; but I bit my lips, and vowed I would not show the white feather.

"Do you think you are all right, sir?" said my guide. "Will you go? You must decide now finally?"

"All right," I said.

And then the bell rung, and down we went. I saw the little face—it was the very last thing I saw—and upon my honour I really and truly felt that I should never see that little face again except by a miracle.

But there was no time then to think of anything but my own safety.

The daylight at the top of the shaft had scarcely disappeared five minutes, leaving us in awful darkness, before a splodge of water extinguished the rushlight on my hat. There was no return now. I must change when I was told to change, or die. I could see nothing. My eyes were blinded with beads of cold perspiration, and when the diabolical man-engine rested for a few seconds to enable me to crawl from one parallel bar to the other, from one ledge to the next, I had to grope my way with the desperation of a dying man, and to pray each change for safety. Into one half hour was concentrated the agony of a lifetime. Once lose pluck and nerve, I should be dashed to atoms. Once get faint or dizzy, and my corpse would have been mangled by the fiendish engine. Once neglect the ghastly summons "Change," coming up to me from the bowels of the earth, and I should never see the dear light of day again. It was maddening.

Each second, as it appeared to me, that terrible monotonous word "Change" came ringing out from the dark depths of the shaft, uttered by the sub-captain on the next ledge below me. And I knew that my life depended upon every change.

Hours, days, years, yes, and centuries, seemed to pass between every change. It was like a hideous nightmare. The awful suspense between every word of command; the feeling that something terrible might happen next time; the loneliness of my situation, the darkness of the shaft, the rush of the water, the glimmer of the rushlights going down; the sad hollow echo of the Captain's voice giving the word of command, and exhorting me to be careful, now kindly, now fearfully—all these things combined made up as hideous a day-dream as it is possible to conceive.

For full five and twenty minutes I was in this awful suspense, and in that time went through about five hundred changes. The preservation of my life was a miracle.

At last, half-blinded with beads of cold perspiration, and nearly dead with fright, I heard the welcome bell ring again, and I was safe on the first ledge of the mine.

The man-engine went no further, and the rest of the journey had to be accomplished by ladders. I never told the men what I suffered, but in a rough kindly way I was congratulated on my feat.

"I never thought you would have come, sir," said one. "It frightens most after the first turn."

"Can't you signal up that we are all safe?" said I, thinking of the little face.

"Yes, sir, to be sure."

And they did.

The signal came back again, "Thank God!" and all the miners took off their hats at the last signal. They are pious fellows, these Cornish miners.

I was quite two hours away from my friends, groping about, now on my hands and knees, now down ladders from ledge to ledge, now in a stooping position, now erect in the dark mysterious corridors I found in the heart of the earth. It was hot—stifling hot; hotter than the very hottest room in a Turkish bath. But the stalwart, half-clad men working away at the ore were so interesting, and the metal sparkled so on the ground, and the scene was so strange and fascinating, that I could not tear myself away.

On and on I went, still for ever walking on. I was very thirsty, and would have given anything for a draught of beer. But no stimulants of any kind are found in the heart of the earth. I was allowed, however, to put my mouth to the bung-hole of a water-barrel, and very refreshing was the draught.

"You can walk on like this for hours, sir," said the Captain, seeing I was tired, and still determined not to give in.

"Is it pretty much the same?"

"I think you have seen all now," said he.

So we went back.

"Which way will you go?" said my guide.

I *was* very tired.

"In the bucket," I said, without any hesitation.

With my pockets laden with copper ore, and in the rough embrace of a stalwart miner—for it was close quarters for two in the bucket—we were swung up to the daylight.

Dash went the bucket against the sides of the shaft, through which the water oozed and trickled and splashed. Lighter and lighter it became, until, at last, I saw above me the clear, blue, cloudless sky; and half-dazzled with the glaring light, and blinking like an old owl, I arrived safe and sound on terra firma.

They greeted me with another loud peal of laughter, louder and merrier than the last. My appearance was certainly not prepossessing. I was covered with red mud from head to foot, hot, dishevelled, wild, and weary. And then "I smelt so pah!" as Hamlet says. However, a refreshing cold bath, a hair-brush, rough towels, and a change of clothes soon made me presentable; and after an excellent luncheon in the board-room of the owners of the Wheal Isabel, we were all very soon trotting away towards Falmouth.

* * * * *

One word more. A brooch made from the copper ore I brought up from the mine rests on the neck of the owner of the little face which is looking at me as I write from a distant corner of the room. Sometimes when I am out of sorts—often when I am bilious—always when I have a nightmare—I wake up suddenly from a disturbed dream in my old arm-chair, and fancy somehow that the little face is gone, that there is a strange singing in my ears, and from a dark unearthly vault a voice keeps moaning, " Change."

HOME!

I have known men who have relinquished the habit of smoking solely, as it appears to me, with the view of revelling in the pleasure of taking to it again. There are always children who gobble down the fat that they may tickle their palates with the delight of the lean. We know of pedestrians who, on a long, hot, dusty, tiring walk, have, with Spartan severity, passed by tavern after tavern, rejected the tempting offer of a mug of ale under a wide-spreading tree in order that at the end of the journey they might be lost in the delightful ecstasy of a tankard of cool-drawn Bass or Allsopp; and there are, no doubt, innumerable instances of self-inflicted pain with the ultimate view of intensifying pleasure. We like to be pinched very hard in order that we may feel the delicious sense of departing pain. We love to be frightened and startled in order that we may be alive to the relief of being told it is all a joke. We are not indisposed to perspire and toil over a nightmare in order that we may wake up and gratefully ascertain it is not true. *Amantium iræ amoris integratio est.* Renewed love springs out of lovers' quarrels. One of the best joys of life is reaction.

And there is no better time the whole year round to experience the full thrill and pulse of reaction than now, when we have come back to London, our home, and our best friend after all. Going out of town is an affectation. Coming home again is a reality; of the two sensations, the latter is immeasurably the more intense. We never love London better than when we are away from her. We never love her so much as when we return to her arms. "There is none like her, none." It has not yet, perhaps, been decided whether London is masculine or feminine. I prefer the latter, because the worship is necessarily more sincere, and there are many just now who are literally revelling in the pleasure of revived friendship. We make it a rule to be delighted when we leave London for our holiday. We part from our homes and our chimney corner. We are weary and tired, perhaps, and overworked and harassed. We only desire to be left alone—just a little alone—from daily care, and letters, and business, and newspapers, and worry. The relief would probably be effected if we pretended to go away, if we deluded the matutinal butcher, and threw dust into the eyes of the postman. The advantage would be gained if we wrote round to our little world, and "made believe" that we were taking our holiday with as much faith as the dear little Marchioness. But as we must sooner or later be caught we do not do this, but really pack up our traps and take ourselves off.

It is all delightful, and intense, and beautiful—for

a few days. The foreign steamer going down the river, the passage across the Channel, the railway train rushing through the summer country, the inn life, the hotel life, the mixing with strangers, the provincial instead of the London paper, the sense of freedom, the relief from the mill—all these work the cure in a marvellously sudden and complete manner. But how soon we experience the sense of what we have lost; how very soon we despise the fickleness of our nature! At night, and when the sun has sunk, we feel the loss of home. We are so dreadfully and completely alone out here, or over there. We are outcasts and wanderers on the face of the earth. No one knows us; not a soul takes interest in us. Our bedrooms are strange; and there is no welcome for us at the inn. Day after day we have to pack up our portmanteau and be off again. Our very clothes and brushes and boots seem friends, for they are old familiar objects. We should be distressed, and honestly cut up if the train arrived at some out-of-the-way place at night, and we were denied the companionship of our faithful portmanteau and familiar hat-box. It is all that is left to us, and we have no one else to talk to.

This intense longing for home grows each step we take, and if we were not cowards we should take the return train and relinquish the rest of the appointed holiday. The recovered invalid pitches his medicine into the dust-hole; why should not the refreshed traveller come home? He would if he only dared. So many things may have happened. Those left at home may have sickened or died. The old dame left in charge of the house may have had a fit, or blown up the establishment. We may have lost work, missed opportunities, been slandered or wanted. Fickle as ever, we desire a letter; we would give a shilling for an English newspaper; we require to be doing something, and to be at work. The first week or so was delightful. The rest is torture. We see sights which we long to share with others. There is no one to lean upon or to sympathize with. This sunset or that daybreak would so delight some old chum separated from us inevitably; this deep wood or cool grove would be health and life to another possibly by fate bottled up in an uninteresting town. This specimen of rare antiquity—an old church, an old carving, a picture, a pulpit, a reredos, some quaint china, a brass dish, a blue plate—would be so deeply appreciated by many who are not here. We are compelled to enjoy it all alone, and we know that any description or allusion to it by-and-by will fall very short of the original charm. As a rule, we generally go away with the wrong man; and, if alone, the longing for sympathy becomes almost painful in the end. There is, we believe, no welcome so soon worn out as the hospitality of holiday time. But, as a relief to many annoyances, a change from dull evenings, constant alteration of residence, unsympathetic companions, and a wonderful isolation in the heart of thousands, comes the best part of the holiday—the return to home when the home is in London.

The joy of the return is immeasurably superior to the delight of departure. Our heart leaps up when we behold the first garret and chimney-pot. How delightfully familiar and pleasant is the roar and rattle of London. The advertisements on the walls as we roll home in the cab are as fresh and inspiriting as half the sights we have seen. Who cares if we have the worst conveyances, the most miserable streets, and the most detestable arrangements in the universe?—they belong to London, and London we love. Oh yes! we know all about it; we have been in Paris, or Vienna, or Liverpool, or Dublin, or Manchester, or Brussels, or where you like, but, thank God! we are in London. There is no place like it in the world. We have been in penal servitude in a provincial town, where the secrets of all the inhabitants are public property; where, if you sit at the window with an old lady, you know all the tittle-tattle "up-street;" where Mrs. Jones knows if Miss Smith goes to church; where Miss Vavasour knows the cut of Miss Jenkins's bonnet; and where solitude and secresy are literally impossible. We have been in so-called freedom in a provincial city, where any John Styles or Tom Brown is known—so directed at the post-office—and where Mr. Mayor is button-holed by an alderman when he walks along the principal street of the place.

When we see a stray farmhouse in the country,

just at the right moment, with the full sun focused on the roses and the honeysuckle, we think we should like to live there for ever. When we are introduced to a cottage by a waterfall, or a hut in the mountains, we envy the miller or the chamois hunter; but where in the whole round world is it possible to find such variety and delights as in London? It ruins you for any other place? Of course it does. The man next door to you does not know or care about your name. You can be domestic or a vagrant. You can live a dozen lives in one day. The instant you are outside the door you are precisely your own master until the key is put into the latch again. There is no scrutiny into your movements, and, so long as you are not tipsy or offensive, you are simply lost daily in a wilderness of humanity.

But there are pleasures and privileges more closely identified with the returned Londoner, who loves his home with a more intense idolatry each time the prodigal returns. The cosy little roof-tree is better, after all, than any hotel or boarding-house that ever was erected. You can get your bath in the morning without ringing for it, your breakfast without ordering it. Here is the dressing-room, where you are always alone night and morning for lounging or for thought. Here are the drawers and corners where you can put your hand precisely on what you require. Down below are the books you have longed for, the papers you have desired, the pictures you love, the treasures you have collected, the furniture you have picked up at odd times, the servants glad to see you, the dog barking at your heels, the cat purring round your legs, and, over all and above all, a delicious sense and smell of home.

There is no joy like that of the returned Londoner. A traveller from New Zealand or Australia could not more intensely appreciate the welcome. The morning omnibus driver greets him with pleasant enthusiasm. The porter at the club chirrups at him as he presents a packet of unanswered letters. He revisits the theatre with the surprise and delight of a schoolboy. He goes eagerly to the promenade concerts to pick up a friend and have a chat. The grave old club is lively with the anecdotes of returned travellers. Night is turned into day with the telling of adventure and romance. Dinner parties are got up for the welcoming of old friends, and conversation is brightened with the fruit of miscellaneous travel.

But above all, and beyond all to the true Londoner, a pleasure superior to the natural excitement of grasping the hands of old friends and settling down into old ways, is the indescribable pleasure of coming back to this huge world, where all our hopes, our ambitions, our trials, and our affections are centred. We have dined, but not as in London. We have slept, but not as in our own bed. We have seen sights, but few so pleasant as those associated with the struggle of life. We have made friends, but none like the old ones. This is our centre, our workshop, our universe, our playground. Here we have struggled and fallen, and been picked up again; here we have complained, and hated, and have loved; here we have had our chance, missed and succeeded; here we have derived all that is good or worthless in our composition. Conscious of London's pain, we would not go hence for all the pleasures of all the capitals of the universe; for there is no home like that in London, and London is our home!

THE END.

TINSLEY BROTHERS'
NEW PUBLICATIONS.

A SUMMER IN SPAIN. By Mrs. RAMSAY, Author of a Translation of Dante's "Divina Commedia." 1 vol. 8vo, with Vignette and Frontispiece.

COURT AND SOCIAL LIFE IN FRANCE UNDER NAPOLEON THE THIRD. By the late FELIX WHITEHURST. 2 vols. 8vo.

"Not only was Mr. Whitehead received from time to time ceremoniously at the Tuileries and Compiègne, but he may be said to have known Cæsar 'at home' and in his slippers; and upon the whole he made good use of his opportunities in the service of his employers. For ten years he reflected for us English people, effectively and agreeably, certain aspects of Paris under the Second Empire."—*Athenæum.*

Spirit Faces, Mediums, At a Dark Circle, The Walworth Jumpers, &c.

UNORTHODOX LONDON; or, Phases of Religious Life in the Metropolis. By the Rev. C. MAURICE DAVIES, D.D. 1 vol. 8vo.

"Mr. Davies, in the most plain, simple, matter-of-fact way, tells us exactly what he saw on each occasion. The result is a most interesting volume. We have left many of Mr. Davies's fifty-nine chapters unnoticed, but all of them will repay perusal."—*Athenæum.*

A Silent Service, Watch-night, Midnight Mass, Extraordinary Services, &c.
Now ready, uniform with "Unorthodox London,"

ORTHODOX LONDON; or, Phases of Religious Life in the Church of England. By the Author of "Unorthodox London."

"It reflects in a very comprehensive way some of the leading aspects of religious thought in the Church of England at the present time, and contains a number of literary photographs—if the phrase may be allowed—of eminent clergymen. . . . . The author knows his subject, and has the art of instructing his readers."—*Daily News.*

Recuerdos de Italia.

OLD ROME AND NEW ITALY. By EMILIO CASTELAR. Translated by Mrs. ARTHUR ARNOLD. 1 vol. 8vo.

"The man whose ardent love of humanity and passion for intellectual freedom, expressed in this volume, render it one of the most satisfying that has ever been written on the subject of Italy, is now—with probably a greater influence than any member of the Government—one of those to whom the destinies of the Spanish people are intrusted."—*Echo.*

Mr. J. Ashby Sterry's New Book.

THE SHUTTLECOCK PAPERS: a Book for an Idle Hour. By J. ASHBY STERRY. 1 vol. crown 8vo.

"It is, above all, in the geniality of this book—in the author's power to establish a sort of confidential relationship with his readers—that its great charm is to be found."—*Morning Post.*
"A gem that ought almost to entitle its author to take a permanent position in the rank of such essayists as Addison, Steele, Goldsmith, and Lamb."—*Morning Advertiser.*
"The book is full of sunshine, and there is not a page of it that cannot be read with interest."—*Standard.*

Life of Madame Sevigne.

MADAME DE SÉVIGNÉ, her Correspondents and Contemporaries. By the Comtesse de PULIGA. 2 vols. 8vo. With Portraits.

"Madame de la Puliga has diligently studied her subject in all its bearings; she is thoroughly imbued with the spirit of the period of which she treats; she is at home with both correspondents and contemporaries; she has made a judicious selection from the embarrassing abundance of materials accumulated to her hands; treading frequently on very delicate ground, she is never wanting in feminine refinement or good taste."—*Quarterly Review.*

Alexander of Russia, Sir Francis of Assisi, Joseph de Maistre, &c.

FOREIGN BIOGRAPHIES. By WILLIAM MACCALL. 2 vols.

TINSLEY BROTHERS, 8, CATHERINE STREET, STRAND.

TINSLEY BROTHERS' PUBLICATIONS.

THE CONQUEROR AND HIS COMPANIONS. By J. R. PLANCHÉ, Author of "The Recollections and Reflections of J. R. Planché," &c.
[*In the press.*

THE RECOLLECTIONS AND REFLECTIONS OF J. R. PLANCHE (*Somerset Herald*): a Professional Autobiography. 2 vols. 8vo.

"Besides illustrations of social and dramatic life, of literature, and of authors, Mr. Planché gives us record of travels, incidents of his *other* professional life as a herald, and reflections on most matters which have come under his notice. . . . There are few men who have amused and delighted the public as long as he has done: and perhaps there has never been a dramatic writer who has been so distinguished as he has been for uniting the utmost amount of wit and humour with refinement of expression and perfect purity of sentiment."—*Athenæum.*

"So many and so good are the anecdotes he relates, that two or three could not be taken from the rest by any process more critical than the toss of a halfpenny."—*Saturday Review.*

Beethoven, Handel, Haydn, Malibran, Mozart, &c.

MUSICAL RECOLLECTIONS OF THE LAST HALF CENTURY. 2 vols. 8vo.

"And music shall untune the sky."—*Dryden and Handel.*

"Such a variety of amusing anecdotes, sketches of character, bits of biography, and incidents in the career of famous *artistes* have never been crammed in a couple of volumes before. . . . 'Musical Recollections of the Last Half Century' is the most entertaining and readable book on musical matters that has been published for many years, and deserves to become very popular."—*Era.*

The Life and Times of Algernon Sydney.

THE LIFE AND TIMES OF ALGERNON SYDNEY, Republican, 1622-1683. By ALEXANDER CHARLES EWALD, F.S.A., Senior Clerk of Her Majesty's Public Records, Author of "The Crown and its Advisers," "Last Century of Universal History," &c. 2 vols. 8vo.

"We welcome this biography as the means of making an illustrious Englishman better known to modern readers, and because it will bring the noble letters and other writings of Algernon Sydney within the easier reach of a great mass of people."—*Athenæum.*

The Life and Adventures of Alexander Dumas.

THE LIFE and ADVENTURES of ALEXANDER DUMAS. By PERCY FITZGERALD, Author of "The Lives of the Kembles," "The Life of David Garrick," &c. 2 vols. 8vo.

"If the great object of biography is to present a characteristic portrait, then the personal memoir of Dumas must be pronounced very successful."—*Times.*

UNEXPLORED SYRIA. By Captain BURTON, F.R.G.S., and Mr. C. F. TYRWHITT-DRAKE, F.R.G.S., &c. With a New Map of Syria, Illustrations, Inscriptions, the "Hamah Stones," &c. 2 vols. 8vo. 32s.

"The work before us is no common book of travels. It is rather a series of elaborate, and at the same time luminous, descriptions of the various sites visited and explored by the authors, either together or singly, and of the discoveries made there by them."—*Athenæum.*

"While these magnificent volumes, with their original plans and sketches by Mr. Drake, the unrivalled map of Northern Syria, and the luxurious print, are triumphs of typography, they are at the same time enduring monuments of the energy and enterprise of our countrymen."—*John Bull.*

"The book must be pronounced to be valuable for its information."—*Spectator.*

TINSLEY BROTHERS, 8, CATHERINE STREET, STRAND.

TINSLEY BROTHERS' NEW NOVELS.

FRANK SINCLAIR'S WIFE. By Mrs. J. H. RIDDELL, Author of "George Geith," "City and Suburb," "Too Much Alone," "The Race for Wealth," "Home, Sweet Home," &c. 3 vols.

A YOUNG MAN'S LOVE. By Mrs. GEORGE HOOPER, Author of "The House of Raby," "Little Maggie and her Brother," "Arbell," &c. 3 vols.

THAT LITTLE FRENCHMAN. By the Author of "Ship Ahoy." 3 vols.

PUNISHED AND PARDONED; or, How Does it End? A Tale of the Nineteenth Century. By Mrs. ALEXANDER S. ORR, Author of "The Twins of St. Marcel," &c. 3 vols.

A CANADIAN HEROINE. By the Author of "Leaves from the Backwoods," &c. 3 vols.

THE OLD CROSS QUARRY: a New Novel. By GERALD GRANT, Author of "Coming Home to Roost." 3 vols.

A TWISTED LINK. By Mrs. C. CROW, Author of "Spencer's Wife," "Heathside Farm," &c. 3 vols.

LAURA ERLE. By the Author of "Blanche Seymour," "Erma's Engagement," &c. 3 vols.

THE GOOD OLD TIMES: a New Novel. By WILLIAM HARRISON AINSWORTH, Author of "Boscobel," "Old St. Paul's," "Rookwood," "The Tower of London," "The Miser's Daughter," &c. 3 vols.

THE AMUSEMENTS OF A MAN OF FASHION: a New Novel. By NORMAN NUGENT. 3 vols.

NOR LOVE: NOR LANDS. By the Author of "Victory Deane," "Valentine Forde," &c. 3 vols.

A HUNT CUP; or, Loyalty before All: a Novelette. By WAT BRADWOOD, Author of "O. V. H.," "Ensemble," &c. 1 vol.

THE SQUIRE'S GRANDSON: a Tale of a Strong Man's Weakness. By ROBERT ST. JOHN CORBET, Author of "The Canon's Daughters," "Church and Wife," &c. 3 vols.

"Enough has been said to indicate our opinion of this novel; and no more need be added than a distinct recommendation of it for general perusal."—*Morning Post.*

A PAIR OF BLUE EYES. By the Author of "Under the Greenwood Tree," "Desperate Remedies," &c. 3 vols.

"It is one of the most artistically constructed among recent novels; and, from considerations affecting higher matters than mere construction, we would assign it a very high place among works of its class."—*Saturday Review.*

"We are very careful how we use the word 'genius;' but we have no hesitation in saying of the author of 'A Pair of Blue Eyes' and 'Under the Greenwood Tree,' that he is distinctly a man of genius. There is in these books more inborn strength, more inborn knowledge, more of that fine humour which is the mark and test of genius, than we are able to detect in any English living novelist of our acquaintance, one only excepted."—*Pall Mall Gazette.*

TINSLEY BROTHERS, 8, CATHERINE STREET, STRAND.

TINSLEY BROTHERS' TWO-SHILLING VOLUMES,

UNIFORMLY BOUND IN ILLUSTRATED WRAPPERS,

To be had at every Railway Stall and of every Bookseller in the Kingdom.

EVERY-DAY PAPERS. By ANDREW HALLIDAY.

THE SAVAGE-CLUB PAPERS (1868). With all the Original Illustrations.

THE SAVAGE-CLUB PAPERS (1867). With all the Original Illustrations.

THE DOWER-HOUSE. By ANNIE THOMAS (Mrs. Pender Cudlip), Author of "Denis Donne," &c.

SWORD AND GOWN. By the Author of "Breaking a Butterfly," "Anteros," &c.

BARREN HONOUR. By the Author of "Guy Livingstone," &c. &c.

THE ROCK AHEAD. By the Author of "A Righted Wrong," &c. &c.

BLACK SHEEP. By EDMUND YATES. Author of "The Rock Ahead," &c. &c.

MISS FORRESTER. By the Author of "Archie Lovell."

THE PRETTY WIDOW. By CHARLES H. ROSS.

THE WATERDALE NEIGHBOURS. By JUSTIN MCCARTHY, Author of "My Enemy's Daughter," &c.

NOT WISELY, BUT TOO WELL. By the Author of "Cometh up as a Flower."

RECOMMENDED TO MERCY. By the Author of "Sink or Swim."

MAURICE DERING. By the Author of "Guy Livingstone," &c. &c.

BRAKESPEARE. By the Author of "Sans Merci," "Maurice Dering," &c.

BREAKING A BUTTERFLY. By the Author of "Guy Livingstone," &c. &c.

The ADVENTURES of DR. BRADY. By W. H. RUSSELL, LL.D.

SANS MERCI. By the Author of "Guy Livingstone," "Sword and Gown," &c.

LOVE STORIES OF THE ENGLISH WATERING-PLACES.

NETHERTON-ON-SEA. Edited by the late Dean of Canterbury.

A RIGHTED WRONG. By EDMUND YATES, Author of "The Forlorn Hope," "A Waiting Race," &c.

MY ENEMY'S DAUGHTER. By JUSTIN MCCARTHY, Author of "The Waterdale Neighbours," "A Fair Saxon," &c.

A PERFECT TREASURE. By the Author of "Lost Sir Massingberd."

BROKEN TO HARNESS. By EDMUND YATES, Author of "The Yellow Flag," "Black Sheep," &c. &c.

GRIF. By B. L. FARJEON, Author of "Joshua Marvel," &c.

GASLIGHT AND DAYLIGHT. By GEORGE AUGUSTA SALA, Author of "My Diary in America in the Midst of War," &c.

PAPERS HUMOROUS AND PATHETIC. Selections from the Works of GEORGE AUGUSTA SALA. Revised and abridged by the Author for Public Readings.

ANTEROS. By the Author of "Guy Livingstone," "Barren Honour," "Sword and Gown," &c. &c.

JOSHUA MARVEL. By B. L. FARJEON, Author of "Grif," "London's Heart," "Blade-o'-Grass," and "Bread-and-Cheese and Kisses."

UNDER WHICH KING? By B. W. JOHNSTON, M.P.

THE CAMBRIDGE FRESHMAN; or Memoirs of Mr. Golightly. By MARTIN LEGRAND. With numerous Illustrations by PHIZ.

LOVER AND HUSBAND. By ENNIS GRAHAM, Author of "She was Young and He was Old."

OLD MARGARET. By the Author of "Leighton Court," "Silcote of Silcotes," "Geoffrey Hamlyn," &c.

HORNBY MILLS; and other Stories. By the Author of "Ravenshoe," "Austin Elliot," &c. &c.

THE HARVEYS. By HENRY KINGSLEY, Author of "Ravenshoe," "Mademoiselle Mathilde," "Geoffrey Hamlyn," &c.

SAVED BY A WOMAN. By the Author of "No Appeal," &c.

A WAITING RACE. By EDMUND YATES, Author of "Black Sheep," &c.

JOY AFTER SORROW. By Mrs. J. H. RIDDELL, Author of "George Geith," "City and Suburb," &c.

AT HIS GATES. By Mrs. OLIPHANT, Author of "Chronicles of Carlingford," &c.

UNDER THE GREENWOOD TREE. A Rural Painting of the Dutch School. By the Author of "Desperate Remedies," &c.

THE GOLDEN LION OF GRANPERE. By ANTHONY TROLLOPE, Author of "Ralph the Heir," "Can You Forgive Her?" &c.

THE YELLOW FLAG. By EDMUND YATES, Author of "Broken to Harness," "A Waiting Race," "Black Sheep," &c.

NELLIE'S MEMORIES: a Domestic Story. By ROSA NOUCHETTE CAREY.

MURPHY'S MASTER; and other Stories. By the Author of "Lost Sir Massingberd," "Found Dead," "Cecil's Tryst," "A Woman's Vengeance."

HOME, SWEET HOME. By Mrs. J. H. RIDDELL, Author of "George Geith," "Too Much Alone," "City and Suburb," &c.

May also be had, handsomely bound in cloth gilt, price 2s. 6d. each.

TINSLEY BROTHERS, 8, CATHERINE STREET, STRAND.

www.ingramcontent.com/pod-product-compliance
Lightning Source LLC
Chambersburg PA
CBHW020218240426
43672CB00006B/353